Elizabeth Barrett Browning's Spiritual Progress

Elizabeth Barrett Browning's Spiritual Progress

Face to Face with God

Linda M. Lewis

UNIVERSITY OF MISSOURI PRESS   Columbia and London

Copyright © 1998 by

The Curators of the University of Missouri

University of Missouri Press, Columbia, Missouri 65201

Printed and bound in the United States of America

All rights reserved

5 4 3 2 1   02 01 00 99 98

Library of Congress Cataloging-in-Publication Data

Lewis, Linda M., 1942–

    Elizabeth Barrett Browning's spiritual progress : face to face
with God / Linda M. Lewis.

      p.   cm.

    Includes bibliographical references (p.   ) and index.

    ISBN 0-8262-1146-1

    1. Browning, Elizabeth Barrett, 1806–1861—Religion.
2. Christianity and literature—England—History—19th century.
3. Christian poetry, English—History and criticism.   4. Women—
Religious life—England.   5. God in literature.   I. Title.

PR4197.R4L49   1997

821'.8—dc21   97-35039

                                          CIP

∞™ This paper meets the requirements of the

American National Standard for Permanence of Paper

for Printed Library Materials, Z39.48, 1984.

Designer: Stephanie Foley

Typesetter: BOOKCOMP

Printer and Binder: Thomson-Shore, Inc.

Typeface: Adobe Garamond

For my mother, Thelma Cogburn Battles,
and my grandmother Maggie Cogburn Powell

Contents

❁

Acknowledgments ix

Abbreviations xi

Introduction 1

1. Prometheus and Jesus as "Free-souled, Reverent Love" 16

2. Eve in Exile 49

3. The Politics of "Planting the Great Hereafter" 86

4. Death and Resurrection 132

5. Prophetess of Divine Love and Wisdom 171

Conclusion 212

Works Cited 235

Index 249

Acknowledgments

"Bards would write worse, if critics wrote no more," commented young Elizabeth Barrett when she was an apprentice bard. Although she would no doubt take exception to many of my insights, I think that she would endorse this enterprise. She would doubtless take issue also with some of the feminist theologians whose work I explore as paradigm to examine the Barrett Browning canon, but she would probably be fascinated with the notion of a *female* theology as legitimate discourse. Certainly she would rejoice over the explosion of feminist criticism that for over two decades has been reexamining and reevaluating the works of nineteenth-century female poets.

I am indebted to several people who took an interest in this critical project. Chief among them are scholars and critics who read the manuscript or parts thereof and offered valuable commentary: Beverly Taylor, Helen Cooper, Marjorie Stone, Jane K. Vieth, Trudy Lewis, Michael Barrett, and an anonymous (and very insightful) reader who like Beverly Taylor evaluated it for the University of Missouri Press. Others generously listened to ideas and approaches with which I struggled and suggested points for me to consider. Among those are Eugene Bales, Ronald MacLennan, Paul A. Olson, Joy Ellis McLemore, and Patricia Murphy. Needless to say, much of the strength of the book comes from the insights of these fine critics, scholars, theologians, and poets. Needless also to say but I shall add nonetheless, any flaws of the book are all my own.

Financial and research assistance from several institutions was invaluable. My sincere gratitude goes to Bethany College for a sabbatical leave in which I produced the first draft of the manuscript; the Armstrong Browning Library (ABL) of Baylor University, which awarded me a research fellowship; and the Evangelical Lutheran Church of America (with which Bethany College is affiliated) for a research grant. Invaluable assistance also came from the Alexander Turnbull Library of the National Library of New Zealand, Te Puna Mātauranga o Aotearoa, and the Margaret Clapp Library of Wellesley College. I single out for special gratitude the following librarians: Denise Carson of the Bethany Library, Rita Humphrey and Cynthia Burgess of ABL, Betty Coley Fredeman (formerly of ABL), Roger Brooks (Director Emeritus of ABL), and Robert Petre of the Alexander Turnbull Library. A version of parts of Chapters 2 and 4 appeared as articles in *Victorians Institute Journal* and *Studies in Browning and His Circle,* respectively. I thank those journals for permission to reprint segments of the essays.

The University of Missouri Press has been patient, considerate, and supportive. I am especially indebted to Clair Willcox, Acquisitions Editor; Beverly Jarrett, Director and Editor-in-Chief; Jane Lago, Managing Editor; Annette Wenda, copyeditor of *Elizabeth Barrett Browning's Spiritual Progress;* Karen Caplinger, Marketing Manager; and Megan Scott, Publicity Manager.

Geneve Selsor will be surprised to find her name listed here, but in a sense she is behind the entire enterprise in that one day years ago, over a leisurely lunch and fine bottle of wine at her home, she quoted some lines from *Aurora Leigh.* At the time I knew little more of Elizabeth Barrett Browning than "How do I love thee? Let me count the ways," but I left the luncheon table hungry to know more. Thank you, Geneve, for this particular literary discussion and for so many more.

Finally, my greatest love and appreciation go to my family—my husband, Frank, and our children and grandchildren, as well as to my mother and grandmother, who have consistently and lovingly demonstrated female spirituality and to whom this book is dedicated.

Abbreviations

Elizabeth Barrett Browning

BC *The Browning Correspondence.* Ed. Philip Kelley, Ronald Hudson, and Scott Lewis. 13 vols. Winfield, Kans.: Wedgestone Press, 1984–1995.

CWEBB *The Complete Works of Elizabeth Barrett Browning.* Ed. Charlotte Porter and Helen A. Clarke. 6 vols. New York: Thomas Y. Crowell, 1900.

The following are used for major works in *CWEBB:*
AL	*Aurora Leigh*
CGW	*Casa Guidi Windows*
DE	*Drama of Exile*
IW	"Italy and the World"
N	"Napoleon III. In Italy"
PB	*Prometheus Bound,* by Aeschylus (EBB's translation)
RSPP	"The Runaway Slave at Pilgrim's Point"
S	*The Seraphim*
SM	"A Sea-side Meditation"
SP	*Sonnets from the Portuguese*
T	"The Tempest"

LEBB *The Letters of Elizabeth Barrett Browning.* Ed. Frederic G. Kenyon. 2 vols. New York: Macmillan, 1898.

LHS *Letters to Her Sister, 1846–1859.* Ed. Leonard Huxley. London: John Murray, 1929.

LMO *Elizabeth Barrett Browning's Letters to Mrs. David Ogilvy 1849–1861.* Ed. Peter N. Heydon and Philip Kelley. Quadrangle/New York Times Book Company and the Browning Institute, 1973.

LMRM *The Letters of Elizabeth Barrett Browning to Mary Russell Mitford 1836–1854.* Ed. Meredith B. Raymond and Mary Rose Sullivan. 3 vols. Waco: Armstrong Browning Library, 1983.

Milton

PL *Paradise Lost,* from *John Milton: Complete Poems and Major Prose.* Ed. Merritt Y. Hughes. New York: Odyssey Press, 1957.

Shelley

PU *Shelley's Prometheus Unbound.* Ed. Lawrence John Zillman. Variorum Edition. Seattle: University of Washington Press, 1959.

Elizabeth Barrett Browning's Spiritual Progress

Introduction

.... O angels, let your flood
Of bitter scorn dash on me! do ye hear
What *I* say who bear calmly all the time
This everlasting face to face with God?

—Elizabeth Barrett, "An Apprehension"

I

When Elizabeth Barrett wrote these words, she expected shortly to face God in death, because she had already discovered that—as Emily Dickinson says—the heads of the horses speeding the carriage of life face toward eternity. Not that Elizabeth Barrett had attempted to rein the horses in. Rather, in early poems she "calmly" anticipated eternal life as alternative to this present existence punctuated, as it is, with human loss and suffering. When she was reborn to life and love, however, death withdrew its visage and the "face to face with God" was postponed. The locution therefore suggests other nuances: a spiritual quest for truth and light; the hubris of spiritual pride (elevating oneself to God's height); and a questioning of theological doctrines such as predestination, grace versus works, and the purpose and necessity of human suffering (together with human responsibility to alleviate the suffering of other humans).

The recurring "face to face with God" in the canon of Elizabeth Barrett Browning is intriguing, especially inasmuch as Moses was told that "seeing" Yahweh is prohibited, that no human can look upon the face of God and live. Dolores Rosenblum points out, however, that the expression "face to face" is a relatively common figure in nineteenth-century writing, resonating as it does with the Pauline text, "For now we see through a glass, darkly; but then face to face: now I know in part;

but then shall I know even as also I am known" (1 Cor. 13:12). Thus, the expression denotes death and immortality, as Barrett Browning says, "Death is a face-to-face intimacy" (*LEBB* 2:140).[1]

Barrett Browning was in her lifetime widely known as a devout, deeply religious poet, elevated almost to sainthood in popular esteem. After death she was canonized by editors, critics, and a generation of women poets. For example, a memorial tribute to Barrett Browning in *Last Poems* calls her "more devout than George Herbert, more fervid than Charles Wesley," the Sir Thomas Browne and Blaise Pascal of women, her works "more meditative than Hervey's *Meditations,* more devotional than Hannah More's *Private Devotions.*" To Isa Blagden, the Brownings' friend and confidante, Barrett Browning was a haloed saint and her poetic witness to God as divine as the song of angels. Blagden depicts her friend's entry into heaven:

> . . . The seraph chorus bowed
> And leant entranced from jasper thrones to hear
> A mortal's voice so nigh the throne of God.

Within the growing body of recent criticism on the works of Barrett Browning, however, surprisingly little attention has been paid to Barrett Browning as a religious poet. Perhaps the interest in mesmerism and spiritualism that she shared with other prominent writers, artists, and intellectuals (Harriet Beecher Stowe, for example) seems rather too bizarre for serious speculation. (How could a classical scholar, a reader of contemporary letters and philosophy, believe in the hocus-pocus of miraculous healing, séance, and table rapping?) Perhaps too the modern critic finds Barrett Browning's religion too conventional. Dorothy Mermin, for example, comments that "Elizabeth Barrett's religious poems do not doubt, and rarely struggle. Nor do they pay attention to the great religious questions of the time. They give an almost childishly literal picture of a heaven inhabited by a tender Christ, adoring

---

1. Rosenblum, "Face to Face: Elizabeth Barrett Browning's *Aurora Leigh* and Nineteenth-Century Poetry," 323; also in the early poem "An Essay on Mind" (*CWEBB* 1:81.662–63) Barrett comments that "face to face" souls see as they are seen, an allusion to 1 Cor. 13:12. She also uses the expression to mean directly confronting God, death, and eternity, but in *Sonnets from the Portuguese* she revises the figure as face to face with the beloved, as noted in Chapter 4.

angels, and a paternal deity who reminds us rather too much of Edward Moulton-Barrett."[2]

Then there is the further problem of a twentieth-century critic's respecting the religion of *any* Victorian woman. After all, traditional religions bind women in servitude to the patriarchy and male-power hierarchy. Simone de Beauvoir says that women are denied transcendence in the social and political world; therefore they seek it in the religious. At all ages girls and women are more religious than their brothers, de Beauvoir notes, because they sense that God's Transcendence surpasses male transcendence and through religion alone can women partake of such Transcendence. Naturally man, who has power and meaning in the present world, abandons God to woman, who

> is asked in the name of God not so much to accept her inferiority as to believe that, thanks to Him, she is the equal of the lordly male; even the temptation to revolt is suppressed by the claim that the injustice is overcome. Woman is no longer denied transcendence, since she is to consecrate her immanence to God; the worth of souls is to be weighed only in heaven and not according to their accomplishments on earth.

Mary Daly insists that this is a bogus hope for transcendence: if God is male, then only a male can be God. Daly suggests an alternate salvation for woman: "[I]f we perceive the good as . . . *not* identical with the intentions of . . . [the] Heavenly Father, but rather with Be-ing in which we participate actively by the qualitative leap of courage in the face of patriarchy, the magic collar that was choking us is shattered." Barrett Browning accepted the doctrines of the patriarchy of God, the Incarnation and Resurrection of Christ, and the divine inspiration of Scripture. Therefore one might well conclude that she was choked by the "magic collar." And if this is the case, then the religious words and works of such an enslaved victim may have limited intellectual or aesthetic interest to a contemporary critic—except perhaps to document victimization. To the degree that Barrett Browning's ideas are original or a deliberate

---

2. Tilton, "Memorial to *Last Poems*," in *Poems by Elizabeth Barrett Browning*, by Elizabeth Barrett Browning, 4:63, 64; Blagden, "To George Sand on Her Interview with Elizabeth Barrett Browning," in *Victorian Women Poets: An Anthology*, ed. Angela Leighton and Margaret Reynolds, 170.55–57; Mermin, *Elizabeth Barrett Browning: The Origins of a New Poetry*, 69.

revision, however, they most certainly deserve attention. And to the degree that they seem derivative, one should note that they may very well have represented a remarkable breakthrough for the poet. As historian Gerda Lerner observes, women of succeeding generations often had the same or similar insights in theology and philosophy because they had no "shoulders of giants" upon which to stand, their male peers having refused to include them in the ongoing dialogues across the centuries.[3] It is to Barrett Browning's credit that she sought out the giants and engaged them in philosophical and religious debate. I shall argue not only that she faced theological issues of her own time but also that her religious convictions colored every aspect of her ideology—politics, gender, sexual love, social activism—and that apart from the religious context, one cannot adequately interpret many works of the Barrett Browning canon.

II

There are several angles from which to observe the very phenomenon of female spirituality. Recently, feminist theologians and cultural historians have speculated about woman's unique religious experience, confronted the sexism in Western religious thought, reinterpreted religious doctrine as it is perceived by women, and recovered empowering myths of the feminine already encoded (though often suppressed) in Judaism and Christianity. Elisabeth Schüssler Fiorenza, Nehama Aschkenasy, Marina Warner, Susan Haskins, and Elaine Pagels, for example, have illuminated the accounts of Eve, the Virgin Mary, Mary Magdalene, and the Old Testament prophetess figure—*as they speak of female spiritual experience.* Rosemary Radford Ruether, among others, has explored the dualistic thought in Christianity and what it means for woman as Other. Ruether interprets the womanly (and empowering) aspects of the "spiritually feminine" Jesus as commonly envisioned in Victorian pietism. Elizabeth A. Johnson suggests that the christology of Sophia-creator shatters the male dominance carried in the language of Jesus as Logos. With such a Jesus, woman—prohibited from participating in the *"imago dei"*—finds the possibility of transcendence in becoming *"imago Christi."* Some, like Judith Plaskow, have undermined the very notion of sin as it pertains to

---

3. de Beauvoir, *The Second Sex,* 621; Daly, *Beyond God the Father: Toward a Philosophy of Women's Liberation,* 189; Lerner, *The Creation of Feminist Consciousness,* 166.

females. The New Testament text and the theological tradition are male produced, speaking of male experience, and defining sin in such terms as pride, separation, will to power, and exploitation because men exist in the hypermasculine culture, a culture that imperfectly expresses female religious experience. Thus, female "sin," Plaskow suggests, is perhaps not hubris but rather the passivity that prohibits her transcendence.[4]

Admittedly, Barrett Browning is to a degree bound by the myths and doctrines of the patriarchal Bible and the theological and poetic tradition, but she appropriates myth and dogma to her own ends. This book will explore her revisionism of classical and biblical myth, uncover her sources for religious doctrine, and scrutinize her modification of the theological "fathers" (St. Paul to Swedenborg). Issues to be addressed are transcendental mysticism, female androgyny as response to a "feminine" Jesus, and the poet's reaction to institutionalized misogyny in the Christian religion. Major works will be studied as encoding her insights on grace and works, death and resurrection. Of especial importance is the tension between pride and humility that is potentially unsettling to any Christian but especially nettlesome to the Victorian woman poet aspiring to excel in the divine calling of poet and prophet. Boldly she affirms—in her letters and especially in the poetic canon—her role as a prophet, wisdom figure, teacher for God. Recent critics have apologized for Barrett Browning's orthodoxy and ignored her unorthodoxy, but have paid little attention to her struggles of faith. Yet tracing such a woman's uniquely spiritual quest for transcendence is an intriguing journey, whether or not one aspires to a similar destination.

III

In the nineteenth century's rough seas of growing skepticism about religion, intellectuals and poets attempted to anchor their souls and minds in different harbors. For some, it was nature and beauty (or culture and beauty); for others, philosophical agnosticism or despair. Religion may well be the opiate of the masses, as Marx claims, but Matthew Arnold

4. Ruether, *New Woman, New Earth: Sexist Ideologies and Human Liberation,* 24, 77; Johnson, "The Maleness of Christ," in *The Special Nature of Women?* ed. Anne Carr and Elisabeth Schüssler Fiorenza, 113; Plaskow, *Sex, Sin and Grace: Women's Experience and the Theologies of Reinhold Niebuhr and Paul Tillich,* 23, 51, 68, 93.

suggests that upper classes and intellectuals are free from the "want of intellectual seriousness" necessary to accept the mysteries, myths, and doctrines of religion. More poetically, in "Dover Beach," the persona discovers that:

> The Sea of Faith
> Was once, too, at the full, and round earth's shore
> Lay like the folds of a bright girdle furled.
> But now I only hear
> Its melancholy, long withdrawing roar . . .

Florence Nightingale calls hers an age in which atheism and indifference are man and wife, and "we do not believe in a type of perfection into which each man is to be developed, we do not believe in social progress, we do not believe in religious progress, we do not believe in God." Thomas Carlyle complains that God's absolute Laws have been replaced by Moral Philosophies, computations of Profit and Loss, considerations of Pleasures, Virtue, and the Moral Sublime: "There is no religion; there is no God; man has lost his soul, and vainly seeks antiseptic salt. Vainly: in killing Kings, in passing Reform Bills, in French Revolutions, Manchester Insurrections, is found no remedy." Carlyle apparently believed that Christianity as doctrine had run its course, for one day when he and Robert Browning were walking together in Paris, they came upon an image of the Crucifixion, and—glaring at it—Carlyle remarked, "Ah, poor fellow, *your* part is played out!"[5]

Of the established church in England, Ralph Waldo Emerson as foreign observer reports, "The spirit that dwelt in [the national] church has glided away to animate other activities, and they who come to the old shrine find apes and players rustling the old garments." He goes on to add that the church has nothing left but tradition and possession, that it is merely reduced to "good breeding" and national pride, and implies that the members of the clergy are appointed by connections rather than because of piety or erudition. Emerson further notes how the lower classes stay

5. Arnold, *God and the Bible*, in *The Works of Matthew Arnold in Fifteen Volumes*, by Matthew Arnold, 8:xlii; "Dover Beach," in *The Poems of Matthew Arnold*, 256.21–25; Nightingale, *Searchers after Truth among the Artizans of England*, in *"Cassandra" and Other Selections from "Suggestions for Thought,"* 118, 114; Carlyle, *Past and Present*, in *The Works of Thomas Carlyle in Thirty Volumes*, 10:137; Orr, *A Handbook to the Works of Robert Browning*, 250–51.

away from the English church in droves; he remarks that the poor have no incentive for churchgoing, that one gentleman in the House of Commons reportedly said he never saw a ragged coat inside the walls of the English church. From within the church, clergyman/novelist Charles Kingsley takes a similar view of the church's relevance; precisely at midcentury he notes, "The place breathed imbecility, and unreality, and sleepy life-in-death, while the whole nineteenth century went roaring on its way outside."[6]

Not only the poorest of the poor and the most privileged of intellectuals but also the informed of the working class apparently vested little faith in the church. In *Hard Times,* Charles Dickens wonders who belongs to the eighteen denominations of fictional Coketown. Whoever does, the narrator adds, they are surely not of the laboring classes. Of that class Nightingale comments, "most of the educated among the operatives, especially in the northern manufacturing towns, have turned their faces to atheism or at least to theism—not three in a hundred go to *any* place of worship; the moral and intellectual among them being, almost without an exception, 'infidels.'" In Elizabeth Gaskell's novel *North and South,* such an infidel laborer from a northern manufacturing town points out to the Dissenting pastor from the south of England that the English industrialist or worker may *claim* for form's sake to believe in the Bible but most certainly does not ask himself each day upon rising, "What shall I do to get hold on eternal life?" but "What shall I do to fill my purse this blessed day?" No doubt the behavior of the so-called religious persons among the capitalist class prejudiced the workers against involvement with the established church. In an "address" by the radical Felix Holt, George Eliot exposes the "abomination of men calling themselves religious while living in splendour on ill-gotten gains."[7] Thus, if neither aristocrat nor commoner, capitalist nor worker, intellectual nor ignorant took an interest in religion, one wonders just who were the people in church on a Victorian Sunday.

Finally, it was generally assumed that, whatever religion should be, it should *not* be a field in which women dabble. For example, in 1854

---

6. Emerson, "English Traits and Lectures and Biographical Sketches," in *Essays and Lectures,* 886–90; Kingsley, *Yeast,* 313.

7. Dickens, *Hard Times,* 26–27; Nightingale, *Searchers after Truth,* in *"Cassandra" and Other Selections,* 8; Gaskell, *North and South,* 289; Eliot, *Address to the Working-men by Felix Holt,* in *The Writings of George Eliot Together with the Life by J. W. Cross,* 21:269.

the English clergyman John Angell James published *Female Piety; or, The Young Woman's Friend and Guide through Life to Immortality*, in which he argues that neither reason nor Christianity "invites women to the professor's chair, or conducts her to the bar, or makes her welcome to the pulpit," or suffers her to teach or speak in the Church of God. But reason and Christianity both "bid her beware how she lays aside the delicacy of her sex" and listens to doctrines that make a dupe of her. Even John Ruskin says theology is the one "dangerous science" for women, though they seem determined to plunge headlong "without one thought of [their] incompetency" in a field in which the wisest of men have erred.

> Strange, that they will complacently and
> pridefully bind up whatever vice or folly
> there is in them, whatever arrogance, petulance,
> or blind incomprehensiveness, into one bitter bundle
> of consecrated myrrh. Strange in creatures born to
> be Love visible, that where they can know least, they
> will condemn first, and think to recommend themselves
> to their Master, by crawling up the steps of His
> judgement-throne, to divide it with Him.

To inhibiting and compartmentalized thinking of this type, Barrett Browning responds:

> There is a feeling abroad which appears to me (I say it with deference) nearer to superstition than to religion, that there should be no touching of vessels except by consecrated fingers, nor any naming of holy names except in consecrated places. As if life were not a continual sacrament to man, since Christ brake the daily bread of it in His hands! (*CWEBB* 2:146)

The "[un]consecrated fingers"—whatever else they might be—are certainly feminine fingers. Yet Barrett asserts (here in the preface of *A Drama of Exile* in which she challenges the religious and poetic paradigms of *Paradise Lost*) that religious speculation is decidedly within her reach. She is devoted both to intellectual speculation and to religion, pursuits that, to Arnold, make odd bedfellows, even in the nineteenth century. Deirdre David, in her study of the "intellectual women" Barrett Browning, George Eliot, and Harriet Martineau, notes that in Victorian England, "[s]ome women intellectuals . . . vigorously interrogated an ideology that mandated the discipline of female mind by male authority."[8] I find it significant that, of the three female intellectuals in David's book, two grew away from the faith of childhood, and only Barrett Browning remained devoted to God and Christianity. It may not have been easy, given that religion was as controlled by male ideology as was the secular world, with the added power of God's voice to sanction the control. Nevertheless Barrett Browning's poetry concerns itself with the struggle to know God and truth, as well as to know her own soul and to transcend spiritual limitations. She always maintains that art and faith are inseparable, that "Christ's religion is essentially poetry—poetry glorified" (*BC* 5:220).

IV

The young Elizabeth Barrett's religious education began early; her first teacher was her mother, Mary Moulton-Barrett, of whom the young Barrett writes in a birthday ode: "she . . . turned my infant thoughts to a redeeming God!" (*BC* 1:92).[9] With her father the young Elizabeth attended the nearest dissenting chapel of the Congregationalists; she especially appreciated the simplicity, the "arid, grey Puritanism in the clefts of their souls," and the fact that they knew clearer than state churches the meaning of the "liberty of Christ" (*BC* 11:10). This liberty of faith remains an important credo. By her own testimony, at the age of twelve, Elizabeth Barrett was declaring her religious independence. She notes, "I was in great danger of becoming the founder of a religion of my own. I revolted at the idea of an established religion—my faith was sincere but my religion was founded solely on the imagination. It was not the deep persuasion of the mild Christian but the wild visions of an enthusiast" (*BC* 1:351). Though she read several theologians (especially the English divines and the Greek Christian Fathers), her

---

8. James, *Female Piety,* in *Women in English Religion 1700–1925,* ed. Dale A. Johnson, 129–30; Ruskin, *Of Queens' Gardens,* in *Sesame and Lilies,* 143–44; David, *Intellectual Women and Victorian Patriarchy: Harriet Martineau, Elizabeth Barrett Browning, George Eliot,* 24.

9. Her mother continued to offer religious counsel; on the sacrament, she notes: "May it be now, & *ever* to my beloved child, her strength in weakness, her comfort in sorrow . . . as long as sin & suffering belong to humanity" (*BC* 1:229).

primary theological education came from the Bible. As a matter of course, she read seven chapters of the Bible daily,[10] and of her religious reading, she announces:

> although I have read rather widely the divinity of the Greek Fathers, Gregory, Chrysostom, & so forth, & have of course informed myself in the works generally of our old English divines, Hooker's, Jeremy Taylor's, & so forth, I am not by any means a frequent reader of books of theology as such . . . I have looked into the Tracts from curiosity & to hear what the world was talking of; & I was disappointed *even* in the degree of intellectual power displayed in them—From motives of a desire of theological instruction I very seldom read any book except God's own. (*BC* 8:107)

It might be assumed that the early reading in the Bible, the Greek Fathers, and English divines (Richard Hooker and Jeremy Taylor) had a lasting effect on the aspiring young poet, and such is the case. Hooker she compliments for his high "compositional *art*," Taylor for his genius (*BC* 4:131). In an unpublished childhood poem, "On laying Hooker under my pillow at night," she testifies to her attraction to the great man's spiritual teachings; Taylor's words she apparently kept by her side throughout life. In any case, his *Rules and Exercises of Holy Living* was sold in the Browning Collections. The Greek Christian Fathers she encountered later, and her diary of 1831–1832 contains multiple references to them as well as to other Greek Fathers and to Hooker, whom she was still studying. In 1832 she had memorized 1860 lines of the "noble and tender" Gregory Nazianzen and 640 of "eloquent" Chrysostom.[11] But in addition to Chrysostom and Nazianzen, Hooker and Taylor, she also studied Martin Luther (whom she found a "schoolman of the most scholastic sect; most offensive, most absurd" [*LEBB* 2:426]), Newman, Pusey, and the "Tracts *against* the times" (as she called them in *Aurora*

---

10. Barrett Browning, *Diary by EBB: The Unpublished Diary of Elizabeth Barrett Browning, 1831–1832,* 19.

11. The manuscript "on laying Hooker under my pillow" is in the Armstrong Browning Library of Baylor University; the sale of the Jeremy Taylor volume is recorded in *BC* 4:134–35; readings and discussion of Chrysostom and Gregory in Barrett Browning, *Diary by EBB,* 4, 26, 97, 105, 113, 123, 125, 128, 132, 140, 162, 163, 168, 179, 183, 187, 240; Hooker's discourse on justification by faith or works in ibid., 177; memorization in Barrett Browning, *Hitherto Unpublished Poems and Stories with an Inedited Autobiography,* 2:134.

Leigh [*AL* 1.394]), the great poet Milton (whose doctrine of Christian liberty she advocated but whom she called "a great bigot" in regard to his anti-Papist views),[12] as well as Christian socialists such as Charles Kingsley, whose humanism she admired but whose socialism she detested. Like her fictional Aurora Leigh who has read "moral books," "genial books," "merry books," "melancholy books," the poet herself studied theorists of ethics, morality, theology, and philosophy. Aurora says:

> I read books bad and good—some bad and good
> At once (good aims not always make good books)
> . . . .
> . . . books that prove
> God's being so definitely, that man's doubt
> Grows self-defined the other side the line,
> Made atheist by suggestion . . .
>
> (*AL* 1.779–85)

Further, Barrett Browning avidly read the heretical mystic Emanuel Swedenborg, in 1842 referring to him as a "mad genius" and a "madman," a writer of beautiful things but manifold absurdities. But in the final decade of her life she read Swedenborg hungrily as her body weakened and she felt her soul growing nearer to the spirit world that she again longed yet dreaded to encounter.[13] Increasingly in these final years she filled her mind with Swedenborgian mysticism, as she pondered the "luminous side" of death, which is, after all, a "face-to-face intimacy; age, a thickening of the mortal mask between souls" (*LEBB* 2:140).

Barrett Browning claimed that she was not a controversialist, that she would not debate the intricacies of doctrine and liturgy (issues that she believed mainly concerned the Anglo-Catholic, or Tractarian, movement). Although she classified herself as an Independent or Dissenter, by early adulthood she had taken to avoiding the religious services of her father's

---

12. Barrett Browning's annotation is handwritten in her personal copy of *The Prose Works of John Milton: Containing His Principal Political and Ecclesiastical Pieces*, 2:186–87. (This copy is in the Alexander Turnbull Library, National Library of New Zealand, Te Puna Mātauranga o Aotearoa. Transcription by Robert Petre.)

13. She objects that Swedenborgianism was detected in her writings even before she knew Swedenborg well (*LEBB* 2:157). However, the letters of the 1840s reveal that she was immersed in Swedenborg's doctrine and could point out the central tenets of his *Heaven and Hell.*

church. (She was highly critical of most sermons, and in the years before her marriage her frail health provided a convenient excuse to skip them.) Besides, why should she attend holy services when—late in life as well as early—they held little meaning to her. She comments, "In truth, I can never see anything in these sacramental ordinances except a prospective sign in one (Baptism) and a memorial sign in the other . . the Lord's Supper, & could not recognize either under any modification, as a peculiar instrument of grace, mystery, or the like" (*BC* 7:211–12). She agreed to marry Robert Browning in an Anglican church (so long as it was not Puseyite), and they baptized their only child in the French Lutheran Church; she records sharing Communion with the Presbyterians; and when in Rome on Christmas Day, the Brownings attended mass at St. Peter's. But for the most part, however, she avoided established religion, though she defended the good works of Bible societies and missionary societies. She considered her views by no means conventional, saying, "I have been called orthodox by infidels, and heterodox by church-people . . ." (*LEBB* 2:420). To a Predestinarian she notes that "Arminians in general w^d. call me a Calvinist,—while Calvinists w^d. call me an Arminian" (*BC* 8:22). She steadfastly refused to be pinned down by the dogma of any church, once saying, "I find it impossible to believe that God *cares* to what church a man belongs" (*LMO* 160)[14] and speculating whether the best Christians are outside of the churches rather than within them. To her, Dissenters are too narrow; Evangelicals should have broken with the state church and had done with it; Methodists—though devoted to preaching Christ's truth—have "strange contractive opinions on the subject of literature & the arts . . . a contracted spirituality as well as a contracted taste" (*BC* 5:278); Calvinists teach a doctrine of reprobation, "a very evil one certainly, & pestiferous with the fruit of its cruelty" (*BC* 5:306);[15] Unitarianism is "ice-bound" (*BC* 5:277), no religion at all, and especially objectionable because it does not accept the divinity of Christ (a doctrine that, if she ceased to recognize, she would have to "throw up revelation altogether" [*LEBB* 2:156]); Catholicism with its altars and votive candles is "religion sensualized" (the opera in place of the tragedy, dancers in the place of the poet, theatrical effects in the place

14. Actually, she is quoting Harriet Beecher Stowe, but adds, "I entirely agree with her."

15. Barrett Browning writes that in her view "the saved are saved by grace . . . the Lost are lost by their choice of free will" (*BC* 6:192).

of "God's great scenery") (*BC* 5:182); Tractarianism is but a step away from Catholicism ("Puseyism is the consummation of High-Churchism, even as Romanism is of Puseyism . . . if I held High-Churchism today at noon, I sh^d. be a Puseyite by break of day, and if I were a Puseyite in the morning, the twilight w^d. find me at confession . . . infallibly as any pope!" [*BC* 5:236]). Rather than some individual church, she claimed membership in "Christ's invisible Church as referred to in Scripture," a church broad enough to include all humankind who accept the Savior's "humanity and divinity" (*LEBB* 2:156) and set about following truth as they understand truth.

It is an error to suggest that Barrett Browning evaded difficult issues—religious or otherwise. The purpose of this book is to examine her ideology, her "everlasting face to face with God." All her literary life was a religious quest, the several stages of which were: 1) the rejection of pride and acceptance of grace, 2) the affirmation of the gospel of Suffering and the gospel of Work, 3) the internalization of the doctrine of Apocalypse (rejecting the doctrine of the end of the world in favor of the injunction to renovate and resurrect this present world), and 4) the ascent to divine love and divine truth (the final consummation of the Apocalypse thus internalized).

My method will be in each chapter to focus upon a major work of the Barrett Browning canon and explore the theological issues in that work: how and where the poet followed and took issue with the tenets she inherited from the Christian theological tradition and the male poetic tradition in Christianity, John Milton being the poet she most elaborately, consciously, and even laboriously undertook to revise. In the separate chapters I shall study Barrett Browning's Christ as Promethean hero in *The Seraphim;* her Eve exiled from spiritual paradise in *A Drama of Exile;* the apocalypse of the present political world (chiefly in Italy) in *Casa Guidi Windows* and *Poems before Congress;* glorious resurrection in *Sonnets from the Portuguese* and incomplete, thwarted resurrection in *Aurora Leigh;* Woman as Wisdom, prophetess for God in advocating the social gospel and Swedenborgian Love and Wisdom (especially in *Aurora Leigh*).

In *The Seraphim,* Barrett revises Aeschylus in presenting Jesus as Christian counterpart of the "free-souled reverent love" for humankind that Prometheus has demonstrated in classical tradition. Chapter 1 focuses upon the Incarnation and redemption evident in *The Seraphim* and upon Prometheanism in the poet herself as compared to Milton's in *Paradise Lost* and Shelley's in *Prometheus Unbound.* In the person of Mary

Magdalene, at the feet of the crucified Jesus, Barrett finds an analogue for her own struggle with selfhood; finally she rejects Prometheanism as ungodly pride.

The central work of Elizabeth Barrett's 1844 volume is *A Drama of Exile,* in which Eve (as central figure) presumes to take upon herself the role of Adam's tutor, teaching him (and by extension their descendants) the gospel of Work (that is, working *for the sake of grace* as opposed to the dichotomy of grace versus work). In Chapter 2 the Victorian role of Ideal Woman as sacrificing wife/mother/nurse/caregiver versus the role of woman as reformer/activist/idealogue is further explored via several manifestations of exiled Eve, especially in the ballads and monologues of the 1844 volume.

In *Casa Guidi Windows* and *Poems before Congress,* the poet argues that this present world is a worthy object of love, that the Apocalypse means bringing the "Great Hereafter" to this present political world, and as such it is the responsibility of all true Christian reformers. In Chapter 3 I explore this "internalization" of Apocalypse and the manner in which Barrett Browning takes issue with the political ideology of Carlyle, Fourier, Owen, Proudhon, Blanc, and Kingsley on various issues of heroism and reform.

If the Incarnation affirmed in *The Seraphim* is a central tenet of Barrett Browning's faith, certainly the doctrine of Resurrection is just as central. Her letters and poems are permeated with the Lazarus/Resurrection motif: the rebirth of art and the artist, of love, of slain republics, of individual lives. Chapter 4 examines the rebirth of love in *Sonnets from the Portuguese* and of a murdered nation in the political poems. *Aurora Leigh* is studied in terms of its successful and failed resurrections, the most notable failure being the case of Marian Erle, a striking depiction of rape as "murder" from which there is no resurrection. I contend that, in spite of Barrett Browning's Swedenborgianism (or perhaps because of it), not every soul has promise of resurrection to complete love and blessedness, in this world or the next.

In Barrett Browning's personal mythology woman as prophet is represented as Miriam, Eve, Mary Magdalene, the Pythian, Cassandra, and Godiva. Invoking the figure of woman as Wisdom (the Sophia/Minerva/Diotima paradigm), both Aurora Leigh and her creator presume to serve as prophetess of God and to teach a social gospel of Love. Draped in the mantle of the prophetess, Barrett Browning condemns social evils (such as child labor, prostitution, and slavery) and preaches a Swedenborgian gospel of "Divine Love and Divine Wisdom," a gospel that she sees as but an extension of New Testament teachers such as St. Paul and St. John. The final chapter analyzes the poet's skillful manipulation of the icon of Woman as Wisdom, together with the "wise" doctrines that she professes.

Elizabeth Barrett Browning asserts that "any work of Art, however vivid & consummate, which excludes the sense of a soul within us & of a God above us & takes life in its conventionality denuded of its inner mystery,—*will* be felt in the end to be one-sided & unsufficing,—& deficient in the elements of greatness" (*BC* 7:214). Striving to be great as Christian, as teacher, and as poet, she is ever aware of the "inner mystery" that this book attempts, in a small way, to elucidate.

1

Prometheus and Jesus as "Free-souled, Reverent Love"

> . . . Prometheus preferred a
> solitary agony: nay, he even
> permitted his zeal and tenderness
> for the peace of others, to
> abstract him from that agony's
> intenseness.
>
> —Barrett Browning, preface
> to *Prometheus Bound*

> You leave Saint Paul for Aeschylus?
> —Who made his Titan's arch-device
> The giving men *blind hopes* to spice
> The meal of life with, else devoured
> In bitter haste, while lo, death loured
> Before them at the platter's edge!
>
> —Robert Browning, "Easter-Day"

I

*P*ublishing *The Seraphim* in 1838, at the comparatively young age of thirty-two, was for Elizabeth Barrett a bold step taken out of the expected order. Imagine John Milton publishing *Paradise Regained* before *Paradise Lost,* and doing so in his thirties rather than his sixties. That is a fair comparison for *The Seraphim* and *A Drama of Exile* (1844), because the former is about Christ's redemptive act on Calvary (Barrett fixed the dramatic moment of triumph at the hour of his victorious death, rather than his victory over Satan's temptation in the wilderness, as Milton had done), while the latter is a sequel to *Paradise Lost,* following Adam and Eve into exile from Eden. And just as the 1844 revision of *Paradise Lost* could have been considered presumptuous, so could *The Seraphim* have been considered a brash effort because of both the poet's age and her gender. In her presentation of the choir of seraphim witnessing Jesus' death in Judea and adjudicating between human and angelic love for the dying god, she no doubt anticipated that she would be compared with Milton. And compared she was. The *Quarterly Review* of September 1840 criticized that Barrett had chosen a subject "from which Milton would have shrunk, and which Miss Barrett would not have attempted, if she had more seriously considered its absolute unapproachableness" (*BC* 4:415). But Barrett does not shrink from spiritual and religious themes because, like Milton, she considers them the most grand and universal, beautiful and good—in a word, poetic. In the preface to *The Seraphim* she says that the irreligious poet is no poet at all and "The poetic wing, if it move, ascends" (*CWEBB* 1:169).

Yet a more obvious similarity than *Paradise Lost,* a comparison openly invited in the poem's preface, is that to Aeschylus's *Prometheus Bound,* which Barrett had recently translated. She loved Aeschylus from the time of her first acquaintance with him, committing to memory some eighteen hundred lines of his verse, and she believed Aeschylus's Prometheus to be "one of the most original, and grand, and attaching characters ever conceived by the mind of man" (*CWEBB* 6:85).[1] Numerous parallels exist between the Greek Titan and the Jewish teacher/martyr. As Prometheus, the thief of fire, benefactor of man, and iconoclast of Olympian order, was suspended on Mount Caucasus in full view of earth, sky, and ocean, the iconoclastic Jesus was suspended on a cross planted on a hill, and (although God turned away) onlookers gathered to revere or revile him. Both works are written as dramas that focus upon the suffering,

---

1. In her diary Barrett Browning writes, "I quite love the Prometheus. It is an exquisite creation: & besides,—I was *so* happy when I read the *first* scenes of that play!" (*Diary by EBB*, 91). The 1832 record of memorized lines is from *Hitherto Unpublished Poems,* 2:134.

courage, nobility, and sublimity of the martyr. And in both, the gift of hope is the final (and finest) gift that humans receive from the divine benefactor—Promethean hope through fire/knowledge coupled with the inability to foreknow one's fate, Christian hope of restoration to the Christian equivalent of the Golden Age—reforging the golden chain "to join, in mysterious union, the natural and the spiritual, the mortal and the eternal, the creature and the Creator" (*CWEBB* 1:59). Both works end in a victory: for Prometheus a victory in defiance by refusing to grant Zeus the foreknowledge of the overthrow of his realm, for Jesus victory over sin and death, thereby ushering in a new age in which God's realm would extend over all races and include all people.

Prometheus Bound presents the *rhetoric* of a "sublime" god-turned-mortal (who says he finds it hard to brave the curse upon him "in silence or in speech" [*PB* 20], but who retorts or otherwise responds to the taunts of Force and Strength, the pleas of Oceanus, the sophistry of Mercury, and the plaints of Io); *The Seraphim,* on the other hand, presents the *silence* of a god "in Adam's clay" (*S* 239). Barrett speculates that had Aeschylus known of Christian redemption, he would have chosen Jesus as the more poetic and sublime subject, for "the gravitation of poetry is upwards" (*CWEBB* 1:169); and just as Milton selected as the noblest possible topic for his epic the Fall of the human race and the redemption to a paradise "happier far," Barrett believes her (Christian) topic more noble than that of (pagan) Aeschylus. *Her* Jesus will suffer pain, contempt, and abandonment, just as Prometheus did, but without hint of guile, pomposity, or revenge, traits that she sees in Prometheus on the rock ("vast, melancholy, beneficent, malign" [*CWEBB* 1:165]). Instead of the "Titanic 'I can revenge,'" he will demonstrate to the universe "the celestial 'I can forgive'" (*CWEBB* 1:165). The 1838 volume *The Seraphim, and Other Poems* is an important step in Barrett's developing poetic career because in it she seeks her way through her adolescent Promethean stage and into the adult spirituality that marks her later works. She flirts with Satanic/Promethean romanticism, but in *The Seraphim* she switches the focus of her *identity* from the suffering heroic martyr Prometheus to the suffering penitent Mary Magdalene, who represents for Barrett humility and love, as well as the role of female witness of the divine message, a role that Elizabeth Barrett intends to perform in her own age.

II

Barrett says that Aeschylus was on her mind when she composed *The Seraphim* because she had just recently finished a translation of *Prometheus Bound.* Written in twelve days, the translation was considered a failure—both by the translator and by the critics. Barrett, who always possessed a gift for self-criticism, was later to pronounce it "cold as Caucasus on the snow-peak, & as flat as Salisbury plain" (*BC* 10:66). Around 1845, Barrett completed a second translation (published in her *Poems,* 1850). If, as Dorothy Mermin says, she had outgrown her Promethean stage and *The Seraphim* is "a repudiation of Prometheus, Byron, and the idea of heroic rebellion," why expend energy on translating Aeschylus once more when she could just wipe the slate clean and go forward with original works? The possibility of a second translation had been in mind for a while; she notes in 1841 that she has, in her translation, bound the Titan to a colder rock than was intended and she wishes to "vindicate [her]self by doing it again" (*BC* 5:26). Later she says the second translation is an act of "[w]ashing out my conscience—effacing the blot on my escutcheon—performing an expiation" (*BC* 10:105). She must have loved her own reputation enough to perform the expiation, or loved Aeschylus ("divinest of all the divine Greek souls" [*BC* 10:111]) enough to make atonement, or Prometheus enough to regret that she had sinned against him. In any case, generations of critics have noted that Barrett's early works are Promethean: Tricia Lootens remarks that—in the canonization and decanonization after her death—the recognition of Barrett Browning as a "Promethean intellectual" was the first stage of the poet's reception into the canon.[2]

Essentially, Barrett finds the myth of Prometheus "original . . . grand . . . attaching." At an early age she must have found him so: an unpublished notebook in the Wellesley College collection contains a translation of Goethe's "Prometheus" in Elizabeth Barrett's handwriting.[3]

---

2. Mermin, *Origins of New Poetry,* 61; Lootens, *Lost Saints: Silence, Gender, and Victorian Literary Canonization,* 128. According to Lootens, subsequent stages are the pure wife/mother/poet (a "secular trinity"), the romantic heroine ("Andromeda of Wimpole Street"), and the shrieking "spasmodic" Pythian (129–57).

3. Pocket notebook 1:6–7 Manuscript D70, Wellesley College Library Special Collections. A review of *The Seraphim* notes Barrett's indebtedness to Goethe (*BC* 4:383), whom she admired for his "essential genius" (*BC* 4:120).

But she was not alone in her attachment. In her century, Coleridge proclaims Prometheus as theoretical reason; Goethe, as creativity in the face of repression; and Nietzsche, as the Titanic artist finding in himself the daring belief and wisdom to create and destroy. Both Shelleys, Percy and Mary, were obsessed by Prometheus and treated the myth in *Prometheus Unbound* and *Frankenstein,* respectively. The Promethean demeanor—dramatic, solitary, defiant, noble, unyielding—had captivated the imagination of the romantic movement in England and on the Continent and the girl-poet Elizabeth Barrett had, in her formative years, admired the Prometheanism of romantic poetry, especially that of Lord Byron, who once commented that Prometheus influenced "all or any thing that I have written."[4] In a letter to her friend Miss Mitford (in a response to the comment that Prometheus is the "new science"), she says, "Surely 'he is the sign of this great ruined struggling Humanity, arising through the agony & the ruin to the renovation & the spiritual empire. I cant consent to desecrate him with the badge of a lower symbol" (*BC* 5:227). Thus, Prometheus was the Ur-myth of the romantic age, and the young Elizabeth Barrett—a child of that age—was appropriately fascinated with the grand Titan.

One of the many attractions to Barrett was that she connected Prometheus's creation of mortals with the creative act of making art, especially poetic art. Such classic writers as Aesop, Hyginus, Apollodorus, Lucian, Ovid, Martial, Propertius, Horace, and Pausanius all name Prometheus as the creator of mankind, some versions suggesting that creation was of his own volition, others implying that he worked under the direction of Zeus, who more hastily repented of his erstwhile creation than did Jehovah in the Noah story. The myth of Prometheus as creator of the species came to represent human creative genius. Ernst Kris and Otto Kurz, for example, posit that Prometheus's breathing of life into mortals is the animating power of the artist.[5] We know that Barrett considered

---

4. Coleridge, "On the Prometheus of Aeschylus," in *Coleridge's Prose Works (Miscellanies, Aesthetic and Literary),* 5:77; Goethe, *Goethe's Popular Works,* 2:212; Nietzsche, *The Birth of Tragedy or Hellenism and Pessimism,* 77; Byron, *The Works of Lord Byron: Letters and Journals,* 4:175.

5. Aesop, *Aesop without Morals: The Famous Fables and a Life of Aesop* 136, 193; Hyginus, *Poetica Astronomica* 2.15, in *The Myths of Hyginus,* 201; Apollodorus, *The Library* 1:7; Lucian, *Lucian* 2:249; Ovid, *Metamorphoses* 1.78–83; Martial, *Selected Epigrams of Martial* 10.39; Propertius, 3.5.8–11 in *Poems of Propertius,* 135; Horace, *Odes*

her thwarted creative/artistic self as a Prometheus in chains, for when she declined to write a work on behalf of the Corn Law League on the grounds that her father and Mr. Kenyon did not approve, she says to Miss Mitford that she is "chafing against a bit, like my Prometheus" for having given in (*BC* 10:66).

One memorable precedent for viewing Prometheus's "animating fire" as literary genius is in Madame de Staël's *Corinne; or, Italy* (which Barrett terms "an immortal book, & deserves to be read three score & ten times—that is, once every year in the age of man" [*BC* 3:25]). In her recitation at the capitol, Corinne sings:

> Imagination gave [Italy] back the world
> Which she had lost. Painters and poets shaped
> Earth and Olympus, and a heaven and hell.
> Her animating fire, by Genius kept,
> Far better guarded than the Pagan gods,
> Found not in Europe a Prometheus
> To bear it from her.[6]

Although Corinne uses the myth for the genius of Italian art, naturally she (as poet, artist, and "improvisatrice") includes herself among the bearers of that animating flame (as Barrett Browning put herself in the company of notable poets such as Byron and Pope and at a later stage Wordsworth, Milton, and Dante). Barrett suggested that her beloved Lord Byron, in spite of hating de Staël, esteemed her *Corinne* and was himself "ignited" by the fire of her art, that Childe Harold spoke with the voice of Corinne (*BC* 3:25). To Barrett the artistic genius of Promethean fire was inspired and beautiful, but dangerous inasmuch as the creator loves the creation too much.

> Eternal Genius! fashion'd like the sun,
> To make all beautiful thou look'st upon!
> Prometheus of our earth! whose kindling smile
> May warm the things of clay a little while;
> Till, by thy touch inspir'd, thine eyes survey'd

1.16.13, in *Horace's "Odes" and "Epodes,"* 75; Pausanius, *Guide to Greece* 1:411; Kris and Kurz, *Legend, Myth, and Magic in the Image of the Artist: A Historical Experiment,* 84–89.

6. de Staël, *Corinne; or, Italy,* 25.

> Thou stoop'st to love the glory thou hast made;
> And weepest, human-like, the mortal's fall,
> When, by-and-bye, a breath disperses all.
> (*CWEBB* 1:64.119–26)

In "To a Poet's Child" (probably addressed to Lord Byron's daughter), she advises that the child live a bland life, avoiding art, fame, and genius because genius is fatal fire, immolating poets young and making orphans:

> And, as a flame springs clear and bright,
> Yet leaveth ashes 'stead of light;
> So genius (fatal gift)! is doom'd
> To leave the heart it fired, consumed.
> (*CWEBB* 1:143.53–56)

The Prometheus myth obviously has special appeal to writers and rebels as a mirror for the self, especially those who see themselves as bold and brilliant, satanic and proud. Shelley's Prometheus is a pacifist, atheist, iconoclast, and idealist, just like Shelley himself. Goethe also sees himself as Promethean: "The old Titan web I cut up according to my measurement," he says. Byron does well to say Prometheus is in everything he has written; Byron is himself an incarnation of the Promethean existence as he sees it, the Byronic (or Promethean) character in life as well as in verse. Not only does Barrett compare herself to Prometheus in a moment of indignation about the Corn League poem, but she also recognizes (as the romantics in general had done) that Milton's Satan is Promethean, a claim she makes in her preface to the 1850 translation of Aeschylus's work as Shelley had done in the preface of his *Prometheus Unbound* (*CWEBB* 6:85). Although she does not say it outright, so is her own Lucifer a Promethean character in *A Drama of Exile,* in which fallen Adam is attracted to the rebellious charisma and magisterial "kingship" still apparent in the fallen angel. Alice Falk says that Barrett Browning was preoccupied with Prometheus because she too was self-willed, self-absorbed, and defiant, just like the romantic version of the Titan.[7] Barrett, who wanted as a child to be Byron's page (*CWEBB* 1:115) and in her 1826 volume described him as a Promethean savior, a "great Deliv'rer" of Greece

---

7. Falk, "Elizabeth Barrett Browning and Her Prometheuses: Self-Will and a Woman Poet," 74–75.

(in "Stanzas on the Death of Lord Byron" [*CWEBB* 1:104.7]), loves Prometheus because he is Byronic, and Byron because he is Promethean. In fact, she refers facetiously to her own "early association with '*Fire-thieves!*'" (*BC* 4:34).

Second, while many artists had adopted Prometheus the creator/artist as a figure for their own creativity, both Prometheus's creation and his theft prove especially provocative for late-eighteenth-century and nineteenth-century female writers in that they feel an injunction against writing. Marjorie Stone comments that Prometheus held a special attraction for Barrett because of his defiance in the face of the "conventionally female attributes of confinement, physical passivity, and self-sacrifice." Thus, to create art or enter into the world of discourse is a Promethean act—defiant and rebellious. Not only is de Staël's Corinne associated with Prometheus, so too is the feminist Mary Wollstonecraft. To Wollstonecraft, as to Coleridge, Promethean fire refers to the "celestial fire of reason," a theft that she readily commits in entering the Enlightenment discourse on education, morals, and sexual politics in *A Vindication of the Rights of Woman*. For Wollstonecraft's daughter Mary Shelley, the creating of human life—however deformed—by Dr. Frankenstein ("The Modern Prometheus") no doubt represents, among other things, the monstrous act of female creativity, with Shelley's psyche depicted as the Promethean/Satanic hero, the "hideous phantasm." British poet Felicia Hemans uses the motif of fire for artistic creativity in "Properzia Rossi," a dramatic monologue for an Italian artist who is, like Corinne, multitalented, in Properzia's case as both poet and musician but chiefly as sculptor. In reference, no doubt, to Prometheus's creation of humans and his animating gift of fire, Properzia laments of her sculpture of Ariadne, "I might have kindled with the fire of heaven, / Things not of such that die." The poet LEL (Letitia Landon) in her poem dedicated to Hemans, uses the Prometheus myth to represent the woman and the poet (and especially the poet who is also woman); the vulture feeding upon the Titan's liver as the "careless tongues and ungenerous words."

> The fable of Prometheus and the vulture
> Reveals the poet's and the woman's heart
> Unkindly are they judged—unkindly treated—[8]

8. Stone, *Elizabeth Barrett Browning*, 72; Wollstonecraft, *Vindication*, 13; Shelley, *Frankenstein; or, the Modern Prometheus*, introduction; Hemans, "Properzia Rossi," in

And Barrett may have had LEL's Promethean allusion in mind in responding to her monody on the death of Hemans. In "Felicia Hemans," Barrett asks: "Would she have lost the poet's fire for anguish of the burning?" (*CWEBB* 2:82.18). The generation of female novelists and poets who came to artistic maturity during the romantic age were aware of the resonance and power of Prometheus, and they readily stole the radical myth as icon of their own radical artistic activity.

Barrett also became wedded to the Prometheus myth because it was analogue for her courtship with Robert Browning. Her first translation was a Promethean act (so bold that for a time she concealed it from Hugh Stuart Boyd, the blind Greek scholar who was her mentor in 1831 and 1832 and whom she was helping to memorize a segment of Aeschylus's drama).[9] But she was undertaking a second translation when Robert Browning entered her life. In 1846, when Browning notes, "I love your verses with all my heart, dear Miss Barrett" (*BC* 10:17), her Caucasus was 50 Wimpole Street, her father, Jove the tyrant (whose oppression seemed even more tyrannical the more attached to Robert Browning she became), and her situation as represented by the bondage of Prometheus was illness, bereavement, and grief, and seclusion in the "great tawny weltering fog" of urban London as opposed to freedom in rural Herefordshire. She felt death a close companion, and—aside from art—she had nothing to make her life worth living. Then Browning appeared, sharing her love of poetry and the classics, assisting her in her work of translating the second *Prometheus,* calling to her attention certain lines from Shelley's *Prometheus Unbound* (*BC* 12:256), and suggesting she create the lost Aeschylus sequel: "[I]n your poem you shall make Prometheus our way" (*BC* 10:120). Together the poets wove a mythology of their own relationship, usually with Elizabeth as Mariana or some other imprisoned maiden and Robert as the rescuer and/or dragon slayer (Orpheus, the Redcrosse Knight, St. George, Perseus, or the angel of the Lord who rescued Peter and his cohorts in Acts 5), but with the implied subtext that (in Promethean terms) he is also Hercules, who sets Prometheus free. Of course, Mr. Moulton-Barrett is cast as Zeus

---

Mrs. Felicia Hemans, 371 (line numbers not included in this edition); Letitia Elizabeth Maclean, "Felicia Hemans," in *The Poets and the Poetry of the Nineteenth Century,* ed. Alfred H. Miles, 8:110–11 (LEL is Letitia Elizabeth Landon, but the Miles anthology uses her married name).

9. Barrett Browning, *Diary by EBB,* 91, 212.

(the "[o]nly one person [who] holds the thunder" [*BC* 11:238]) or as the dragon. Ann P. Brady argues that Elizabeth Barrett is no passive Andromeda, that the so-called rescue is a "heroic natural deliverance" of the type that reaches its potent idealization in *Aurora Leigh*. Brady is correct in that Barrett does not wish always to be the passive maiden; in fact the lovers occasionally turn the myth about, as when Elizabeth jests that in her forceful hold on Robert, she binds him like a Prometheus (*BC* 12:132). Yopie Prins makes a compelling case that the work of translating allowed the poets to place themselves in secondary relation to *Prometheus Bound* and that the myth itself allowed them to negotiate their courtship, invoking Aeschylus to justify their rebellious elopement while, conversely, the Promethean bondage was also the bond of love.[10]

But Barrett did not know Browning when she first fell in love with the myth. Of greatest importance to Barrett in 1838 was the correlation between Prometheus and Christ. Prometheus had been compared with Christ long before Barrett wrote *The Seraphim* or before Percy Bysshe Shelley, in *Hellas,* proclaimed Christ as "Promethean conqueror" and before he drew numerous parallels between the Titan and the Christian deity in his *Prometheus Unbound.* The parallels as benefactor and savior of the human species, together with the iconic similarities of hanging on a cross and being transfixed on a mount, make the comparisons inevitable. As early as 1567, Puritan poet Arthur Golding in a commentary on *Metamorphoses* says that the Prometheus who first created humans then stole fire to contrive that they flourish, represents the providence, the word, and wisdom of God (all terms that refer to Jesus). In 1612 Prometheus was depicted in crucifixion iconography in the popular *Minerva Britanna, or a Garden of Heroical Devices,* that is, lashed to a tree trunk with cross beam rather than to a mountain crag.[11]

In the Christian era, St. Augustine, Fulgentius, Marsilio Ficino, George Sandys, and Dante all cite the myth received from the classic age that Prometheus created the species, attributing to the mythological creator

10. Brady, *Pompilia: A Feminist Reading of Robert Browning's "The Ring and the Book,"* 8; Prins, "Elizabeth Barrett, Robert Browning and the *Différance* of Translation," 435–51.

11. Shelley, *Hellas: A Lyrical Drama,* in *The Complete Works of Percy Bysshe Shelley,* 3:26.211–20; Golding, "Epistle," in *The XV Books of P. Ovidious Naso, entytuled Metamorphoses, translated oute of Latin into English meeter by Arthur Golding, Gentleman,* lines 434–54. For the Christianizing of the Prometheus myth, see Olga Raggio's "The Myth of Prometheus: Its Survival and Metamorphoses up to the Eighteenth Century."

divine foresight (Fulgentius), wisdom (Augustine), contemplation (Ficino), and providence (Sandys), all traits that are attributed to the Christian deity.[12] Thus, he allegorically prefigures Jesus, and thus the Church Fathers and the Christian tradition endorse the Promethean myth because it exemplifies, prophesies, or allegorizes certain ideals of the Christian faith. A reviewer of Barrett's *The Seraphim* comments that the parallel between Prometheus and Jesus is "increasingly attracting the meditation of the poets and thinkers of Europe," and that the parallel is of long standing:

> an ancient commentator upon Eschylus—the Englishman, Stanley, remarked that the founders of Christianity addressed themselves in this manner to interpret the allegory of Prometheus . . . they have not ceased to associate this tradition with the spirit of the most sacred mysteries of the church. They have often compared the torture upon Caucasus with the passion upon Calvary,—thus making of Prometheus a Christ before *the* Christ. Among these authorities that of Tertullian is, above the rest, striking. . . . he exclaims, *"Behold the real Prometheus—the omnipotent God! transpierced by blasphemy!"* (*BC* 4:376)[13]

In her second translation of *Prometheus Bound,* the one on which she and Robert Browning worked together, Barrett translated Prometheus's name as meaning Providence (*PB* 96), while in the previous translation she had termed him "Prometheus the Provider," a term less theological; she says he became a martyr because of "free-souled, reverent love" for humankind (*PB* 624), words and phrases that sound more Christian than classical, more like Jesus than Prometheus.[14] Falk has noted that Barrett translates from the Greeks in theological terms such as "sin" and "soul," and "our Father" in place of "the father"—"language with Christian resonance." In one instance, for example, Jove is "Sire" in the first translation, while Zeus is "Father" in the revision (*PB* 1206); the transgressions of both

---

12. Augustine, *City of God* 18.8; Fulgentius, *Mythographies* 2.6, in *Fulgentius the Mythographer,* 71–72; Ficino, *The Philebus Commentary* 244; Sandys, *Ovid's Metamorphoses Englished, Mythologized and Represented in Figures;* Dante, *The Convivio of Dante Alighieri* 4.15.

13. The reviewer is quoting Edgar Quinet from the preface to the *Prométhée,* suggesting, however, that Barrett probably did not know this work.

14. Comparisons are based upon the Porter and Clarke edition of Barrett Browning's works (volume 6) and *Prometheus Bound Translated from the Greek of Aeschylus. And Miscellaneous Poems, by the Translator.*

Prometheus and Io are usually called "sins" in the second translation, more frequently "crime" or "offense" in the first. Barrett also uses terms that recall Milton's Christian epic; for example, Prometheus's wish that Zeus be "thrust . . . headlong from his gerent seat / Adown the abysmal void" (*PB* 1078–79), a fall that recalls Satan's falling "headlong flaming from th' Ethereal sky . . . To bottomless perdition" (*PL* 1.45–47). Yet among central tenets of Barrett's Christian religion are humility and obedience, qualities foreign to classical Prometheus. According to Falk, it was "precisely because [she] did not perceive the incoherence of a Prometheus made simultaneously Christ-like and defiant, she was able to recover the myth for herself," but in truth the metamorphosis of Prometheus into Jesus had been occurring for several centuries in Western culture, especially in English poetry.[15] The tension between Prometheus as savior and Prometheus as rebel had colored the myth almost from the beginning, and—like Shelley and others—Barrett examined various nuances of the myth. One might say that she loved Prometheus and Christ because both embody the characteristic of human-directed godly love, which was central to Elizabeth Barrett's religious faith. Increasingly, however, she abandoned the rebellious and proud aspect of Prometheanism to endorse the penitent and humble aspect of Christianity.

III

"The Tempest," the opening piece in Barrett's 1833 volume, is a Promethean work, as are several short works in both *An Essay on Mind, with Other Poems* (1826) and *Poems* (1833), though none as overtly as "The Tempest." In Browning's terrifying and nightmarish tempest the sky is red like blood, yellow like fire, and black "like plumes at funerals" (*T* 28), but the speaker, inebriated with the wine of violence and danger, gladly encounters the storm with its sulfureous lightning, whirlwinds, and roaring thunder like that which Prometheus calls up at the conclusion of Aeschylus's drama. Instead of frozen towers of Dis as in Dante's *Inferno*, huge shaggy trees take the role of Titans (in the Greek succession myth Prometheus's siblings who eventually lose in celestial warfare to Zeus and the Olympians because they will not heed Prometheus's advice that the

15. Falk, "Browning and Her Prometheuses," 78, 82.

wiles of strategy are more effectual than the strength of arms). Barrett's work employs martial metaphors and epic similes to recall Zeus and the Olympians' war with Titans and Giants or Messiah and the angels' battle with the rebel forces of Satan in *Paradise Lost,* the latter a revision of classical myth with the Judeo-Christian God cast as the "Thunderer" and Satan's hosts as the Titans.

A close reading of "The Tempest" reveals several parallels between Barrett's work and that of the "godlike Milton" (*CWEBB* 1:93.1048), parallels that—traced closely—reveal the persona's dead "familiar" (*T* 90) as none other than Satan (or Satan's offspring Sin), the Promethean conception that also emerged when it also "sank deeply into the soul of Milton" (*CWEBB* 6:85). This Satan is the poet's "reptile moods" (*T* 201) and deep anxieties, as well as her human proclivity for sin and rebellion. "The Tempest" is an acknowledgment of Barrett's Prometheanism and her attempt to negate it.

In Milton's epic the angelic-demonic war produces discord and mayhem in heaven and catastrophic storms in the universe.

> . . . Arms on Armor clashing bray'd
> Horrible discord, and the madding Wheels
> Of brazen Chariots rag'd; dire was the noise
> Of conflict . . .
>   . . . all Heav'n
> Resounded, and had Earth been then, all Earth
> Had to her Centre shook.
>   (*PL* 6.209–19)

In "The Tempest" Barrett makes use of similar details and imagery, sometimes even the same terminology:

> The footsteps of martial thunder sound
> Over the mountain battlements . . .
> . . . behold the lightning faintly gleam
> Amid the clouds which thrill and gape aside,
> And straight again shut up their solemn jaws,
> As if to interpose between Heaven's wrath
> And Earth's despair . . .
> As brazen chariots rushing from the war,
> As passion'd waters gushing from the rock . . .
>   (*T* 24–47)

Dorothy Mermin posits that heaven, thunder, lightning, energy, wrath, and power are the male aspect of Barrett's imaginative world; while earth, passivity, despair, stooping, and death are the female.[16] Certainly in her Promethean stage the young poet is drawn to the masculine imagery.

In Milton's epic battle Satan's hosts take up mountains to fling at God's warriors, a battle strategy like that of Zeus and his cohorts against the Titans in Hesiod's *Theogony:*

> Light as the Lightning glimpse they ran, they flew,
> From thir foundations loos'ning to and fro
> They pluckt the seated Hills with all thir load,
> Rocks, Waters, Woods, and by the shaggy tops
> Uplifting bore them in thir hands . . .
>
> (*PL* 6.642–46)

As the Empyrean shakes, the Messiah attacks in his indomitable chariot, "[g]rasping ten thousand Thunders" (*PL* 6.836), his celestial weapon entrusted to him by the Father. He returns triumphant once the battle is won and Satan's Titanic hosts are plunged into the "fiery Gulfe" of "bottomless perdition" (*PL* 1.52, 47), just as in the Greek myth the sky god Zeus with his "headlong bolt of thunder breathing flame" (*PB* 420) hurls the Titans down into Tartarus.

Barrett is well aware that Milton's fall of rebel angels deliberately mirrors the titanic fall in classical myth; she says, "during the whole of his description [Milton] has so evidently in his head the sublime of the immortals in the *Theogony* . . ." (*BC* 2:48). In Barrett's own work the forces of the elements and destruction of nature echo the celestial warfare of *Paradise Lost,* as well as the battle of Olympians versus Titans in Hesiod or Olympians versus Giants in Claudian's *Gigantomachia:*

> As thousand crashëd woods, the thunder cried:
> And at his cry the forest troops were shook
> As by the woodman's axe; and far and near
> Stagger'd the mountains with a mutter'd dread.
>
> (*T* 48–51)

Amid the flames of the "fiery Deluge, fed / With ever-burning Sulphur unconsum'd," Milton's fallen demons lie outstretched on the floor of

16. Mermin, *Origins of New Poetry,* 51.

Hell, "o'erwhelm'd / With Floods and Whirlwinds of tempestuous fire" (*PL* 1.76–77), and thus the Arch-Fiend revives and rallies his troops, not dead like the figure that Barrett describes lying in the forest after the storm, but only stunned and supine from the thunderbolts of triumphant Messiah. A similar image is found in *Prometheus Bound,* in which Typhon, the hundred-handed serpent of the Titan generation who does battle with Zeus, is struck with Zeus's "sleepless arrow" (*PB* 419) or flaming thunderbolt, his strength withered to ashes, his helpless trunk outstretched beside the strait of ocean where—according to Greek myth—he becomes the flaming source of the volcano Ætna.[17] In Milton's epic Typhon is associated with chthonic powers of the underworld (the volcano Ætna), and, by implication, the demonic:

> . . . whose combustible
> And fuell'd entrails thence conceiving Fire,
> Sublim'd with Mineral fury, aid the Winds,
> And leave a singed bottom all involv'd
> With stench and smoke
>
> (*PL* 1.233–37)

The persona of "The Tempest" finds the lightning's victim even as she breathes the lightning's "sulphur stench" (*T* 55), recognizing her familiar by the fire leaping from the "entrails of the firmament" (*T* 75) as Satan recognizes fallen Beelzebub by hell's tempestuous flames. The dead figure rivets her with his unblinking gaze of hatred, and she is shocked to recognize "I knew that face— / His, who did hate me—his, whom I did hate!" (*T* 78–79).

Angela Leighton has suggested that the dead figure whom Barrett hates and who hates her is probably Edward Moulton-Barrett, her father. Peter Dally, who subjects "The Tempest" to a Freudian reading, says the dream makes psychological sense only if we read it as the younger Edward Moulton-Barrett, the all-powerful father slaying his rival son for the possession of his daughter. But the iconography and allusions of the poem suggest otherwise. The shock is not in realizing that she hates the "Papa" or "Bro" whom she has steadfastly claimed to love, but in recognizing that in looking into the face of evil, she sees as her

---

17. In Hesiod, Typhon is a serpent whose eyes flash fire; in Apollodorus his body consists of huge coils of hissing vipers. Thrown down into Tartarus with his brothers the Titans, he is, like Prometheus, often associated with Satan.

"familiar" a mirror image of herself, both the rebellious Satan and all the implications of sinfulness. As a Christian, Barrett is describing the horror of one's initial realization of death as the fruit of sin: that she is capable of hatred, that there is an evil aspect of her being. Certainly she acknowledges her own sinfulness. For example, in an 1845 letter to Robert Browning, she writes for the first time of Bro's death by drowning and her own grief, explaining, "When grief came upon grief, I never was tempted to ask 'How have I deserved this of God,' as sufferers sometimes do: I always felt there must be cause enough . . corruption enough, needing purification . . weakness enough, needing strengthening . . ." (*BC* 11:177). A non-Christian might well express this recognition of the "familiar" as the suppression of the unconscious, which rises to the level of consciousness to undermine the worthy intentions of the conscious will-to-good—something close to Jung's shadow figure, or his analogy of the repressed Prometheus in bonds. (Jung interprets the myth of Prometheus as unconscious powers subordinated to the whim of conscious mind.) The reference to "low anxieties" and "reptile moods" that wait upon the flesh would support the interpretation of the figure as an aspect of the poet's own consciousness (and conscience), and recall too the fallen Typhon whose imprisonment Prometheus regrets. Further, the image also mirrors that of Gregory Nazianzen whose "Soul and Body" Barrett translated and published in 1842 (revised and published posthumously in 1863 in *The Greek Christian Poets*). To Gregory, who incorporates the Christian dualistic model into this thought, the fleshly nature demands of the soul to take its ease, but the spiritual nature repulses the reptilian sensual nature:

> . . . I have not leisure so
> To warm thee, Sweet, my household foe,
> Until, like a serpent frozen,
> New-maddened with the heat, thou loosen
> Thy rescued fang within mine heart![18]
>   (*CWEBB* 6:194)

Another aspect of the human conscious from which Barrett shrinks in horror then acknowledges as her "familiar" is Satanic, arrogant pride,

---

18. Leighton, *Elizabeth Barrett Browning*, 47; Dally, *Elizabeth Barrett Browning: A Psychological Portrait*, 23; Jung, *Phenomena Resulting from the Assimilation of Consciousness: Two Essays on Analytical Psychology*, 318; of Gregory, her favorite among the Greek Christian poets, Barrett Browning says, "We kiss the feet of Gregory's high excellences" (*CWEBB* 6:237).

the flaw that as a young poet she considered her besetting sin. In an early autobiographical essay she notes, "My mind is naturally independent and spurns that subserviency of opinion which is generally considered necessary to feminine softness! But this is a subject on which I must always feel strongly for I feel within me an almost proud consciousness of independence . . ." (*BC* 1:355). And when her father severely criticized a draft of an early work as Byronic and boring, she says, "I have hardly ever been mortified as I was last night—but perhaps this also will do me good. I was growing a little too exalting in myself, a little too full of myself . . ." (*BC* 1:360). In "Idols" (from the 1833 volume) the persona identifies three distractions that separate her from complete devotion to Christ: natural Beauty, Moloch Fame, and human Love. Of these, only the second could be considered as a manifestation of pride, and it is namesake of one of Milton's devils, the "fiercest Spirit / That fought in Heav'n" against God's divine monarchy (*PL* 2.44–45). The young Elizabeth Barrett, in her reading of the Bible and the English divines would have known that "God resisteth the proud, and giveth grace to the humble" (1 Pet. 5:5), and would have recalled the warning of her childhood favorite Richard Hooker, to whom pride was the greatest of sins, an "[i]mmoderate swelling, a token of very imminent breach, and of inevitable destruction: pride a vice which cleaveth so fast unto the hearts of men, that, if we were to strip ourselves of all faults one by one, we should undoubtedly find it the very last and hardest to put off." Much later in her writing career Barrett Browning has her poet hero of *Aurora Leigh* admit that, in regard to her career and fame, she has been "very vilely proud," and "so wrong, so proud, so weak . . ." (*AL* 9.619, 712). Like the poet Aurora, the poet Elizabeth Barrett was concerned about excessive pride. In "The Tempest" the persona's "sympathy with power," violence, and grandeur put her in the company of the romantic spirit—"tameless, and swift, and proud."[19]

It is significant that Barrett identifies her personal shortcoming as that great wrong that precipitated the fall of Satan, deadliest of the Seven Deadly Sins, and parallel to the hubris that brought down the tragic heroes of classical drama and epic. If the "good Christian woman" is active only in her self-abnegation, then the woman who takes up her

---

19. Hooker, *A Learned Sermon of the Nature of Pride*, in *The Works of That Learned and Judicious Divine, Mr. Richard Hooker: With an Account of His Life and Death by Isaac Walton*, 3:602; Shelley, "Ode to the West Wind," in *Shelley's Poetry and Prose*, 223.56.

pen to follow in the tradition of Milton, Wordsworth, and Byron is guilty of colossal presumption. (Is she, by implication, neither Christian nor good?) Barrett's particular form of remorse over her sin of pride is familiar to the brilliant (and aspiring) nineteenth-century literary woman who happens also to be deeply religious. For example, twenty-year-old Mary Ann Evans, later to reject Christianity and to become famous as George Eliot, says in 1839, "I feel that my besetting sin is the one of all others most destroying, as it is the fruitful parent of them all,—ambition, a desire insatiable for the esteem of my fellow creatures."[20]

The "anxiety of influence," which Harold Bloom has identified as a great tension for the male writer (especially the male Romantic poet), is but a slight problem as compared to the anxiety of sin, the teaching of the Reverend Mr. Hooker that if Christ be within one, then pride must be beaten down and subjected. Especially problematic, then, is the spiritual danger of the *female Christian poet* up against the apostle Paul's injunction to silence, yet wishing to follow the same poetic models who produce an anxiety of influence in nurtured, pampered male egos (specifically, Milton as the model who produces the greatest anxiety for English Romantics, Bloom says). Women were not supposed to seek after the "Moloch Fame." Even John Stuart Mill, who vindicates the rights of Victorian women, was under the impression that, "whether the cause be natural or artificial, women [artists] seldom have this eagerness for fame. Their ambition is generally confined within narrower bounds."[21]

Judith Plaskow argues that, although pride is sin and forgiveness comes through love, woman *always* lives a life of sacrificial love; female sin therefore must be perceived as self-abnegation ("leaving the sin of pride to men") and grace as reconstitution of the female self. Even Barrett's contemporary Florence Nightingale notes in her theological speculations that great harm is done by striving after what is called humility and checking what is called pride: "It is a cry of nature to wish to be something—to do something. To check it is to check the appetite for activity which God has placed in our nature."[22] Barrett, however, adheres to the male theological interpretations she has inherited and does not

---

20. Cross, *George Eliot's Life as Related in Her Letters and Journals,* in *Writings of George Eliot,* 1:39.

21. Bloom, *The Anxiety of Influence: A Theory of Poetry,* 107; Mill, *The Subjection of Women,* in *The Collected Works of John Stuart Mill,* 21:320.

22. Plaskow, *Sex, Sin and Grace,* 93; Nightingale, *"Cassandra" and Other Selections,* 54.

question that biblical and Christian doctrine place a high premium on humility. Her avowal of pride and ambition is unsettling, frightening whether pride be alive and cursing (as the dead familiar was formerly) or suppressed and dead (as he now is). It should be borne in mind that the Prometheus of female literary tradition *always* sinned the sin of pride: for example, the presumption of assuming God's creating and animating role in Mary Shelley, of doing battle by means of stolen Enlightenment rationalism in Wollstonecraft. Perhaps Barrett and her predecessors realized how potentially lethal is the undertaking. And for Barrett, whose religion was certainly more personal and more intense than that of either Wollstonecraft or her daughter Mary Shelley, the temptation to pride, the presumption of the professional *woman* writer is all the more terrifying. It might easily destroy her Christian soul. Since Barrett lived in an era in which—as Mill says—women artists were all amateurs, her choice to be a professional and furthermore to excel in the exclusively male genres such as the poetic drama or the epic (as opposed to the prose novel) might seem all the more arrogant.

Also speaking as Christian, Barrett believes that realization of one's proclivity for evil is universal, or, put another way, that the good God allows evil to exist in the microcosm of individual existence as well as in the macrocosm. Not only Elizabeth Barrett but also every person within the "deep Eleusis" of the heart struggles in solitude with the contrary spirits of power versus passiveness, humility versus pride, good versus evil, soul versus flesh, life versus death—the dualistic forms of Gregory. The Promethean enemy of "The Tempest" threatens the Christian soul as Milton's Promethean Satan does.

The persona spends the remainder of chaotic night clasping to her living self the dead victim; then in the "idiocy" of morning light in the shaggy forest lays to rest her familiar, her counterpart, her evil genius, under a titanic tree that has also been stricken by lightning—the burial suggesting repression of the rebellious aspect of self—the "self-will" of which Alice Falk speaks. "The Tempest" is a fragment; therefore one cannot guess what transition Barrett might have included between the burial of the titanic victim and her apostrophe to "pale-steedëd Death" (*T* 158). As the poem stands, the omission is problematic. Because of the "MAN who died and lives" (*T* 193), "only Death shall die" (*T* 202), a conclusion that alludes to the last line of John Donne's familiar sonnet and suggests resurrection. But whether the buried unconscious or doppelgänger—the dark Satanic side—will remain dead until Death's death the poem does not answer. Nor does it speculate. When the poet shall "enter the eternity to come, / Where live the dead" (*T* 202–3), where will the dead familiar be? When the radical Prometheanism of oneself has been buried, one questions whether it will arise unto life like Dr. Frankenstein's creation.

"A Sea-side Meditation," published in the same volume, could be read as a gloss on "The Tempest" in that it links Prometheus with the romantic Satan more than with Christ. "The Tempest" ends with the slaying of Death; "A Sea-side Meditation" with the overthrow of Satan, probably at the end of the thousand years' reign in the "latter days of earth." If the former work is Promethean/Miltonic, the latter is Wordsworthian. In Barrett's description of the "fresh-toned gushings" (*SM* 16) and the "cataract's / Deep passion" (*SM* 18–19), one recalls the atmosphere of Tintern Abbey or scenes from *The Prelude*. For Barrett as for Wordsworth the "mighty being" is awake, reminding her of the sublime within nature and within humankind. But we are oblivious to the sublime. Wordsworth would say we have laid to waste our powers in getting and spending; Barrett says we are chained by the physical, by sensation, and—unlike Prometheus—we are in love with our bondage. This is not the golden chain of mysterious union binding creature to Creator, but rather "corroded brass" (*SM* 41) binding humans down by the weight of hours—"work-times, diet-times, and sleeping-times" (*SM* 44). We mortals are like Milton's Archfiend "Chain'd on the burning Lake" (*PL* 1.210), our corroded brass forged, in a sense, by the demonic, certainly by the sensual:

> . . . mean and heavy links
> Within the pandemonic walls of sense,
> Enchain our deathless part"
> (*SM* 45–47)

The walls allude to Satan's capitol in Milton's Hell. Like Satan condemned to go on his belly rather than erect as he had done before the successful temptation of Eve, we "eat / Dust, like the serpent" (*SM* 61–62). In "A Sea-side Meditation," the enslavement of spirit by flesh is an ironic reversal of the divine intention—humans linked to God by the great chain of being.

Also as in "The Tempest" Barrett makes a leap in intent from sublime nature to enchained humans to "Hell's angel" (Satan), "Lift[ing] his scarr'd brow, confirm[ing] his rebel heart" (*SM* 145). In an image that again echoes that of Milton's Satan, the rebel is overcome by the blast of God, which hurls him back. This Satan, boldly defiant like the idealized Prometheus of Byron, Goethe, and Hartley Coleridge, exists to counteract "God's holy plan" (in either the Wordsworthian sense or the Miltonic). He is the Promethean aspect of oneself ("Selfhood" in Blake's mythology and Swedenborg's theology) that must be rejected.

The triumph of the Godly over the demonic parallels for Barrett the spirit struggling against the flesh, the "heav'n born" versus the "earthborn" (*SM* 69). "A Sea-side Meditation" renounces Promethean power and energy, here rebellion, ambition, even forbidden wisdom and knowledge (accepting, as Raphael says to Adam, that it is not given to man to know all things). In subjecting the physical to the spiritual dominance, the poet subjects herself in humility before the one whose feet walked upon the Sea of Galilee. Therefore, the poet Barrett puts herself in the same position in which we find the woman at the closure of *The Seraphim,* a Magdalene figure at the feet of Jesus. But the cost is, as "The Tempest" suggests in its imagery and mythic motif, the burial of an aspect of the self.

IV

The Seraphim treats the theme of Christ the Promethean savior as his martyrdom is witnessed by God's angelic hosts. But Barrett knows that "pomp angelical" (*S* 18) is dangerous material for a poet to handle. In *The Book of the Poets,* Barrett Browning faults the divine Milton for his depiction of angels in *Paradise Lost;* his spiritual beings are merely "humanities, enlarged, uplifted, transfigured—but no more." They have a "ponderous materialism," and Shakespeare displays more of fairyhood in *A Midsummer Night's Dream,* Barrett Browning adds, than Milton does of angelhood in *Paradise Lost* (*CWEBB* 6:289). Believing in Milton's genius and knowing that if Milton failed, Barrett might be likely to do so as well, it is no surprise that she was in "two panics" about the publication of *The Seraphim:* "First—because it seems to me a very daring subject—a subject almost beyond our sympathies, & therefore quite beyond the sphere of human poetry. . . . Secondly—because all my tendencies towards mysticism will be called into terrible operation by this dreaming upon Angels" (*BC* 3:198). And in the "Epilogue," the poet makes a final apology: "Forgive me, that mine earthly heart should dare / Shape images of unincarnate spirits . . ." (*S* 1035–36). She is aware that celestial topics put her in the category of such notables as Milton and Dante, whose unincarnate spirits appeared in their most mature works. In addition, *The Seraphim, and Other Poems* was Barrett's first volume of work published under her own name; therefore, laying claim to a work with only suprahuman actors is an act bolder still. She seizes Milton's Promethean fire and in the end asserts her right as poet and woman to treat the most "daring subject" of poetry. The act of witnessing/writing is at once animating Promethean fire and holy celestial song. Therefore, the poet is ambivalent and insecure about seizing illicit power, and she finally discovers her own identity not through a Promethean hero, but through the weeping woman at the foot of the cross.

The Seraphim is a masque (or a "dramatic lyric" Barrett says in the preface) involving the observation of Jesus' crucifixion by two seraphim, Ador the Strong and Zerah the Bright. Although Barrett does not assign gender to the seraphim, they seem to be male and female, as Mermin has noted.[23] In fact, Ador is much like Adam in *A Drama of Exile,* and Zerah— "more newly made, / More feeble, more afraid" (*S* 118–19) is even a closer parallel to Eve. There is in *The Seraphim* a static quality similar to that of Aeschylus's *Prometheus Bound,* Milton's *Paradise Regained* and *Samson Agonistes,* and Shelley's *Prometheus Unbound* in that the principal heroic figure remains stationary and others (or in *Paradise Regained* the Other) approach and respond to him. Unlike the protagonists of its predecessors, however, the figure in *The Seraphim* is—except in the final moments— absolutely silent, and the commentary on humans and sin, forgiveness and redemption, is principally the discovery of Ador and Zerah. Their central revelation seems to be that humans experience greater love than even the angels and therefore can return greater love, for angels have not sinned and therefore cannot know expiation. Just so, the earth's celebratory song of redemption will eventually rival the music of the spheres.

The Seraphim recalls Aeschylus, but in some ways a more obvious parallel is the revisionist Prometheus myth in Shelley's *Prometheus Unbound.* There is no conclusive proof that Barrett had, at this time, read Shelley's *Prometheus,* although it would be highly unlikely that she would have overlooked it, considering that her 1831–1832 *Diary* reveals her to be reading through the Shelley poetic canon, and mentions works

---

23. Mermin, *Origins of New Poetry,* 62.

less well known than his *Prometheus Unbound*.[24] Also the attraction of
Prometheus and Aeschylus would no doubt have drawn her to Shelley's
famous revisionism. With the eagle piercing his side and the crown of
icicles on his brow, Shelley's Prometheus in agony mirrors Jesus' passion.
For Shelley, Prometheus is Love, as Jesus is for Barrett. Like Barrett's Jesus,
Prometheus brings peace and harmony to the universe by realizing he
can forgive, rather than revenge. Shelley's design in *Prometheus Unbound*
is to reveal that Jesus' sacrifice has failed, that Christianity has become
a curse, that Jesus' modern disciples are responsible for much of the
world's grief, and that another sacrifice of love is required. To demonstrate
this, Shelley compares Jesus' ineffectual martyrdom with Prometheus's
efficacious suffering. Shelley's Prometheus, in his agony on Caucasus,
sees in a vision a "woeful sight" (*PU* 1.584), the other youth in crucified
agony, and he dismisses the martyrdom:

> Fix, fix those tortured orbs in peace and death
> So thy sick throes shake not that crucifix,
>
> . . . .
> O horrible! Thy name I will not speak
> It hath become a curse. I see, I see
> The wise, the mild, the lofty, and the just,
> Whom thy slaves hate for being like to thee . . .
>
> (*PU* 1.600–606)

The agony of Prometheus, "Hung here in fetters, 'neath the blanching
sky" (*PB* 127) is, in Shelley,

> Three thousand years of sleep-unsheltered hours
> And moments aye divided by keen pangs
> Till they seemed years, torture and solitude,
> Scorn and despair . . .
>
> (*PU* 1.12–15)

24. Among those she notes are *Revolt of Islam, Queen Mab,* and *Adonais;* Barrett
Browning acknowledges Shelley as a great poet, his works rooted in air instead of earth
and "perfectly exquisite" (*Diary by EBB,* 102, 138). In a letter to Miss Mitford in 1841
she notes that Shelley's works "glitter" but are cold (*LMRM* 1:229), and in 1840 she
informs her brother that she has finished reading Shelley's prose and would have been
"very deeply delighted" were it not for his defiled and atrocious opinions (especially on
religion and Plato) (*BC* 4:233).

In Barrett's work, Jesus also experiences torture and solitude, scorn (in the form of "Scornful Voices from Earth") and seeming despair (in his cry "My God, My God / Why hast Thou me forsaken?" (S 931–32). Like Shelley, Barrett stresses the incomprehensible pain:

> No crown! the woe instead
> Is heavy on his head,
> Pressing inward on his brain
> With a hot and clinging pain
> (S 711–14)

These lines seem to echo the curse of Prometheus upon Jove in Shelley's drama: "And thine Omnipotence a crown of pain, / To cling like burning gold round thy dissolving brain" (*PU* 1.290–91). Suffering as Shelley's Prometheus does for the entire race, Jesus bears the weight of collective human sin; he "feels the billowy griefs come up to drown, / Nor fears, nor faints, nor fails, till all be finished" (S 630–31). For Barrett, reconciliation with God can be accomplished only by Jesus' death and humans' obedience ("not obeisance," she insists); for Shelley, humans cannot be reconciled with *humans* until the collective human conscious concludes that "most vain [is] all hope but love" (*PU* 1.807).

Several of Barrett's contemporaries who criticized *The Seraphim* note its supposed indebtedness to Shelley, but *whether or not Barrett knew Shelley's revisionism,* I posit a surprisingly similar revisionism in both poets—each revealing a course of Prometheanism.[25] Certainly, the similarities indicate that Barrett is probably responding not only to Aeschylus and Milton, but also to Shelley's drama. Either way, her cosmic treatment of Jesus' love and sacrifice bears remarkable resemblance to Shelley's adoration of Prometheus. Even the imagery parallels. For example, both poets make much of the suffering of Earth, just as Barrett does in "The Tempest." In Aeschylus's tragedy the parent of Prometheus to whom he cries out in agony is "Earth, mother of us all . . ." (*PB* 101). While Aeschylus glosses over Earth's travail, Shelley and Barrett dramatize it, Shelley because he envisions an Earth tortured, rolling on a "wheel of pain" (*PU* 1.141) not to be mitigated until human love replaces human revenge as basis for human society and politics, Barrett because she believes that only

---

25. See Appendix III in *BC* 4:383, 400, 409. No reviewer mentions *Prometheus Unbound;* all refer to Shelleyan style and traits such as Shelley's "wild, dreamy spirit" as influences on Barrett.

Godly love can redeem humans and restore to Earth a second Eden. In Shelley, Earth suffers famine and ruin, tyranny and grief; she is stricken by red gulphs of war, famine-wasted cities, thick shapes of human death. Shelley's Earth tells Prometheus of her misery, poison, plague, famine, and contagion, summing up "my breast was dry / With grief . . ." (*PU* 1.176–77). In Barrett, Earth suffers because of human depravity: the Earth Spirit in *A Drama of Exile* accuses Adam and Eve: " . . . ye give me / The thorn to vex, and the tempest-fire to cleave me—"(*DE* 1117–18). And in *The Seraphim,* Earth laments:

> I have groaned; I have travailed: I am weary.
> I am blind with my own grief, and cannot see . . .
> Harkening the thick sobs of my children's heart"
> (*S* 818–24)

Earth, the "God-created and God-praised," has become the "God-curst" and "God-striken," because Earth's occupants strive for profit and gold, crowns and scepters (temptations that Jesus rejects in *Paradise Regained*) and because spiritual things bow to "things of sense" (*S* 159). (This recalls the spirit's enchainment to the pandemonic walls of sense in "A Sea-side Meditation.") Though in the presence of the dying god, Earth feels no pity but self-pity, and the voices of her scornful inhabitants chide the dying god, "If verily this *be* the Eternal's son—" (*S* 836).

In Shelley's drama once Prometheus can "unsay the curse" of spite and revenge on heaven's monarch, the spell of human evil is broken; thrones are kingless; priests, aristocrats, and authority exist no more; and humans are "[e]qual, unclassed, tribeless, and nationless" (*PU* 3.4.195). The subdued music that, like the footsteps of a weak melody (*PU* 2.1.89), has led Asia and Panthea to the portal of Demogorgon (the creature who then deposes the tyrant Jove) now swells to a triumphant universal symphony. Harmony permeates the universe; Promethean man becomes "one harmonious soul of many a soul" (*PU* 4.400). And Earth—formerly wasted and wailing—is made like Heaven (*PU* 3.4.160), experiencing joy defying description (*PU* 3.4.78) and weaving the "mystic measure / of music and dance" of the spheres (*PU* 4.77–78). Music sings in Earth's pine boughs and living grass; it floats through the air in Æolian modulations; it resounds in woodlands, waters, and mountains; it speaks with the "lute of Hope" and "voice of Love" (*PU* 4.65–66). Even human language, the base element of which the poet makes music, becomes "a perpetual orphic song" (*PU* 4.415).

Milton too uses the strains of music to celebrate heroic victory, in this case the Messiah's victory in *Paradise Regained* over the lusts of the eye, the lusts of the flesh, and the pride of life. Satan offers power, knowledge, esteem, wealth, and political kingdoms, but one by one Jesus passes every test. And "Angelic Choirs / Sing Heavenly Anthems of his victory," as previously they had burst forth in "Celestial measures" when the Father prophesied that the weakness of Jesus' humiliation would overcome Satanic strength and as the "Angelic Song" echoed in the fields of Bethlehem upon the occasion of his birth.[26]

The Seraphim, however, contrasts music and silence. Throbbing harp strings, spheric song, God's voice murmuring in harmony with the rivers, and heavenly choirs singing carols at the birth of Jesus are merely memories, and "[T]he golden harps the angels bore . . . Lie without touch or tone / Upon the glass-sea shore" (*S* 5–9). The universe that the seraphim reconnoiter in their search for the God now walking in human clay is like a desert lion shaking "[d]ews of silence from its mane" (*S* 371). Drawing closer to Judea, Ador and Zerah see an empyreal company "circle upon circle, tier on tier" (*S* 347), a formation reminiscent of the heavenly rose in Dante's *Paradiso,* but the songful angelic lips are "divorcèd from all sound" (*S* 352). The seraphim discover three crosses; the crucified human figures "[g]hast and silent to the sun" (*S* 460), and a woman (either Jesus' mother or Mary Magdalene) kneels at the foot of the central cross with "a spasm, not a speech" (*S* 481). As songful cherubs are stricken dumb, even God turns away in silence from the scene, leaving the son "God-orphaned." The "silentness" answers the seraphim query "like a brazen sound" (*S* 550).

In Shelley's work, celebratory music and the epithalamion of Prometheus and Asia mark Prometheus's titanic victory over hatred and emotional violence, and in the calm following the wild mystic music and dance, Demogorgon—who has the final word—says that love and hope alone are "Life, Joy, Empire, Victory" (*PU* 4.578). In Barrett's drama, the seraphim both recall and predict music, but the awed silence of the universe is replaced by noise: wailing winds, desolate cries, earthquake, and thunder (reminding one of the conclusion of Aeschylus's drama rather than Shelley's and presenting a final scene more troubling than

---

26. Milton, *Paradise Regained,* 4.593–94, 1.170, 4.505, in *Complete Poems and Major Prose,* 529, 486, 527.

comforting). The dead arise from "splitting tombs" to witness "victory is the Lord's" (*S* 1000, 1004).[27] The seraphim have called upon Earth to awaken and rejoice in song:

> In all thy vernal noises,
> In the rollings of thine ocean,
> Leaping founts, and rivers running,—
> In thy woods' prophetic heaving
> . . . .
> And with all thy music rolled
> In a breath abroad
> By the breathing God,—
>
> (*S* 752–65)

But Earth can respond only with wails and laments, as she does in *A Drama of Exile*. When Zerah sees love in the eyes of the dying Jesus, he observes that Earth has potential for music greater than that of the Heaven-choirs. In the silence emanating from Judea, however, there is yet no anthem, but only the promise of song as there is promise of redemption. Heaven is thus dull to this Earth, whose "winding, wandering music . . . returns / Upon itself, exultingly self-bound" in everlasting praises (*S* 602–5). Zerah "hears" this music of reconciliation in the tableau of silent suffering.

> My heaven! my home of heaven! my infinite
> Heaven-choirs! what are ye to this dust and death,
> This cloud, this cold, these tears, this failing breath,
> Where God's immortal love now issueth
> In this MAN'S woe?
>
> (*S* 611–15)

In *The Seraphim,* angel tongues can sing only praise, for angels have never experienced sin or death; humans sing the "passion-song of blood" (*S* 656), a song of grief and loss. If the human song of redemption supersedes angelic hallelujahs, then the angels will fall as mute as Earth has been during the moments of Jesus' torture and death, Zerah suggests.[28]

27. Biblical accounts of the crucifixion include an earthquake and the resurrection of saints from the grave (see Matt. 27:51–53).
28. The question of whether sinless angels can fully appreciate the significance of grace as sinful humankind does (suggesting, as it does, various degrees of grace) is more

But in future, Ador responds, the earthly and celestial songs will be blended into one.

Barrett believes that her *Seraphim* lacks a guiding unity and this is nearly so, for the music versus silence motif is not developed as fully or as satisfactorily in *The Seraphim* as it is in Shelley's *Prometheus Unbound*. Barrett leaves the universe in chaos as it exists in Aeschylus's tragedy, rather than presenting peace and promise, retribution and redemption, as Shelley does, and as her drama seems to foreshadow. One might expect Barrett to close *The Seraphim* in the same mood and spirit as a Good Friday service. But the feeling is not silence and expectant waiting; it is chaotic.

Yet music and language (the warp and woof of poet's craft) are also the medium of communication between spirit and mortals. Music (poetry) is, for Barrett, the language with which one speaks to God. As she says elsewhere, "All truth, & all beauty & all music belong to God . . . In poetry, which includes all things, 'the diapason closeth full . . in God' " (*BC* 10:139). The act of writing the poem is an exercise in making music; the poet is singing her or his song. Shelley's drama ends in "perpetual orphic song," while Milton's *Paradise Regained* begins:

> I who once erewhile the happy Garden sung
> By one man's disobedience lost, now sing
> Recover'd Paradise . . .
>
> (*PR* 1.1–3)

Barrett begins her Epilogue "My song is done, / My voice that long hath faltered shall be still" (*S* 1007–8). As singer/poet she has broken the silence with her "hoarse music" (*S* 1039). Earth is deprived of voice and language:

> Without language for the rapture,
> Without music strong to come
> And set the adoration free . . .
>
> (*S* 82–84)

Who, therefore, can better than the poet supply the wanted song? Thus, Barrett validates her own boldness of singing, of creating a mystic song,

---

significant than the question of how many angels can dance on the head of a pin, a parallel query suggested by Virginia Radley in her evaluation of *The Seraphim* (*Elizabeth Barrett Browning*, 39).

as well as her argument that religion is the highest and best subject for poetry. As she puts it in a letter to Sara Coleridge, "Religious truth is high, . . is sublime: but when it acts most sublimely on the religious man . . when his heart melts within him & his eyes are full of tears, . . he is in the sphere of poetic truth . . ." (*BC* 10:129).

Further, in poetry's creation of mystical music, the poet puts herself in the shadow of Jesus, the creating Word who, like the Prometheus of classical myth, created and animated humans. Barrett lays claim to orthodox Trinitarianism. She chooses the aspect of Jesus as Word in the sense of Jesus as the active, creating, agency of God, at the same time a part of the triune spirit of the deity, all presumably present in the beginning and all consenting to the act of creation. In so doing, she refers thematically both to the artistry of Prometheus as creator and to the poet herself. In Genesis, God spoke heavens and earth into existence, and in John 1:1, Jesus was the Word spoken: "In the beginning was the Word and the Word was with God and the Word was God." By tradition this Word of God, who was present in the beginning, is the Jesus who became flesh (or clay) and dwelt on earth. In the seventeenth chapter of John's gospel, which Barrett calls "my system of divinity" (*BC* 6:129), Jesus says to the Father, "I have given them thy word; and the world hath hated them," and "I in them, and thou in me, that they may be made perfect in one" (John 17:14, 23). In *A Drama of Exile*, Lucifer acknowledges the presence of the Word in the beginning as participating in the creation of angels (as Satan does in *Paradise Lost*): "so we / Sprang very beauteous from the creant Word" (*DE* 757–58). The seraphim also name Jesus as creator. For example, Ador refers to the "mystic's word's creative grace" (*S* 560), and notes the silence of the suffering martyr's "creating mouth" (*S* 572). Lamenting humanity's concern for its slain savior, he says:

> Unto Him, whose forming word
> Gave to Nature flower and sward,
> She hath given back again,
> For the myrtle—the thorn,
> For the sylvan calm—the human scorn.
> (*S* 436–40)

And Zerah says that the "Master-word . . . lie[s] / A mere silence" (*S* 771–72). Since Barrett's drama is frequently obscure, one might argue that these references are to God the Father. But this would not be a valid argument because the seraphim never behold God's face, hear God's voice, or remark upon God's martyrdom; rather they focus upon the cross: Jesus' silent suffering and Jesus' passivity as active role in human redemption. Recall that Dorothy Mermin argues that in Barrett's adaptation of the Prometheus myth, the female aspect is passive, the male aggressive. It is Barrett's purpose to equate Jesus' acceptance of suffering with the Christian humility of herself—woman and poet. Helen Cooper posits that *The Seraphim* is a fusion of two traditions, the Victorian woman-as-angel and the Miltonic angel-as-poet.[29] Yet it is more than that: it is also Jesus as Word/Creator parallel to woman/poet as creator through words and the Word.

V

Not only is the poet Elizabeth Barrett the creator of a mystic song of praise, she is also by implication the female figure at the foot of Jesus' cross, the mourner whose only sound is her hoarse weeping. This woman is probably Mary Magdalene, the friend of Jesus who was chosen to bear the news of the Resurrection to his skeptical male disciples. The Magdalene is the only one of the women (including Jesus' mother) named in all four canonical gospels as standing at the foot of the cross and bringing spices to anoint him in the tomb, and, as Susan Haskins notes, in traditional paintings of the crucifixion or deposition, she is the figure crouched or kneeling at the foot of the cross. It is also she, "Apostle to the Apostles," who announces to Jesus' chosen disciples that the tomb is empty.[30] That this Mary was witness to the Resurrection is all the more remarkable, given that in Jewish culture of the time women were not allowed to bear legal witness, and this particular woman was tainted in reputation (perhaps not so tainted in Jesus' day but later known as a woman sexually fallen). Supposedly, she is the woman who anointed Jesus' feet with ointment from an alabaster box (in Luke 7) and wiped his feet with her hair (though conflated too with Mary of Bethany who similarly anointed and wiped Jesus' feet in John 12). In fact, the witness of Magdalene is so troubling that some theologians have explained it

29. Cooper, *Elizabeth Barrett Browning, Woman and Artist,* 28.
30. Haskins, *Mary Magdalene: Myth and Metaphor,* 201–5, 67.

away because Peter, as "first witness," is considered heir to the keys of the kingdom. Chrysostom (whom Barrett had been reading avidly a half decade before publishing *The Seraphim*) says that Mary was privileged to witness the Resurrection because she, being of the feeble female nature, did not believe like the men who had already seen the folded grave clothes and had already departed believing. Rosemary Radford Ruether, who believes that the suppression of Jesus' friendship with Mary Magdalene occurred because early Christians wished to promulgate the view of Jesus as "virgin ascetic," says the Marys of the synoptic crucifixion stories are Mary Magdalene and Mary the mother of James the Younger, but that the single version that has Mary the Virgin at the foot of the cross is to authenticate John as Jesus' heir (in John's gospel) and later dissemination of this version was to establish the Mariology of Mary as mediatrix of all graces (as she emerged in Catholicism). Magdalene was not only the initial witness of the Resurrection, but in medieval legend she also later repented her courtesan's life, living in self-exile and penitence in a grotto in the south of France, where her story evolved through medieval times and the Renaissance as witness that it is never too late to accept forgiveness.[31] With Mary of Bethany, she represents Contemplation, both because by tradition Magdalene lived as a religious ascetic and because Mary of Bethany, in sitting at Jesus' feet, contrasts her sister Martha, who is depicted as busily pursuing household tasks. John Keble in "Advent Sunday" refers to the home of Lazarus and his sisters as:

> The peaceful home, to Zeal sincere
> And heavenly Contemplation dear,
> Where Martha loved to wait with reverence meet,
> And wiser Mary lingered at Thy sacred feet.[32]

In Victorian England, Mary Magdalene also represented Christian service; in the Church of England the name Magdalene refers not only to women of easy virtue as in the title St. Mary Magdalene's (a church institution where Christina Rossetti served as volunteer), but also sometimes to the woman rendering aid—doing womanly works. In the words

---

31. Chrysostom, Homily 86 on John, in Philip Schaff, ed., *A Select Library of the Nicene and Post-Nicene Fathers of the Christian Church,* 14:323; Ruether, *New Woman, New Earth,* 47–49; Warner, *Monuments and Maidens: The Allegory of the Female Form,* 257.
32. Keble, *The Christian Year,* 15.

of Mother Lydia Sellon, a founder of an Anglican sisterhood in 1848, women of the age are cautioned to leave theological arguments to others and to be active "in action and in love." Woman's distinct role is to imitate "Mary Magdalene of blessed memory [who] has taught us our place; we are to lie at the Feet of our Lord, in silence, in tears, in love; or we may press amid the crowd to touch His garment, and hear the comforting words—Daughter, thy *faith* hath saved thee, go in peace. Life is short enough for penitence; let us not waste it in aught beside."[33]

The humility that Barrett associates with the weeping woman suggests that she is Mary Magdalene. Further, the figure of Magdalene as contemplation, penitence, service, and testimony serves to parallel the poet's role. Zerah speculates that "[s]uch a music, so clear" as the woman's hoarse weeping might well be richer to God's ear than the song of angels (*S* 508–11).

The humility and contrition of Mary Magdalene, in fact, attracted several female Victorian poets. Jean Ingelow, in "Brothers, and a Sermon," stresses Magdalene's love and repentance, together with a sense of guilt for Jesus' suffering:

> Sore in her soul to think, to think that she,
> Even she, did pierce the sacred, sacred feet,
> And bruise the thorn-crowned head.

And in Christina Rossetti's "Divine and Human Pleading" the "blessed Mary Magdalene" serves as intercessor for a contrite sinner, bearing testimony that when she cast off her jewels and rich attire and threw herself at the feet of Jesus, the "heavy chain" of guilt that bound her to earth was broken.[34] In Barrett Browning's *Aurora Leigh* the humble Marian compares her adoration of the angelic Romney in terms of the nard of ointment with which Mary anointed Jesus' feet; in *The Seraphim* the silently weeping woman so impresses Zerah that he comments that not even angels uplift such music as that woman's "hoarse weeping" (*S* 511). If that hoarse weeping be music to angels' ears expressing as it does grief, love, and adoration, then also the poet's "hoarse music" and thought

33. Sellon, "A Few Words to Some of the Women of the Church of God," in *Women in English Religion 1700–1925*, ed. D. Johnson, 179.

34. Ingelow, *The Poetical Works of Jean Ingelow*, 163; Rossetti, *The Complete Poems of Christina Rossetti*, 3:88.3, 89.51.

"[c]old with weeping" (*S* 1039, 1038) is music in the divine ear. Barrett vows her own humility, saying she has, like Moses, "worn no shoes on this holy ground" (*CWEBB* 1:166), but has stood there and caught the shadow of the cross. Through humility and adoration, obedience and love, she suffers for his suffering. At present her song is the "passion-song" of Ichabod (inglorious [*S* 655]), but she anticipates a time when it will merge with the praise song of angels. In *The Seraphim* she takes care to put herself in the camp of the woman at the Savior's feet, a position of humility. Since Barrett believed that pride is her own worst sin, she deliberately attempts (both here and elsewhere, though especially as Eve in *A Drama of Exile*) the better choice by equating woman's position as nearer that of Christ's humility than Satan's hubris. Yet that figure in the "shadow" of the cross creates and animates too, although her work is but a reflection (a shadow) of that of Jesus—wisdom and Word.

In *The Seraphim,* Barrett sheds light and warmth on Shelley's "glittering coldness" to exemplify the heights of divine grace and human (more than angelic) love, and to express the bond between deity and disciple, in this case, the disciple being a Magdalene-like woman poet. She has found the Promethean myth useful, but in trying to soar above it, she feels she has sunk beneath it.

Elsewhere Barrett Browning notes, "We want the touch of Christ's hand upon our literature, as it touched other dead things—we want the sense of the saturation of Christ's blood upon the souls of our poets, that it may cry *through* them in answer to the ceaseless wail of the Sphinx of our humanity, expounding agony into renovation" (*CWEBB* 6:176). Though occasionally uneasy about the patriarchy, Barrett seemingly has no reservations about the centrality of Christ's redemption to everything she believes and values—including her creative self. In "The Dead Pan" the gods of Hellas are supplanted because " 'Twas the hour when One in Sion / Hung for love's sake on a cross . . ." (*CWEBB* 3:154.182–83). The loving—free-souled, reverent love—seems to be the answer to human pain, making restitution for sin, binding up human wounds, reforging the broken chain linking earth and heaven. And, for herself, the poet must affirm a symbolic role as her century's Mary Magdalene the witness, not its modern Prometheus.

2

Eve in Exile

❀

Where the apple reddens
Never pry—
Lest we lose our Edens,
Eve and I!

—Robert Browning,
"A Woman's Last Word"

Sorely the mother of mankind
Longed for the garden left behind;
For we still prove some yearnings blind
Inherited from Paradise.

—Jean Ingelow, "Scholar and Carpenter"

I

A Drama of Exile is the central work of Elizabeth Barrett's 1844 *Poems* and, according to the poet in the preface, her most important work to that date. The drama takes up Eve's story (and to a lesser extent Adam's) where Milton leaves off and follows the spiritual awakening of Eve as she faces exile in a strange and dangerous world. Naturally Barrett feels an identity with Eve; among the female poets and novelists of nineteenth-century England, such an identity was common. Frequently Barrett refers to herself as Eve: on one occasion, she jests in pronouncing herself "curious beyond the patience of my Eve-ship" (*BC* 6:162), and to her sister she remarks, "You must remember that I was always of an Eveish constitution" (*BC* 4:141). An identity with Eve's mythic and theological role suggests an identity too with the religious doctrines taught by Eve in *A Drama of Exile*. Eve's theology is Elizabeth Barrett's theology as well. As loss (and the lost) is the central theme of the biblical fall of (wo)man, so also is loss the focus of many of the works in the 1844 volume: loss of naïveté, of life and lover, of the bower of childhood, of happiness, of safety and innocence—in a word, of Eden. This motif of loss and grief is apparent not only in *A Drama of Exile* but also in the sonnets, the Wordsworthian nature reflections, and numerous ballads.

Again Barrett's position is on the perimeter, an onlooker. As the seraphim hover *above* the scenes on Calvary, Eve and Adam find themselves in the sword's glare *outside* Eden. In fact, just as the 1844 works are about loss, they are also about the obstructions to one's restoration, presented in the ballads by images of doors, gates, walls, casements, windows, and barriers that prevent the wanderer from returning to innocence, forcing numerous Eves to walk where "Hades rolls deep on all sides" (*CWEBB* 3:114.97). In spite of the recognition that woman (like man) brings loss upon herself by sin and knowledge, Barrett insists upon enlightenment as the key that opens the door once more: "KNOWLEDGE BY SUFFERING ENTERETH" (*CWEBB* 2:348.1004). Furthermore, exiled Eve of *A Drama of Exile*—once "schooled by sin"—learns lessons in humility and Christian service that she presumes to teach her fellow sufferer, Adam, who has not yet assimilated these lessons. Not only does Barrett take issue with the traditional presentation of Eve (in Christian tradition and among the Church Fathers, but especially in the epic of Milton), but she also, in *speaking through Eve*, establishes the role of the woman poet (especially herself) as a prophet and instructor in her own right. Eve's teaching in *A Drama of Exile* is the Gospel of Pity for all things, the message that one must be compassionate in order to merit grace. A Gospel too of Humility and of Suffering, the acceptance that human suffering is a necessary outcome of human sin. And finally, a Gospel of Work.

II

A Drama of Exile is a bold revision of John Milton's *Paradise Lost*, directing one's attention to Eve rather than to Lucifer or Adam as the center of the drama of the Fall. A reborn Eve takes her place in the postlapsarian world as the mother of promised new life and the messenger, as well as example, of Godly grace. Barrett's revisionism makes important claims for Eve: 1) that she is reclaimed from sin to become the preeminent figure of divine grace—not as perfect innocence—but *because she has sinned* and as a result experiences, understands, and demonstrates God's salvational role of forgiveness (as in *The Seraphim* when Ador explains to Zerah the mystery of redemption) and 2) that the woman so enlightened becomes man's true partner in the world, rather than his slave. She is therefore liberated for holy works, including the work of a poet, which is to Browning the highest calling in God's realm of works. Browning not only justifies the ways of God to man, but also finally proves that the anxiety of Miltonic influence will not silence her poetic voice.

Virtually every major British poet of the nineteenth century was haunted by Milton's great epic. Admittedly, many a woman writer called up Milton's specter to curse and scorn it. Mary Wollstonecraft, for example, in her 1792 *A Vindication of the Rights of Woman,* suggests that Milton meant to "deprive us of souls" and that he considered woman "complete" if she were skilled merely at the *"frivolous* accomplishments."[1] (It should be noted that Elizabeth Barrett was—from girlhood—an admirer of Wollstonecraft.) Barrett is, nevertheless, unique among Victorian women writers in composing a direct revision to *Paradise Lost,* a work that she had studied thoroughly in the three decades since she had begun reading it at a precocious age eight (*BC* 1:350). The poet excuses her temerity by suggesting that Eve's allotted grief had yet to be dealt with in literature, and furthermore it might be more expressible by a woman than a man. Barrett rejects the expected role of the female confined within the drawing room, nursery, and parish, while her brothers tread the great outdoor world of quest and exploration. In her preface, she deliberately juxtaposes the inside/outside metaphor of freedom and confinement: Milton is closed *within* the gates of Eden, and Barrett—by virtue of her bold poetic endeavor—is *outside* the gates with fallen Eve and Adam: "I also an exile!" (*CWEBB* 2:144). And as exile, she raises her voice together with her fellow exiles.

Deliberately looking beyond Milton's bogey (as Virginia Woolf was to name the act in *A Room of One's Own*), Barrett anticipates and counters

---

1. Wollstonecraft, *Vindication,* 19, 59.

objections, just as she had done in *The Seraphim*.[2] "Milton is too high, and I am too low," she says in her preface to *A Drama of Exile,* to render it necessary that she "disavow any rash emulation of his divine faculty" (*CWEBB* 2:145). Her apology may well be explained by the "anxiety of influence" as defined by Harold Bloom, or more specifically by an "anxiety of authorship" noted by Sandra M. Gilbert and Susan Gubar in *The Madwoman in the Attic,* who add that several women writers have, nonetheless, devised revisionary myths and metaphors in an effort to "come to terms" with the institutionalized and metaphorical misogyny that Milton's epic expresses—or, Joseph Wittreich would say, *exposes.*[3] Certainly, Barrett had lived with the anxiety at least since the time of writing *The Seraphim,* when critics compared her unfavorably with Milton. She was well aware of the risks involved, and for her the ultimate risk was *literary* exile.

A Drama of Exile, a work that Dorothy Mermin describes as a cross between Greek and Renaissance form,[4] ends not with the tragic catharsis of the Greek classic drama, but with the promise of spiritual rebirth. The play begins where a Greek tragedy would end; Lucifer, Adam, and Eve have all experienced catastrophe. In the first movement fallen Lucifer confronts unfallen Gabriel. Boasting of his strength and free will, Lucifer proclaims his tyranny on earth where cares and sorrows will "increase and multiply" (*DE* 196) and jeers at the divine pity of which Gabriel speaks. Next Eve and Adam confront the Earth Spirits, who pronounce that the exiles will be deprived of the sounds, sights, and fragrances that "expire at Eden's door" (*DE* 298, 324, 350, 384), blessings to remain enclosed *within* Paradise while fallen humanity is forever exiled *outside.* Eve and Adam are confronted by their fellow exile Lucifer, who first insults them, then sarcastically sues for pardon. Eve, feeling pity for Lucifer as she does for the wailing Earth Spirits, forgives him, whereupon Lucifer mocks her pity as he has mocked Gabriel's and God's. The woman and man depart

---

2. She does not refer to Milton by name, but attributes influence to Aeschylus's *Prometheus Bound.* But in the preface she quotes from *Paradise Lost:* "[F]rom the height of this great argument," Prometheus is diminished in comparison with Jesus (*CWEBB* 1:164).

3. Bloom, *Anxiety of Influence,* 5–7; Gilbert and Gubar, *The Madwoman in the Attic: The Woman Writer and the Nineteenth-Century Literary Imagination,* 48–51, 189; Wittreich's *Feminist Milton* is a defense of Milton's treatment of the feminine, and of feminist responses to Milton.

4. Mermin, *Origins of New Poetry,* 88.

from Eden, Eve leading the way but soon despairing. She proposes that they return to be smitten to death at Eden's gate, but takes courage from Adam and prays to God for divine pity. When the spirits of Organic and Inorganic Nature upbraid Adam and Eve for their suffering, Adam vows perpetual enmity with them, but Eve begs that they avoid strife and asks pity of the "spirit of the harmless earth" (*DE* 1053) and of the "harmless beasts" (*DE* 1067) whom she has harmed. In her eloquent sermon on pity and forgiveness, she as fallen mortal exercises pity on all fallen beings in God's universe. Of the vengeful spirits she pleads:

> . . . And, so, pity us,
> Ye gentle Spirits, pardon him and me,
> And let some tender peace, made of our pain,
> Grow up betwixt us . . .
> . . . .
> For the poor sake of our humility,
> Breathe out your pardon on our breathless lips,
> . . . .
> . . . perceive your love
> Distilling through your pity over us . . . [5]
>
> (*DE* 1305–16)

When Eve stoops in penitence, the exiles hear in the wind the voices of infants, youths, poets, philosophers, revelers, lovers, and the aged, all of whom speak for life, dispelling the "cruelty" of time and seasons symbolized in the zodiac that encircles the world, "curl[ing] round . . . like a river cold and drear" (*DE* 1146). At last the fallen humans encounter Christ, who calms the spirits, comforts the exiles, and promises redemption for humankind. At the conclusion Lucifer realizes that Christ will voluntarily become exile from heaven for humans' salvation, rather than (as Lucifer has done) become infiltrator from hell for their ruin, that Christ will be crowned first with the crown of sorrow and finally the crown of majesty. Adam and Eve go forward into the fallen world, accompanied by an angelic chorus that comforts them by singing: *"Exiled is not lost!"* (*DE* 2258).

---

5. Eve uses the term *pity* some nine times in the drama, each time implying love and forgiveness unmerited by the recipient (that is, grace). Only the angel Gabriel defines and demonstrates pity as eloquently as Eve does. Lucifer himself uses the word five times, each time in contempt and scorn.

In Barrett's revisionist reading of the Fall, she is less interested in the education of Adam (at the feet of Gabriel, as Milton depicts him) and more interested in the schooling of Eve (intuitive understanding of the forgiveness Christ will demonstrate in his future redeeming Incarnation). Or, put another way, the poem concerns itself with the lessons first learned, then taught by Eve. That Eve has a message and the drama a theme has been entirely lost upon many critics, such as Gardner Taplin, who in his biography charges that Barrett's work is a burlesque of *Paradise Lost* and the choral passages an (unintended) parody of *Prometheus Unbound* with, unfortunately, "no central idea, no action, no conflict, no development of character."[6]

Writing as Christian and female, Barrett *does* have a plan: the reinterpretation of both Eve's nature and her theological importance. Woman is the last and best gift to man, but first too to enter sin and death, a comment made "over & over," but nobody seems to have said *"first & deepest in the sorrow"* (*BC* 8:117), Barrett alleges, adding that nobody has paid adequate attention to Eve's grief. Intended as a blessing, Adam's bride turns out to be a dubious prize. Milton describes Eve in theological terms: "Grace was in all her steps, Heav'n in her Eye" (*PL* 8.488); in *A Drama of Exile,* she is Adam's "utter life and light" (*DE* 441), "lady of the world, princess of life, / Mistress of feast and favour" (*DE* 1238–39). In spite of Eve's potential as Adam's "light and life," however, Milton holds to the Scholastic (and Milton says, the Pauline) position that only man is in the *imago dei.* In the words of Richard Hooker (which both Milton and Barrett knew intimately), the subalternation of woman is naturally grounded in her inferiority "in excellency" ("the very imbecility of [her] nature and sex"). In the words of Milton, man is cast in the image of God reflecting the glory of the Father; woman is not: she reflects only the lesser glory of the man.[7] Furthermore, Milton—responding to the androcentric ideal of Bible texts and Christian tradition—makes his Eve inherently inferior and intellectually shallow, an easier target for the wiles of Satan. In the postlapsarian world that she effects, Eve emulates Satan's fraud and guile in seducing Adam into tasting the fruit; whereas Adam sins

    6. Taplin, *The Life of Elizabeth Barrett Browning,* 124, 126.
    7. Hooker, *On the Laws of Ecclesiastical Polity* 5.73.2, 5, in *Works of Mr. Richard Hooker,* 2:427, 429; Milton, *Tetrachordon,* in *The Complete Prose Works of John Milton,* 2:389.

against God and self, *she* sins against God, self, and neighbor.[8] Thereafter, the daughters of Eve perpetually sin against neighbors; they become the temptresses who lead the sons of God from the narrow paths of virtue.

Traditionally Eve's sin is considered greater than Adam's because it preceded and prompted his. Elaine Pagels notes that among the Church Fathers, Clement justified patriarchy on the grounds that Eve, not Adam, sinned first. Nehama Aschkenasy observes that, in the Bible and Midrash, Eve's sin is Faustian (a pact with Satan), while Adam's is noble: he would rather die than live without his helpmeet. "And since she was the harbinger of death, Eve, as the eternal woman, was believed to have a demonic side to her being." Diane Kelsey McColley points out that Milton inherited in patristic, puritan, and humanist traditions an Eve who is the sister of Circe and Calypso, Alcina and Armida, and Spenser's Acrasia.[9] In Milton, Eve is in a sense Satan's consort: Satan is the father of lies and Eve the mother of humans' sin and death (paralleling on earth the role played in hell by Sin, Milton's Scylla-like daughter/bride of Satan and mother of shadowy Death).

Tradition also connects Eve and Pandora, that first woman created by vengeful gods to bring innumerable ills upon man. John A. Phillips says that to the Church Fathers the Greek myth of Pandora is preserved as a "commentary on the story of Eve," and Eve, like Pandora, is vain, fraudulent, immodest, self-seeking, and prurient.[10] In *Paradise Lost*, Eve is

> More lovely than *Pandora,* whom the Gods
> Endow'd with all thir gifts, and O too like
> In sad event . . .
>
> (*PL* 4.714–16)

In fact, Milton's Eve herself agrees with the Church Fathers on the issue of who is the greater sinner. After the two moral infants of Paradise have

---

8. Elisabeth Gössmann says that this view of Eve in scholasticism is the outgrowth of the teaching of Augustine that Adam's sin is more trivial in that he sinned out of sympathy with Eve and of Peter Lombard on Eve's arrogance ("The Construction of Women's Difference in the Christian Theological Tradition," in *Special Nature of Women?* ed. Carr and Fiorenza, 52–53).

9. Pagels, *Adam, Eve and the Serpent*, 29; Aschkenasy, *Eve's Journey: Feminine Images in Hebraic Literary Tradition,* 40; McColley, *Milton's Eve,* 13.

10. Phillips, *Eve: The History of an Idea,* 22.

tasted the fruit, she admits to being the one deceived by Satan, as well as the greater sinner, Adam having sinned "[a]gainst God only, I against God and thee" (*PL* 10.931). But Barrett Browning denies that Eve is more in the wrong; in *A Drama of Exile, her* Adam confesses, "I am deepest in the guilt, / If last in the transgression" (*DE* 458–59), adding that his sin is greater because he has sinned against "more complement of gifts / And grace of giving" (*DE* 463–64). Barrett is turning the tables on Milton's argument: while Milton's Adam sins *for* Eve, Browning's Adam sins *against* her.

In *Paradise Lost,* Eve gives in to Satan's temptation to become "A Goddess among Gods, ador'd and serv'd / By Angels numberless" (*PL* 9.547–48), and the "Sovran of Creatures, universal Dame" (*PL* 9.612). Essentially this self-aggrandizement mirrors Satan's hubris in seeking godhead rather than service to God. But the implied admonition against sinful pride is also, according to Judith Plaskow, a most troubling concept of "sin" for female wholeness, inasmuch as the (male) attribute of excessive arrogance when applied to the (female) attribute of excessive servility inhibits the female evolution to independent selfhood, a "centered self."[11] The conventional (theological) wisdom is that in striving to reach beyond *human* limits Eve commits sin; Plaskow's revisionism would imply that, were she to fail to attain her *personal* potential, Eve would be sinner all the more.

The results of hubris for Milton's Eve (and consequently for womankind) are immediate: Eve becomes jealous, guileful, deceptive, and despondent. She fears that she alone will die and Adam will enjoy another Eve newly created for him. She attempts to cast all blame on the serpent, who "me beguil'd and I did eat" (*PL* 10.162). She proposes that the two cheat Death of his prophesied glut and foil God's punishment simply by having no progeny. Finally, she despairs (suggesting to her partner, "Let us seek Death" [*PL* 10.1001]). Once Eve is "[D]efac't, deflow'rd and now to Death devote" (*PL* 9.901), Gabriel brings a deep sleep upon her in order that Adam receive a private vision of the future redemption and the paradise within, happier far. Adam is educated; Eve left ignorant. The woman is then awakened, and as the two exiles "through *Eden* [take] thir solitary way" (*PL* 12.649), a chastened woman humbly vows her submission to God and to man (*PL* 12.614–17).

11. Plaskow, *Sex, Sin and Grace,* 87.

In that vision of the future that the Gabriel of *Paradise Lost* gives to Adam, man (but not woman) is given direct access to Gabriel's prophetic knowledge and divine comfort (which Adam will explain to Eve later), perhaps because Milton believes that Eve's was the greater sin or the weaker intellect (or both), and perhaps because knowledge is the key to power and Milton wants Eve (and her daughters) to remain as subjective as his own Satan perceives her to be and what Barrett's Lucifer calls, "[m]y docile Eve" (*DE* 1323).

Barrett's Eve certainly is docile at the outset of the drama, penitent and humble at the conclusion. She is less narcissistic than Milton's Eve, of whom she says:

> And as fair Eve, in Eden newly placed,
> Gazed on her form, in limpid waters traced,
> And stretch'd her gentle arms, with pleased surprise,
> To meet the image of her own bright eyes—
> (*CWEBB* 1:90–91.972–75)

She is nevertheless empress of Eden and she knows it: she has observed that roses redden and birds sing for her. Once schooled by human sinfulness to understand grace, she grants Lucifer pardon merely because he asks her (*DE* 690), accepts the Earth Spirits' charges against the humans (*DE* 1188), and begs pardon from the Earth Spirits. In other words, she demonstrates forgiveness and grace. She is the first to confront her own sin and to confess her guilt. As Sandra Marie Donaldson puts it, Eve's "first reconciliation is to an awareness of her death-dealing sin."[12] She is also first to accept punishment, and to comprehend human love as reflecting (or emanating from) God's love. Barrett is preparing innocent and ignorant Eve for the anagnorisis of the drama, when enlightened Eve will lead her partner to a fuller recognition of godly grace.

Before accepting Helen Cooper's conclusion that Browning's drama is dominated by male ideologies, it is necessary to compare her to the male exiles, Lucifer and Adam, who represent, respectively, satanic defiance and human courage.[13] Both male images are figures of pride; both preoccupied

---

12. Donaldson, "Elizabeth Barrett Browning's Poetic and Feminist Philosophies in *Aurora Leigh' and Other Poems,"* 134.
13. Cooper, *Woman and Artist,* 60–61.

with titles and power, authority and kingship. Both contrast the virtue of humility, which Barrett depicts in Eve.

Milton's Satan proclaims that it is better to reign in Hell than serve in Heaven (*PL* 1.262–63), and that the earth is his own to rule (*PL* 10.488–93); Lucifer claims the earth as his footstool, saying "my sin is on the earth, to reign thereon" (*DE* 206). He boasts that he has

> Strength to behold Him and not worship Him,
> Strength to fall from Him and not cry on Him,
> Strength to be in the universe and yet
> Neither God nor his servant.
>
> (*DE* 80–83)

This particular type of self-love, the will to control, is, according to Emanuel Swedenborg, the worst form of hellish love.[14] As such it is peculiar to devils.

Lucifer (whom Browning calls in her preface "an extreme Adam" [*CWEBB* 2:144]) recognizes his human counterpart as the world's fallen royalty, exulting, "Unkinged is the King of the Garden, / The image of God" (*DE* 19–20). He scorns Adam as the "clay-king" (*DE* 731), nevertheless fearing all the while that Adam's progeny will, through redemption, "fill the vacant thrones of me and mine" (*DE* 167). Until the last Lucifer defies the monarchy of heaven in terms of his own royal arrogance, boasting that he is

> . . . self-elect
> To kingship of resistant agony
> Toward the Good around me . . .
> (*DE* 1470–72)

Finally, the Promethean Lucifer curses humans to hate one another, depriving them—he believes—of hope. Lucifer's curse on mortals is despair, together with

---

14. Swedenborg, *Angelic Wisdom Concerning Divine Love and Wisdom,* 77. In fact, the love of domineering is lowest Hell, called the Devil, while second and subordinate to the Devil is Satan, the love of possessions (165). To Plaskow, however, woman's great sin is the failure to turn toward the self—to achieve "selfhood" (*Sex, Sin and Grace,* 151). *A Drama of Exile* predates Barrett Browning's period of most intense study of Swedenborg, but she knew his works from 1842 (*BC* 6:128).

This hate which shall pursue you—this fire-hate
Which glares without, because it burns within—
Which kills from ashes . . .

(*DE* 1461–63)

Lucifer, whom Alethea Hayter characterizes as "jeering, boasting, self-pitying, cacophonous" and "a conception perhaps more *theologically* telling than Milton's Satan," shuts himself outside the divine plan for grace and, ironically, deprives himself of all hope.[15] He is, Adam says, "fallen below hope / Of final re-ascent" (*DE* 715–16). Barrett's revisionism is ironic in that the Aeschylean Prometheus (as well as the Shelleyan) is the architect of hope, his last and best gift to humankind, but this Promethean gives despair even to himself. In reversal of the companion myth, Barrett makes Eve the symbol of hope, not as a Pandora who saves hope by accidentally trapping it in an earthen jar or cask, but hope as promise of divine grace and mercy. As mother of infant life and, consequently, of the Messiah, she brings hope to the fallen world, her seed (Jesus) predestined to bruise the head of Satan, as the Genesis writer and Milton note (Gen. 3:15; *PL* 12.623) and as Eve repeatedly echoes in *A Drama of Exile*.

As Eve is Adam's hope, he is her strength, his human strength paralleling Lucifer's demonic strength. She takes strength from Adam, saying love makes her heart strong (*DE* 546), and pleading, "Adam! hold / My right hand strongly!" (*DE* 645–46). On his part, Adam recognizes that without Eve, his own life would be unbearable. ("If I am exiled, must I be bereaved?" [*DE* 541]). Not until the end of the poem, however, does he discover that he can learn from the woman.

Adam by himself is one-sided; his are the masculine virtues of strength, authority, and the will to power. His rhetoric echoes Lucifer's. For example, in praising the " . . . angelic pomps, / Thrones, dominations, princedoms, rank on rank" (*DE* 405–6), he echoes Milton's Satan in *Paradise Lost:* "Thrones and Imperial Powers, off-spring of Heav'n, / Ethereal Virtues" (*PL* 2.310–11) and "Thrones, Dominations, Princedoms, Virtues, Powers" (*PL* 10.460). He admires flashiness and pride (the attributes of Lucifer) more than humility and pity (the attributes of Christ that Eve intuitively understands). When Eve looks at fallen Lucifer, she sees a *sad* spirit in need of pity, but Adam sees a *strong* spirit

15. Hayter, *Mrs. Browning: A Poet's Work and Its Setting,* 76.

(*DE* 704–5) who "one day wor[e] a crown" (*DE* 708). When Eve pities the "Wretched Lucifer," Adam admires Lucifer's magnificence: "How he stands—yet an angel!" (*DE* 1345). Which, of course, he is decidedly not.

If Adam sees Lucifer as fallen monarchy, he sees himself as king of earth, even though he is after the Fall crowned only by the love he sees in Eve's eyes (*DE* 493). He boldly rebukes the spirits: "I charge you into silence—trample you / Down to obedience. I am king of you!" (*DE* 1723–24). The Earth Spirits scorn his claim, just as Lucifer has done, sarcastically pointing out his "sin for a crown, / And a soul undone!" (*DE* 1726–27). Thereupon the exiled humans appeal to God, their rhetoric illustrating their respective attitudes. Adam cries, "God, there is power in thee! I make appeal / Unto thy kingship" (*DE* 1744–45), but Eve pleads, "There is pity in THEE, / O sinned against, great God!" (*DE* 1746–47). Thus, Eve needs Adam because his boldness gives her courage as antidote to the satanic gift of despair (*DE* 1323). And he needs her because she is mother of life and mother of Mary whose seed will bruise the head of the serpent. Eve represents forgiveness, pity, and hope. The respective roles of male and female (strength and tenderness) are demonstrated also in Christina Rossetti's " 'All Thy Works Praise Thee, O Lord,' " in which all creatures in nature testify to their unique form of praise. Rossetti's men proclaim, "God gives us power to rule"; her women speak of work and love: "God makes our service love, and makes our wage / Love."[16] The message of the transfigured Christ in *A Drama of Exile* acknowledges both male and female values: "Take courage, O thou woman,—man, take hope!" (*DE* 1987).

Actually, Eve vacillates between boldness and temerity. As she is first to sin and first to repent, she boldly takes the first step outside the angelic sword-glare protecting Eden and into the outer darkness of the wasted universe. Not only is she sometimes Adam's leader; she is also his teacher. While he vows to wage perpetual strife against Lucifer and the avenging Spirits of the Earth, she cautions:

> Shall I speak humbly now who once was proud?
> I, schooled by sin to more humility
> Than thou hast, O mine Adam, O my king—
> *My* king, if not the world's?
>
> (*DE* 1181–84)

16. Rossetti, *Complete Poems of Christina Rossetti*, 2:137.174, 171–72.

Eve had formerly herself been seduced by pride and power; she admits to "reigning the earth's empress yesterday" (*DE* 1296) and says of her sin,

> Yea, I plucked the fruit
> With eyes upturned to heaven and seeing there
> Our god-thrones, as the tempter said,—not God.
> (*DE* 914–16)

Here Barrett follows the lead of Milton, whose Eve fell for the ploy that she should be "Empress of this fair World," "Goddess among Gods" (*PL* 9.568, 547). The sovereignty that Eve nearly attains is like the selfhood that Emanuel Swedenborg and William Blake condemn, an empty form of self-glorification. (To be empress of earth would be a presumptuous mockery of God's monarchy of heaven.) In *A Drama of Exile* the woman Eve *negates the power myth,* substituting for it the *theology of divine grace and human endeavor.* Barrett's treatment of Eve as teacher, however, has not been admired in the main by her readers and critics, although Antony H. Harrison comes closer than most in noting that Barrett "privileges the female voice in radical ways" to demonstrate that woman can command the "mythologies that have traditionally determined their cultural status and constraints." Even when the poem was newly published, the critical public failed to appreciate the significance of Eve's voice. Edgar Allan Poe, for example, admires Barrett's "wild and magnificent genius," but charges that "Miss Eve" is a "mystical something or nothing, enwrapped in a fog of rhapsody about Transfiguration, and the Seed, and the Bruising of the Heel, and other talk . . . that no man ever pretended to understand. . . ."[17]

This rhetoric of Eve that Poe found nebulous and Harrison finds potentially liberating not only grapples with theological mystery and reshapes myth; it also foreshadows the humility of Mary Magdalene, as well as the grace awarded by Jesus to Mary (if she is a sinner, as tradition suggests) or the endorsement of Mary of Bethany when he tells Judas Iscariot to leave off complaining about the expensive ointment with which she has anointed his feet. Or that awarded the same Mary who sat at the foot of Jesus while her sister, Martha, bustled about as hostess.[18] Like

17. Harrison, *Victorian Poets and Romantic Poems: Intertextuality and Ideology,* 130; Poe, "Elizabeth Barrett Browning," from *Edgar Allan Poe: Essays and Reviews,* 123, 119.
18. Haskins notes that, following the interpretation of Origen, Mary became identified as the contemplative life, Martha as the active (*Mary Magdalene,* 91).

Mary (or the Marys) Eve understands grace and allows herself (and her progeny) to be its recipient. When the vision of Christ approaches, Eve's humble plea, "Lift my soul upward till it touch thy feet" (*DE* 1761), recalls the humility of the Mary who washed Jesus' feet, who learned his teachings while sitting at his feet, who knelt at the foot of his cross. The Mary/Magdalene allusion is summoned in Barrett's work to suggest her own response to the conviction of sin and her own humility before the redeeming Christ. In the sonnet "Comfort," she pleads, "Speak to me as to Mary at Thy feet" (*CWEBB* 2:231.5); in *Aurora Leigh,* Marian Erle humbles herself before her savior Romney "To feel how tenderly his voice broke through, / As the ointment-box broke on the Holy feet . . ." (*AL* 3.1221–22); in "The Rhyme of the Duchess May" the duchess clings to her beloved as "one, withstood, clasps a Christ upon the rood" (*CWEBB* 3:24.367). Also, as noted in Chapter 1, the figure of the Magdalene-like woman weeping hoarsely in the shadow of the cross in *The Seraphim* prefigures the weeping (hoarse) song of the poet herself.

So far, so good. Via the icon of Eve, Browning deliberately reinterprets theological tradition in that Eve learns, then teaches, and finally demonstrates the lessons of repentance and grace. But how is Eve's example different from that of the Victorian heroine in works almost too numerous to mention? Is not the pure woman typically the salvation of erring man?

True enough, Victorian literature is replete with virtuous and self-sacrificing angels who save or enlighten the world—or at least their corner of it—by the traditional female virtues. Examples of this paragon are Dickens's Rose Maylie, Esther Summersun, and Agnes Wickfield, Tennyson's Elaine and Enid, Thackeray's Amelia Sedley, and George Eliot's Mary Garth and Dinah Morris. She represents the virtues of hearth and home; she is a gentle daughter, sister, or wife, a deified Vesta, a goddess of the hearth, and a sinless Madonna. Naturally in her exiled postlapsarian existence Eve the helpmeet, now reconciled to the rule of God and man, will be also Eve the domesticated mother, wife, and housekeeper.

Victorian novelists and poets, however, contrast the idealized woman with her counterpart: woman as monster, witch, or temptress, as the daughter of Circe, Pandora, or traditional Eve. Familiar examples are Hardy's exotic witch-goddess Eustacia Vye, Dickens's heartless Estella, Thackeray's little schemer Becky Sharpe, and Tennyson's Vivien and Isolt. Apparently Victorians categorized women in just the same two extremes. At any rate, Charlotte Brontë's fictional Shirley Keeldar makes this charge: "the acutest men . . . do not read [women] in a true light: they misapprehend them, both for good and evil: their good woman is a queer

thing, half doll, half angel; their bad woman almost always a fiend." Like
Aurora Leigh's mother, they seem "[g]host, fiend, and angel, fairy, witch,
and sprite" (*AL* 1.154). According to Rosemary Radford Ruether, Christianity (especially, it seems, nineteenth-century Protestantism) typically
produces a schizophrenic view of women split into sublimated spiritual
femininity (of the Virgin Mary) and actual fleshly women (fallen Eve).
Thus, spirituality and carnality. Nina Auerbach argues, however, that the
angelic and demonic are not always separated, that "female demons bear
an eerie resemblance to their angelic counterparts." In Robert Browning's
The Ring and the Book, for example, a single woman, Pompilia, fits both
roles in the eyes of the two men who best know her. The avenging
husband, Guido, sees Pompilia as "thief, poisoner and adulteress," while
the adoring Caponsacchi thinks of her as "The glory of life, the beauty
of the world, / The splendor of heaven." To the young priest she is
Marian purity, the representative of God as Beatrice was to Dante, for, as
Caponsacchi says, "Duty to God is duty to her."[19] Guido and Caponsacchi
are a case in point to prove the assertion of Brontë's Shirley.

The Eve of *A Drama of Exile* is different from the Victorian cult of ideal
womanhood, however, precisely because she has been *schooled by sin.* She
has tasted the forbidden fruit. The Victorian angel (or the maiden in her
angelic, rather than her demonic, manifestation) is idealized because she
is untainted by any evil (as Mary is), not because of her bold acquisition
of forbidden knowledge and experience. Barrett's Eve, on the other hand,
has tasted desire, ambition, and pride, followed by guilt, remorse, and
repentance, then salvation. This constitutes the necessary prototype of
all human experience, male and female, and Eve has demonstrated to
Adam, her human helpmeet, that she has been reclaimed and made the
vessel of grace *because of her sin.* In finding a near likeness to Barrett's Eve,
one might look to Christina Rossetti or to William Blake. In *Later Life:
A Double Sonnet of Sonnets,* Rossetti speculates whether Adam and Eve
still loved once they had been ejected from Paradise, and she concludes
that they probably did:

> I think so; as we love who work us ill,
> And wounds us to the quick, yet loves us still.
> Love pardons the unpardonable past . . ."

19. Brontë, *Shirley,* 2:37; Ruether, *New Woman, New Earth,* 18; Auerbach, *Woman
and the Demon: The Life of a Victorian Myth,* 75; Browning, *The Ring and the Book,*
5.1975, 6.118–19, 1030.

In *Jerusalem,* Blake's "polluted" Mary (Blake denies the doctrine of the virgin birth) explains forgiveness to Joseph,

> . . . if I were pure, never could I taste the sweets
> Of the Forgive[ne]ss of Sins! if I were holy! I never could behold the tears
> Of love![20]

Barrett's Eve, like Blake's Mary, understands forgiveness because she has experienced it.

Significantly, Barrett's Christ does not respond to Eve's humility by declaring forgiven Eve the servant of Adam, but the now exiled pair as jointly "masters" of the rebellious Earth Spirits (*DE* 1768). Here, Barrett once more departs from Milton. Before the Fall, Milton's Adam and Eve "seem'd Lords of all, / And worthy seem'd" (*PL* 4.290–91). But man and woman were not equals; they only *seemed* so. Adam was for contemplation and valor formed; Eve for softness and attractive grace, "Hee for God only, shee for God in him" (*PL* 4.299). Thus man was the intended master of woman and nature—also considered as female. McColley denies that Eve is subjected to Adam by God or man, insisting that Milton emphasizes Eve's liberty more than his predecessors had done. In any case, Barrett follows Chrysostom on the initial relationship of the pair in Eden (whether or not Milton does). Chrysostom believes the subordination of woman to man *follows* the Fall and was not inherent in Eve's womanhood.[21] While not proclaiming for Eve's female descendants full political and social rights enjoyed by males, Barrett, however, does illustrate that in some aspects (humility, insight, intuitive faith) woman is rightly the teacher of man, not his student. In this proclamation, she is revising not only Milton's version of the Fall, but also the Pauline version of woman as *follower* of man, whom she is prohibited from teaching. In an epistle to Timothy, the woman is commanded to "learn in silence with all subjection. But I suffer not a woman to teach, nor to usurp authority over the man, but to be in silence. For Adam was first formed, then Eve.

---

20. Rossetti, *Later Life: A Double Sonnet of Sonnets,* in *Complete Poems of Christina Rossetti,* 2:145.15.10–12 (sonnets 14 and 15 ask the same question about Eve and Adam in exile); Blake, *Jerusalem* 3.61.11–13, in *The Complete Works of William Blake,* 211.

21. McColley, *Milton's Eve,* 48–50; Chrysostom, *Homilies on First Corinthians* 26 in *Select Library,* ed. Schaff, 12:150–51.

And Adam was not deceived, but the woman being deceived was in the transgression" (1 Tim. 2:11–14).

In disposing of the quarrel between the exiles and the Spirits, Christ illustrates by means of his own rhetoric that Eve is not Pandora, but symbolic grace and charity, exemplifying the lessons that he will teach in Galilee, that the meek shall inherit the earth, that the least shall be greatest (Matt. 5:5). Or, as Eve says:

> It little doth become me to be proud,
> . . . .
> Only my gentleness shall make me great,
> My humbleness exalt me.
>					(*DE* 1275–79)

Thus Eve teaches her descendants the Gospel of the rejection of pride that her creator Elizabeth Barrett has struggled to achieve.

Mary Daly, in "exorcising" the Eden and Eve myth, says that there is no escaping that in Christianity women are powerless scapegoats of guilt because identified with sin, while (no matter how you cast it) salvation always comes through the male God-made-man.[22] My thesis does not deny the power of the Eden myth; if it were not powerful, Barrett need not have bothered to confront and revise it. I merely argue that Barrett, working *within* the Christian religion to which she subscribed and working *against* the Christian patristic tradition and the rhetoric of Milton that she finds devastating, elevates Eve to a new position of theological insight, making her at once a role model for Adam and a prophetess for God.

III

The Christ of *A Drama of Exile* advocates not only humility but also service as an avenue to greatness. In this Barrett echoes the Jesus of the Gospels: "If any man desire to be first, *the same* shall be last of all, and servant of all" (Mark 9:35) and " . . . whosoever will be chief among you, let him be your servant: Even as the Son of man came not to be ministered

22. Daly, *Beyond God the Father,* 71.

to, but to minister . . ." (Matt. 20:27–28).[23] The service of ministry (the Gospel of Good Works) is a second major value that Eve, now schooled by sin, feels impelled to teach her partner. And in spotlighting this teaching the poet Barrett joins a dialogue (or perhaps more accurately a chorus) on the Gospel of Work currently in vogue in Victorian England.

At the conclusion of *A Drama of Exile,* Christ instructs Adam to "[b]less the woman" (*DE* 1823), and Adam responds by proclaiming to Eve:

> . . . Rise, woman, rise
> To thy peculiar and best altitudes
> Of doing good and of enduring ill,
> Of comforting for ill, and teaching good,
> And reconciling all that ill and good
> Unto the patience of a constant hope . . .
>   (*DE* 1842–47)

In accepting the calling to Christian charity, as here enunciated by Adam, Eve emerges from grief to affirmation, or from Eden into adult participation in the world, as Mermin says. Barrett, who knew the New Testament intimately, would have been aware that the epistles to various churches repeatedly instructed early-day Christians to demonstrate their grace by means of works, that is, ministry to the saints. Among the "works" mentioned in letters to the churches are: admonishing, comforting, edifying, teaching, prophesying, exhorting, nursing, visiting orphans and widows, housing and clothing the destitute. "[W]orkers . . . receive not the grace of God in vain" (2 Cor. 6:1); rather they "labour and travail" in preaching, prophesying, teaching, serving the downtrodden (1 Thess. 2:9).[24] Adam instructs Eve to consider herself blessed in rendering service:

> A poor man served by thee shall make thee rich;
> A sick man helped by thee shall make thee strong;
> Thou shalt be served thyself by every sense

23. Ruether argues that while Christ has been interpreted as king, he saw himself as Suffering Servant (*Sexism and God-Talk: Toward a Feminist Theology,* 29). In *A Drama of Exile,* Barrett incorporates both aspects of Christ: servant and sacrifice in the earthly Incarnation, his brow of "kingly whiteness" to be crowned anew after his triumph over sin and death (*DE* 1979).

24. Mermin, *Origins of New Poetry,* 88; for the litany of Christian "works," see 1 Thess. 5:11–13, Eph. 4:11–12, 1 Thess. 2:7–11, and James 2:15–16.

Of service which thou renderest. Such a crown
I set upon thy head . . .

(*DE* 1871–75)

Such a crown St. John Rivers also invites Jane Eyre to wear in Brontë's most famous novel, and such a crown Aurora Leigh initially rejects from Romney Leigh in Barrett Browning's novel-epic.

If we interpret the drama as meaning women alone are enjoined to care for children, the poor, and the sick as Eve vows to do on behalf of herself and her daughters, however, then we accept the unschooled values of both exiles: the myth that man is king and woman is servant. We close the female back inside the parlor, nursery, and parish, a choice that Barrett rejects. In fact, some years later Barrett Browning expresses strong reservations about the example of Florence Nightingale as nurse in the Crimea on the very basis that the work of caregiver is the work women have always done and there must surely be better use to be made of a gifted and accomplished woman. Nightingale's "retrograde movement" is hardly a solution to the "woman's question," suggests Barrett Browning, revealing, however, that she does not understand the full implications of Nightingale's ideology and her profession (*LEBB* 2:189).

Barrett's definition of work is, nonetheless, a broad definition, including a whole array of works for God and humankind. Deirdre David interprets *A Drama of Exile* somewhat as Barrett Browning interprets Nightingale's work: she argues that Barrett is made twice passive, by Milton and by God, that she effaces herself from the text and that Eve moves to a dignified, noble acceptance of her Miltonic destiny (as man's slave, humanity's servant).[25] But if Christian charity is to manifest godly love to all people, to be "servant of all," then Adam is not exempt by virtue of his gender. In fact, the teachings of the biblical Jesus negate this version of service, and Barrett's Christ tells *both* the penitent exiles, " Live and love . . . Live and work . . ." (*DE* 1995–97). The role of being "servant to all" and doing the good work of humanity is the role of all the sons of Adam as well as the daughters of Eve. In an essay applauding Thomas Carlyle's contribution to the age, Barrett Browning says he taught us that work is "every man's duty." She goes on to query: "Who doubted

25. David, *Intellectual Women*, 108–9.

that among the factory masters?—or among the charity children, when spelling from the catechism of the national church, that they will 'do their duty in the state of life to which it shall please God to call them'?" And, she notes, Carlyle adds the word *soul* to that of *work,* elevating work from a duty to a devotion (*CWEBB* 6:316).

The Victorian Gospel of Work takes on a broader connotation than Christian charity to the impoverished; work is noble in itself, not only in Milton or in the Puritan ethic of "duty" but also in the secular world, a claim that some critics trace from Milton. Joseph Wittreich, who believes that Milton is "of Eve's party and knows it full well," argues that the Eve of Milton's epic was also enlightened to the necessity of activity in the world (even when it is yet unfallen). Wittreich says Eve "values work over idle speculation; she would rather tend her garden than take tea." And Diane McColley suggests that the trope of gardening represents any art or science in which future Adams and Eves might engage.[26] If Barrett reads Milton as Wittreich and McColley do, she has chosen to make her revisionist Eve emphasize the Gospel of Work with more clarity and insistence; if not, Barrett very deliberately chooses the female partner in Eden as her advocate of a value that she everywhere holds. For example, in *Casa Guidi Windows,* Barrett Browning advocates for the political and moral salvation of Italy the prayer and work of its citizens: "Then turn to wakeful prayer and worthy act" (*CGW* 1.223). The poet herself does not swerve from this position of dedication to holy, poetic work. While at work on *A Drama of Exile* she notes, "The poet's work is no light work. This wheat will not grow without labour, any more than other kinds of wheat—and the sweat of the spirit's brow is wrung by a yet harder necessity" (*BC* 8:124). And near the end of her life, she remains steadfastly loyal to the ethic of work: "[God] never made a creature for which He did not make the work suited to its hand. He never made a creature necessarily useless, nor gave a life which it was not sin on the creature's part to hold unthankfully and throw back as a poor gift" (*LEBB* 2:291).

In *Aurora Leigh,* published twelve years after *A Drama of Exile,* Browning's poet-hero Aurora rejects the marriage proposal of her cousin Romney, who sees her as an Eve "with nature's daybreak on her face"

26. Wittreich, *Feminist Milton,* 98, 10; McColley, *Milton's Eve,* 110.

(*AL* 2.159), and she rejects him in part because she does not accept the work he intends for her to do. Like Adam he believes that woman is fit for charity alone, meant to be wife, mother, nurse, and social worker, but not meant for poetry and art. After much suffering, both Aurora and Romney learn God's lesson about work. Aurora says:

> The honest, earnest man must stand and work,
> The woman also,—otherwise she drops
> At once below the dignity of man,
> Accepting serfdom. Free men freely work.
> Whoever fears God, fears to sit at ease.
> (AL 8.712–16)

To this Romney concurs that after human's sin work was cursed, the sweat of labour in God's curse upon Adam having become the sweat of torture (*AL* 2.166–68), but "after Christ, work turns to privilege" (*AL* 8.719). In *A Drama of Exile* even the Earth Spirits exist for work; they upbraid the mortals:

> God gave us golden cups, and we were bidden
> To feed you so.
> But now our right hand hath no cup remaining,
> No work to do . . .
> (DE 237–40)

In the sonnet "Work" (also from the 1844 volume) Browning suggests that work is the true purpose of existence:

> What are we set on earth for? Say, to toil;
> Nor seek to leave thy tending of the vines
> For all the heat o' the day, till it declines,
> And Death's mild curfew shall from work assoil.
> (CWEBB 2:232.1–4)

In another sonnet from that same volume ("Work and Contemplation") she embraces the contemplative life along with active life (the roles of both Mary *and* Martha, one might say), recommending to the "dear Christian church":

> . . . that we may do
> Our Father's business in these temples mirk,

> Thus swift and steadfast, thus intent and strong;
> While thus, apart from toil, our souls pursue
> Some high calm spheric tune, and prove our work
> The better for the sweetness of our song
>   (*CWEBB* 2:235.9–14)

Thus Eve in *A Drama of Exile* is teaching Adam the Christian virtues that Barrett Browning repeats throughout her poetic canon. Not only is this virtuous *behavior*, it is also grounded in a theological understanding. As a child Barrett learned from reading Jeremy Taylor that "God hath given every man work enough to do," and that "[i]dleness is the greatest prodigality in the world." She refused to enter the quarrel whether salvation comes by grace or by works, although the theologians whom she most admired tended to stress the necessity of works. At the same time she distrusted Arminianism, which, she notes, implies that man is saved by *his* works, rather than Christ's works, and she insisted that good works are as absolutely a consequence of faith as salvation is. Richard Hooker, one of the Anglican divines whom she particularly admired, argues for election by grace but adds, paradoxically, "unless we work, we have it not." Thus we are saved both by faith (as Paul says) and by works (as James says); "Habitual" and "Actual" sanctification being, respectively, the holiness with which our souls are endued the moment we accept grace and the "holiness which afterward beautifieth all parts and actions of our lives."[27] In what might be almost a paraphrase of Hooker, Barrett says of salvation that good works are a consequence of faith, adding that only one "work" brings salvation, that of Christ's death, and that work "saves us *that we may work,*—and not *because we work*" (*BC* 8:24).

In her devotion to the doctrine of work, Barrett aligns herself with contemporaries such as John Ruskin and Carlyle, the great teacher at whose feet she is "a devout sitter" (*BC* 10:81).[28] In *Past and Present* (1843), Carlyle claims that there is a sacredness in work and that "all true Work is Religion," and in *Sartor Resartus* the "Everlasting Yea" is an injunction to "Produce! Produce! Were it but the pitifullest infinitesimal

---

27. Taylor, *The Rule and Exercises of Holy Living,* 1:8, 9; Hooker, *A Learned Discourse of Justification, Works, and How the Foundation of Faith Is Overthrown,* in *Works of Mr. Richard Hooker,* 3:491, 507–8.

28. Although admiring Carlyle's doctrine of work, she is annoyed that he advised her to write prose instead of verse, and she fears that he has failed to understand that "song is work."

fraction of a Product, produce it in God's name. . . . Whatsoever thy hand findeth to do, do it with thy whole might. Work while it is called Today; for the Night cometh, wherein no man can work." Ruskin, who—like Carlyle—became a friend to both the Brownings, concurs. He says that although Milton and Dante tried to tell us that religion is a mystery amplified by imagination, and although Shakespeare and Homer tried to exemplify the mystery of life in courage, honor, and integrity, he himself opts for the art (and task) of feeding, housing, and dressing those in need (a secular version of the admonition of the New Testament epistles); he says that in times of national crisis or religious trial, we must do wholesome work and this is the basis for an "infallible religion." Even Florence Nightingale, whose "work" Barrett Browning eschewed, holds a similar belief (although Barrett could not know this since her moral treatise, *Suggestions for Thought to the Searchers after Truth among the Artizans of England,* was not published in Barrett Browning's lifetime). Nightingale, whose religion was unorthodox, believes that the highest good and only source of happiness is but "to do the work of God and mankind," that there is a blessedness in assuming we will work our way into the light, that "[T]hrough work, worlds and firmaments rise to our consciousness." Finally, in Robert Browning's "Prince Hohenstiel-Schwangau," published a decade after his wife's death, the Prince champions the religion of work:

> . . . for religion, works,
> Works only and works ever, makes and shapes
> And changes, still wrings more of good from less,
> Still stamps some bad out, where was worst before,
> So leaves the handiwork, the act and deed,
> Were it but house and land and wealth, to show
> Here was a creature more perfect in the kind—
> Whether as bee, beaver, or behemoth,
> What's the importance? he has done his work
> For work's sake, worked well, earned a creature's
> praise—[29]

29. Carlyle, *Past and Present,* in *Works of Thomas Carlyle,* 10:210, 211; Carlyle, *Sartor Resartus,* in ibid., 1:157; Ruskin, "On the Mystery of Life," in *Sesame and Lilies,* 217–22; Nightingale, *"Cassandra" and Other Selections,* 92, 150, 204; Browning, "Prince Hohenstiel-Schwangau, Saviour of Society," in *The Poems* 1:961.670–79. I am not

Not only a "creature's praise," but also a blessing. Adam says to Eve:

> . . . But go to! thy love
> Shall chant itself its own beatitudes
> After its own life-working.
> (*DE* 1867–69)

Unfortunately Adam does not accept his own role as blessed servant. But as Romney Leigh—a more enlightened Adam—says, "I count that heaven itself is only work / To a surer issue." (*AL* 8.724–25). Not only is Barrett joining other important Victorian thinkers in evolving the Gospel of Work, but she is also expressing an important teaching of Emanuel Swedenborg, whose very angels in heaven work in heaven because the "Lord's kingdom is a kingdom of uses."[30]

In *A Drama of Exile,* Barrett's Eve now knows she is no empress and that she has work to do; Adam still believes he is king and that his role is to receive homage. He must learn by Eve's example that all humans are—as Carlyle says—"blessed" in finding work and doing it. Browning's Eve is not a slave, but an equal worker; no moral simpleton, but a spiritual teacher. She knows that "Noble work / Shall hold me in the place of garden-rest" (*DE* 1899–1900). The crown of service will replace Eve's crown of empress as it must Adam's crowns of authority and of sin. Eve also anticipates (in retrospect) the female Christian disciples of the first century: while many of their male counterparts expected Jesus to rule in kingly glory, the women understood that his true ministry was *diakonia* (service), a value that they demonstrated in witness and ministry, notes Elisabeth Schüssler Fiorenza. Also, for some intellectual women of the nineteenth century, as for some female Christians of the first, faith in a servant Christ proved a liberating faith, enabling them to become activists

---

suggesting that Browning is in sympathy with the Prince (who represents Napoleon III), but merely that the poem (like other Victorian works) expresses the value of work *as religion.*

30. Swedenborg, *Heaven and Hell,* 300. Swedenborg despised Luther because he taught the "pernicious doctrine" of grace without works (Toksvig, *Emanuel Swedenborg: Scientist and Mystic,* 305). Coming under the influence of Swedenborgian spiritualism around 1851, Barrett Browning found nothing in Swedenborg's views on work to disagree with her own: citing his doctrine of work and activity beyond the grave, she says, "I believe in an active, *human life,* beyond death as before it, an uninterrupted human life" (*LEBB* 2:177).

in a male-dominated world. Such was the case for Elizabeth Barrett, called to be a poet—as David says, "a ministering healer to an infected world." So too for Florence Nightingale, no Christian in the traditional sense but nevertheless advocate of Jesus' ministry as example for a radical liberation for women. Nightingale claims that Jesus Christ raised women above the condition of mere slaves, mere ministers to the passions of the man; raised them by his sympathy, to be the ministers of God. He gave them moral activity. But the Age, the World, Humanity, must give them the means to exercise this moral activity.[31]

Alexander Welsh, in *The City of Dickens,* considers the paradoxical nature of the Victorian work ethic. Just as Calvinism advocates work, but denies that works can earn salvation, so the work ethic merely substitutes a "polite agnosticism" in that the "preachment of work is intensified, but its end is obscure." Barrett's advocacy of the Gospel of Work rejects Martin Luther's doctrine of salvation by grace alone. Like many other Victorians, she believes one works for the sake of the work and for the love of God and humans. Like Christina Rossetti, she endorses the necessity of work. Rossetti's Eve calls herself a "fool" and regrets the sin of sloth: "My garden plot I have not kept; / Faded and all-forsaken. . . ."[32] Barrett insists that women are elevated by Christianity to do the noble works of body and spirit. Or, as Aurora Leigh says, woman need not drop below the dignity of the man, accepting serfdom.

IV

As noted at the outset of this chapter, a unifying element of the 1844 volume is suffering a loss of Eden: of love, innocence, happiness, or life. In affirming that exile from Eden serves as unifying motif, however, one should not overlook that the same preoccupation recurs throughout the 1838 *Seraphim, and Other Poems.* In fact, although it is overshadowed in importance by Prometheus and Christ (rebellion and redemption) in *The Seraphim,* the loss of Eden is expressed in that earlier volume in various

31. Fiorenza, "In Search of Women's Heritage," in *Weaving the Visions: New Patterns in Feminist Spirituality,* ed. Judith Plaskow and Carol P. Christ, 30; David, *Intellectual Women,* 117; Nightingale, *"Cassandra" and Other Selections,* 227.

32. Welsh, *The City of Dickens,* 85; Rossetti, *Complete Poems of Christina Rossetti,* 1:208.6–7.

ways. Among ballads and other narratives, for example, are numerous case studies: in "A Romance of the Ganges" the Hindu maiden Nuleeni loses her faith in her beloved, in "The Romaunt of Margret" the deserted Margret dies a suicide upon accepting that all human love is transient; in "Isobel's Child" the young mother, Isobel, must learn to submit humbly to the God who steals away in death her three-month-old infant; and in "The Poet's Vow" the protagonist withdraws from the world not merely to create art but also because the world—infected by Adam's sin—is a bitter place. Indeed, the poet's misanthropy is informed ("haunted") by the knowledge that Adam bequeathed his offspring pride, death, endless labor, and numerous degrees of suffering.

The 1838 poems repeatedly also employ Eden imagery and Edenic rhetoric. Nature scenes in "The Deserted Garden," "The Soul's Travel-ling," "Earth and Her Praises," and "Night and the Merry Man" are used to indulge in nostalgic dreams of an Eden once possessed, but inevitably lost as a child comes to know sin and guilt, remorse and regret. In the pseudo-allegory "Memory and Hope," Hope is a prophet "[c]rowned with an Eden wreath" until slain by Memory (*CWEBB* 2:85.26). In "Earth and Her Praisers," Earth is old, sick, and weary, a church whose dogma is "remorseful melancholy," allowing us to forget that formerly we had "an Eden in thee" (*CWEBB* 2:65.16, 18). In "Night and the Merry Man" the speaker (not a merry man but a man formerly merry because formerly innocent) digs a grave to bury the "past joy" of childhood, a youth in which he vainly believed life was a poem (*CWEBB* 2:62.24–27, 58). In "The Deserted Garden" the exiled adult persona would hardly choose to become once more the happy child in a long since deserted Eden. And in "Isobel's Child" the mother wishes her child to become a nature poet who will guard from decay "Earth's flowers recovering hues of Eden" (*CWEBB* 2:20.294), to which the enlightened spirit of the child responds:

> "Can your poet make an Eden
>   No winter will undo,
> And light a starry fire while heeding
>   His hearth's is burning too!
> Drown in music the earth's din,
> And keep his own wild soul within
>   The law of his own harmony?
>   (*CWEBB* 2:26.476–82)

The dying infant concludes that—although such tasks may be possible—
he would prefer immediate eternal life rather than continue to adulthood
and suffer loss of Eden in this present world.

In *A Drama of Exile,* however, the sorrow is both human and divine.
Christ is crowned with sorrow in order to be crowned with majesty. "We
worship in Thy sorrow, Saviour Christ!" declares Barrett's Eve (*DE* 1926).
And Barrett's Christ responds:

> . . . With my pangs
> I will confront your sin . . .
> . . . .
> And set a holy passion to work clear
> Absolute consecration
>
> (*DE* 1973–78)

If humankind is a suffering creation, it worships a suffering God. Or a
suffering God is required—as George Eliot suggests in *Adam Bede*—to
give meaning for human suffering, to make it endurable.[33] The seraph
Ador comments in *The Seraphim,* "[M]an's victim [is] his deity" (*S* 248),
implying first that Christ died as atonement for human wrongs, but also
perhaps that God must suffer *because* mortals do.

By 1844 Barrett was herself a confirmed sufferer, an invalid who had
mourned the deaths of her mother and two brothers and believed her own
death to be immanent; she had experienced hemorrhage of the lungs,
used morphine and ether to relieve pain, felt her face leaning so near the
tombstone that she forgot on which side of death she languished. Her
grief was—in her words—"bitterness dropp[ing] on bitterness like the
snows" (*BC* 5:18). The doctrine of human suffering is clearly amplified
in Barrett's sonnets of the 1844 volume: in "Past and Future" life's wine is
spilled, the bread of repast scattered and trampled (*CWEBB* 2:228.6–9);
in "Irreparableness" the persona clutches handfuls of decayed blossoms
"Held dead . . . till myself shall die" (*CWEBB* 2:229.14); in "Tears" she
"grope[s] tear-blinded in a desert place / And touch[es] but tombs"
(*CWEBB* 2:229.11–12); in "Discontent" she shoulders "weights of pain"
(*CWEBB* 2:236.11); in "The Prisoner," she counts "the dismal time by
months and years" (*CWEBB* 2:240.1); in "Insufficiency" her imprisoned
soul "throbs audibly . . . yearning to be free" (*CWEBB* 2:240.2–3). And

---

33. Eliot, *Adam Bede,* in *Writings of George Eliot,* 4:107.

in "The Seraph and Poet," she contrasts the sorrowful condition of earth with the beauty of the anticipated new Eden: "Sing, seraph with the glory! heaven is high; / Sing, poet with the sorrow! earth is low" (*CWEBB* 2:227.10–11). In artistic merit these sonnets of the 1844 volume certainly rank well below those yet to come in the *Sonnets from the Portuguese* volume, but they deserve attention at this point because of their kinship to the themes of patience-in-suffering manifest throughout the work.

Human suffering is universal result of human loss of Eden. In "De Profundis" Barrett says that being and suffering are one. She often depicts this loss as an experience with nature, the speaker either being out of tune with nature or having been banished from an idyllic pastoral Eden. In "The Lost Bower," for example, the vanishing of a child's woodland arbor merely prefigures the "suffering of many losses" of "ripened womanhood," losses such as

> Many a hope and many a power—
> Studious health and merry leisure,
> The first dew on the first flower!
> (*CWEBB* 3:46.294, 297–99)

(This loss appeared in similar fashion in the 1838 "Deserted Garden" in which the garden is lost; the speaker now beholds white sepulchres, and "silk [is] changed for shroud" [*CWEBB* 2:46.40].) In "The Romance of the Swan's Nest" (which recalls "The Deserted Garden") Little Ellie in innocent harmony with nature dreams of a dashing lover on a red-roan steed; to this gallant lover she will reveal her own soon-to-be-lost bower. But her dream is dashed when her own Eden is infiltrated, by either lust or the evil One, or by her own impending adult sexuality. Barrett depicts the loss as the desertion of the wild swan and the gnawing of reeds by an invading rat.

In *A Drama of Exile,* Eve's peculiar suffering includes the loss of harmonic understanding with nature:

> . . . I cannot evermore, as once,
> With worthy acceptation of pure joy,
> Behold the trances of the holy hills
> Beneath the leaning stars, or watch the vales
> Dew-pallid with their morning ecstasy,—
> Or hear the winds make pastoral peace between
> Two grassy uplands,—and the river-wells

Work out their bubbling mysteries underground,—
And all the birds sing, till for joy of song
They lift their trembling wings as if to heave
Their too-much weight of music from their heart
And float it up the æther. I am 'ware
That these things I can no more apprehend
With a pure organ into a full delight,—

(*DE* 1194–1207)

Similarly, in "The Prisoner" the speaker is a stranger to Nature's beauties, nearly deaf to Nature's distant lute. In "The Lost Bower" the grief will not be mended until the advent of

. . . God's Eden-land unknown
With an angel at the doorway,
White with gazing at His Throne
(*CWEBB* 3:50.367–69)

This is similar to William Wordsworth's view of there having passed away a glory from the earth, a "splendour in the grass . . . glory in the flower," with the exception that Wordsworth emphasizes the loss, Barrett (especially in the 1844 ballads and in "De Profundis") the grief and suffering attendant to the loss.[34]

In Browning's 1844 poems the suffering seems at times endless, pointless, even godless. Barrett does not, however, succumb to nihilism. Instead of denying God, she persists in the stoicism of a Job or an Isobel, the view, that although God smite me, yet will I serve Him. Instead of accusing God of cruelty, though, she bends to His will, declaring her own insufficiency and shortsightedness (and ours). In "Exaggeration," for example, our grief, of which we complain, cannot begin to approach that of the grieving One; in "Adequacy" we lift up our ills in complaint as if we deserved better.

Works in the 1844 volume consider what is the antidote for grief and suffering—whether grace, love, or patience. Or faith in a God that one cannot always see face-to-face but as yet only through a glass darkly. Or in the passage of time that in conventional wisdom heals all wounds (or at least dulls pain). Or, as Eve suggests, in noble work that will

34. Wordsworth, "Intimations on Immortality," in *The Poetical Works of Wordsworth*, 356.179.

provide "[w]orthy endurance of permitted pain" (*DE* 1902). If there is a motif of consolation that runs throughout the sonnets, it is only partially satisfactory, and it comes in the form of the human's, the poet's, song. In "Perplexed Music," however, we mortals fail to understand celestial harmonies that Experience "like a pale musician" performs for us on the "dulcimer of patience" (*CWEBB* 2:231.1–2); in "The Soul's Expression" the poet "with stammering lips and insufficient sound" vainly tries to deliver the music of her nature (*CWEBB* 2:227.1). Yet suffering is the raw material from which the poet creates.

In making the woman Eve a spokesperson for God, for grace and work, Barrett paves the way for her own life's work, for singing her own song of grief, suffering, and loss. Furthermore, since the greatest work is creative work, God is the best worker. In "The Dead Pan" (the closing poem in the 1844 volume) she says that "God Himself is the best Poet" (*CWEBB* 3:157.248) and in *Aurora Leigh* that God is the "supreme Artist" (*AL* 5.435). Human poets, therefore, are also doing God's work: in "A Vision of Poets" poets are "God's prophets of the Beautiful" (*CWEBB* 2:321.292), and in *Aurora Leigh* they are the "only truth-tellers now left to God" (*AL* 1.859). Barrett believes that woman as well as man is capable of doing the work of a poet, the work of God. Thus she places herself, and Eve, in good company. If Milton can justify the ways of God, why cannot Barrett?

Only women and men who have suffered, however, have earned the right to speak for a suffering God. In "A Vision of Poets," also in the 1844 volume, a poet must drink of the *World's* curse and *World's* cruelty, must be tried in the fires of suffering. Like Eve, poets "[n]eed good and evil, to see good" (*CWEBB* 2:330.522). Presenting her 1844 volume to the public, she notes, "I never mistook pleasure for the final cause of poetry; nor leisure for the hour of the poet. I have done my work . . ." (*CWEBB* 2:148). Like Eve, she has been schooled by suffering to become a poet, a "witness" for God (*AL* 7.838).

Barrett's witness is about human suffering and the call to work in the heavenly vineyard; it is also witness of divine grace. In the words of her Christ, for exiles once closed outside Paradise and grace,

> . . . a new Eden-gate
> Shall open on a hinge of harmony
> And let you through to mercy
> (*DE* 1990–92)

V

Throughout the 1844 volume, the voices of various sadder but wiser Eves often go unheard, voices as ineffectual as that of "Cassandra at the gate" (an allusion in "Wine of Cypress"). Two ballads, "The Rhyme of the Duchess May" and "The Romaunt of the Page," exhibit female behavior that is bold, informed, and instructive—like that of Eve leading Adam out into the smitten world—but in both cases the courageous act of will is misunderstood by audience and auditor. Dorothy Mermin says that the ballads examine with resentment the virtues of self-repression and self-sacrifice seen as heroic in *A Drama of Exile*. But *A Drama of Exile* is about Christian service, which Barrett *does* see as noble, while the tone of the ballads remains more detached, allowing the *reader* to react with resentment or approval. No doubt a feminist critic of the present century would respond differently from Barrett's public, who were more attracted to the brave, self-sacrificing heroines of the ballads than to the theological-minded Eve. In fact, the critical commentary on Barrett's ballads has been largely unfavorable, although Marjorie Stone has recently "resuscitated" them as solidly within the masculine romantic ballad tradition and furthermore eminently adaptable by the female Barrett because of the form's energy, strong heroines, elemental passions, frank physicality, and "sinewy narrative conflicts allow[ing] her to circumvent the ideologies of passionless purity and self-sacrifice confining middle-class Victorian women."[35]

At issue in the case of Duchess May is the female will to dispose her love where she wishes; the duchess wills *not* to marry the churlish Leigh to whom she has been promised but instead Sir Guy Linteged whom she loves. But Sir Guy has reason to rue the wedding day (and the bridal choice) inasmuch as, a few months later, five hundred archers attack his castle to regain the willful bride. Though the valiant bridegroom wills to die alone and spare his retainers the vengeance sure to result in the fall of the besieged castle, he does not seem to appreciate the dangers likely to befall the young widow he leaves behind. Saying that she is young and will love again, he bids her beg grace of the barbaric Leighs in whose hand his suicide will leave her. (Does he think that she will be saved by marital rapture in the bloody arms of the very blackguard who is about

---

35. Mermin, *Origins of New Poetry,* 91; Stone, *Elizabeth Barrett Browning,* 95.

to slay himself and his troops?) But in the last moment before his heroic suicide, his bride proves the tenacity of *her* will: on the castle wall Duchess May leaps into the saddle with Sir Guy and falls to her death with horse and rider. As the teller of the tale observes, the wills of both are now "unwilled," and—in the peaceful churchyard with little birds singing— the reader is asked the unanswerable question, life or death: who knows which is best.

In an equally dramatic ballad of medieval setting, "The Romaunt of the Page," a knight in discussion with his page rejects a hypothetical woman who would (incognito) follow her husband into battle, and never learns that the very page to whom he condemns this bold, assertive, and loyal version of womanhood is none other than his bride, who, out of love and loyalty, has disguised herself and followed him to holy war in Palestine. Angela Leighton speculates that Barrett is, in this disguise, acting out her own fantasy of becoming Lord Byron's page and at the same time alluding to Byron's *Lara,* in which a page accompanies her master into battle.[36] The knight/husband, however, prefers womanhood evidenced by the trappings of femininity ("golden brooch and glossy vest" [*CWEBB* 2:248.200]); he wants a bride high, pure, cool, serene, and unearthly as the cloud that drifts above himself in the calm woodland (and deceptively Edenic scene) in which the conversation between knight and page takes place. When the Paynims attack, the page/bride, reconciled to the knowledge that she has loved her knight too much and that he loves an idealized, not a real, woman, facilitates his escape and becomes a martyr for love. As is the case with the Duchess May, "[t]he Loving is the Dying" (*CWEBB* 2:253.322). Unlike Duchess May, however, in this case the bride dies *for* the groom, not with him. And he will never know that she commits a Christ-like act of sacrificing her life for his literal salvation.

"Bertha in the Lane" is another ballad (or at least ballad in stanzaic form though dramatic monologue in rhetorical paradigm) that capitalizes upon the inside/outside relationship and anticipates the renunciatory works of Christina Rossetti, as well as the fickleness of Rossetti's men who abandon their true loves in such works as "Cousin Kate," "Songs in a Cornfield," and "Light Love." Devoid of the medieval/chivalric trappings of the previously mentioned ballads, "Bertha in the Lane" is somewhat more satisfying. At the very least it puts into practice Aurora Leigh's dictum to

36. Leighton, *Victorian Women Poets: Writing against the Heart,* 81.

write of one's own age, not "trundle back [the] soul five hundred years, / Past moat and drawbridge, into a castle-court" (*AL* 5.191–92). The sacrificial (and perhaps sentimental) display by one sister for another was especially appreciated by Barrett's contemporaries; "Bertha in the Lane" was singled out for praise by several reviews and by discriminating readers such as Harriet Martineau.[37] When—after sewing the wedding gown for Bertha and the shroud for herself—the dutiful older sister of the poem dies, she gives the fickle fiancé Robert to her younger sister (whom he now loves). The entire poem is the dying sister's monologue addressed to the victor in love to whom go the spoils. This elder sister (and now surrogate mother) compares her sacrifice to that of the deity: "Jesus, Victim, comprehending / Love's divine self-abnegation" (*CWEBB* 3:106.232–33). The sacrifice of "Bertha in the Lane" is similar to that in "The Romaunt of the Page," but here the conclusion is drawn, the moral espoused, by the martyr who, Glennis Stephenson believes, in describing her sacrifice and taking her leave also lays upon the young bride a heavy burden of guilt and an insistent demand for gratitude.[38] This sacrifice from a newly enlightened Eve recalls Jesus' martyrdom with a variation: greater love hath no *woman* than this, that she lay down her life for a sister.

The Eden of "Bertha in the Lane" is springtime with its buds, heaving and throbbing hills and vales, winding green hedgerows, and bees inebriated with May blooms—and the imagery is warm, lush, fecund, heavy with promise. But the dying narrator of "Bertha in the Lane" is closed *inside,* not outside. Outside is throbbing life; inside is weariness, duty, and coldness where one should expect warmth. Cold rays emanate from the ghostly mother whose spirit the dying woman imagines in the room; the cold hand of the older sister holds her own suffering heart; a cold answer is given at the family's portal just after the eavesdropper overhears Robert's declaration of love for Bertha. The bride-to-be is "rose-lined from the cold," ready to be claimed by young love (*CWEBB* 3:104.173), while the older sister will be "plucked" by the angel of death (*CWEBB* 3:104.182), whose approach the victim no doubt hears, sees, or otherwise imagines in

---

37. Martineau had a similar idea for a story, she says in her autobiography, but Mrs. Browning precluded her writing it by her "beautiful" "Bertha in the Lane" (Martineau, *Harriet Martineau's Autobiography,* 1:412).

38. Stephenson, " 'Bertha in the Lane': Elizabeth Barrett Browning and the Dramatic Monologue," 6.

the street just outside, although she may think it Robert or the maternal ghost approaching. ("No one standeth in the street?" [*CWEBB* 3:97.12] and "Hush!—look out— / Up the street! Is none without?" [*CWEBB* 3:102.124–25].) But her truly loyal paramour is the Bridegroom Death, who also claims the princess in Rossetti's *The Prince's Progress.* And the only warmth that she anticipates will be the angels' uplifting hands of fire (a Swedenborgian image), while her body lies in the cold and lonely grave.[39] Though the younger sister wins Robert as bridegroom, "Bertha in the Lane" is really about the loss of both sisters, for both lose the innocence and promise of youth and springtime. Both are exiled from Eden. The dying sister's plea for divine mercy ("Cleanse my love in its self-spending" [*CWEBB* 3:106.234]) reveals her own admission that her sacrifice is not untainted by melodrama and spite, plus the irony of what should be required of the living by the dead.

Kathleen Hickok has commented upon the Christ-identified martyr-dom of nineteenth-century fictional females as a predominant theme in the works of nineteenth-century women poets. Womanly sacrifice was not only a theme frequently produced by female (and male?) writers, but also a theme that came to be expected. Judith Plaskow says that female spirituality has been expressed (and no doubt preferred) as activity in passivity, that is, active self-denial, losing the self, renouncing for the good of others, for the God-created order. The elder sister is *active* in her passivity (sewing shroud and gown, for example, as proof of her passive renunciation of Robert, love, and life). This view of sacrificial womanliness and Christianity is rejected both by Plaskow and by theologian Beverly Wildung Harrison, who argues that sacrifice is *not* the central moral goal in Christian life (or in Christ's life) but rather the "radical activity of love."[40] I would suggest, however, that Barrett—like her Victorian counterparts both in literature and in real life—sees no better model (or at least no more dramatic and compelling model) for womanly virtue. Probably no better model of radical love. The sacrifice of de Staël's Corinne, George Eliot's Maggie Tulliver, and Barrett's speaker

39. In Swedenborg's vision all light and fire are emanations from God; love and fire correspond, as do light and wisdom; angels live in spiritual light and heat (*Angelic Wisdom,* 50–51).

40. Hickok, *Representations of Women: Nineteenth-Century British Women's Poetry,* 21, 87; Plaskow, *Sex, Sin and Grace,* 23; Harrison, "The Power of Anger in the Work of Love: Christian Ethics of Women and Other Strangers," in *Weaving the Visions,* ed. Plaskow and Christ, 222–23.

of this monologue have in common the renunciation of a would-be lover to a younger/fairer/milder sister, along with the resulting death of the sacrificial sister. Certainly not all these diverse writers endorse such sacrifice. Indeed, it may be argued that all three use the case study to illuminate the pointlessness of laying down a life for a sister, but all consider it an important literary (and life) motif. It is a recurring paradigm of womanly suffering, of the loss of one type of Eden.

If Eve once schooled by sin is a vessel of grace, then Onora of "The Lay of the Brown Rosary," is in this obvious aspect her opposite: a vessel of death and damnation. Barrett calls it a "wild and wicked ballad" (*BC* 4:169). Mermin says this is Barrett's only ballad in which the heroine's behavior is plainly assumed to be wrong, a stance that she finds awkward and incoherent.[41] Certainly it is a work in which the heroine, like Eve and like folk heroines of medieval ballads, brings suffering upon herself. In this work, though, the voice that goes unheeded is not that of an enlightened Eve but that of an innocent child, Onora's young brother who attempts to inform mother, priest, and bridegroom that his sister has committed an irreversible evil, symbolized by the brown rosary that she wears, which everyone wrongly interprets as a sign of humility and faith.

Specifically, Onora has made a pact with the evil spirit of a dead nun who, mocking a priest and refusing to acquiesce to the patriarchy of church authority, was buried alive as punishment. Exceeding the nun's sin, Onora rejects the patriarchy of God himself, vowing neither to thank God nor to seek him. God has decreed her death, Onora says, but she decides to make God wait, choosing "a love-lit hearth, instead of love and heaven" (*CWEBB* 3:274.382). Angela Leighton points out, however, that Onora's earthly patriarch (now dead) takes God's side and the father's seductive call from the other side is more powerful than that of earthly lover.[42] Like traditional Eve and like bonny Barbara Allan of the medieval ballad, in her dying Onora also effects the death of her true love. Like Eve who cannot bear the thought of Adam wed to a second Eve, Onora protests:

> How could I bear to lie content and still beneath a stone,
> And feel mine own betrothed go by—alas! no more mine own—
> Go leading by in wedding pomp some lovely lady brave. . . .
> (*CWEBB* 2:263.170–72)

41. Mermin, *Origins of New Poetry,* 93.
42. Leighton, *Elizabeth Barrett Browning,* 35–37.

Thus, Onora boldly lives life for herself: "I say . . . no holy hymn," she tells the evil spirit, "I do no *holy work*" (*CWEBB* 2:261.134; italics mine), signifying that in her self-fulfillment she is Eve's opposite or, as Helen Cooper says, an Eve allied with Lucifer rather than Eve who repudiates him in *A Drama of Exile*.[43] Angels "beside the Heavenly Gate" (*CWEBB* 2:264.187) call for Onora to return to God—to enter the gate through which both she and Eve have exited—and renounce her sin (that she has bartered God's love for man's, the angels say), but she decides too late (after the death of her groom at the altar) to cast the brown rosary from her. Onora is an exile from innocence and Paradise, but certainly unlike Barrett's Eve in that she seeks no reconciliation with the good. She neither reenters the gate of heavenly mercy nor advocates charitable ministry (work) in God's name and for humans' sake. It is no wonder that Barrett considered the poem "wild and wicked." Like the nun interred alive, Onora dies not face-to-face with God but with her "face turned from heaven."[44] Bold and courageous Onora certainly is, but dangerously self-willed too. Her cry "Take pity, God" comes too late (after the death of the bridegroom); she dies in suffering and exile, learning the hard way that God's grace is not limitless, that " . . . if she has no need of Him, He has no need of her" (*CWEBB* 2:264.191). Barrett challenges the reader to take sweetness (that is, the religious precept) from the ballad, but, shockingly, the dark threat of a merciless God overshadows the exhortation against willful self-exile from grace.

In the preface to her work *The Greek Christian Poets,* Barrett Browning charges that some poets " . . . not a few, have been guilty of singing as if earth were still Eden; and poets, many, singing as if in the first hour of exile, when the echo of the curse was louder than the whisper of the promise" (*CWEBB* 6:176). For Barrett exile is horrific, but the promise is Christ and redemption. None can accuse her of singing as if earth were still Eden. She knows that the loss of Paradise will not be remedied until the advent of the eternal Eden, "God's Eden-land" still unknown. In the *Poems of 1844* she ponders her own exile from Eden and her affinity with the feminine Jesus who is also teacher, sufferer, benefactor, and servant, self-exiled from paradise for humans' sake. In "A Vision of Poets"

---

43. Cooper, *Woman and Artist,* 83, 79.
44. In "The Lay of the Brown Rosary" the nun's face is turned from God (*CWEBB* 2:257.65); so too is Onora's turned away (*CWEBB* 2:274.375).

a questing poet is taught that Christ consecrated the "temporal sorrows" of existence. No "World-praiser" (that is, no singer that the world is still Eden) can ever be true poet, for a poet of God recognizes her exile, affirms the pain, and works in God's temporal world, always with an eye to the eternal world. It is her only path for reentry into Eden.

3

The Politics of
"Planting the Great Hereafter"

> . . . to believe in no
> other God than him who ordains
> justice and equality among men.
>
> —George Sand, Correspondence

> Peace, you say?—yes, peace, in truth!
> But such a peace as the ear can achieve
> . . . .
> 'Twixt the dying atheist's negative
> And God's Face—waiting, after all!
>
> —Barrett Browning,
> "First News from Villafranca"

I

At the conclusion of *Aurora Leigh*, Aurora and Romney, the reunited lovers and reformers, look toward the new Jerusalem, anticipating an apocalypse in which all class barriers will be leveled like the walls of Jerico and old governments and religions with their various forms of tyranny and oppression will be replaced by

> New churches, new œconomies, new laws
> Admitting freedom, new societies
> Excluding falsehood . . .
>
> (*AL* 9.947–49)

This dawning of a new age will result from the combined agency of human and God: Aurora and Romney will devote their future together to the renovation of human systems through their love (first for one another, then for all humankind), and God will abet in building the foundation of that "new, near Day / Which should be builded out of heaven to God" (*AL* 9.956–57).

While Barrett Browning advocates a form of government that *liberates*, it is compulsion, not liberation, that laws and government provide. At least it had been traditionally so. It was a time-honored truism of classical Christianity that human governments exist because human beings are sinful. The Church Fathers, particularly St. Augustine, held that government is remedy for sin. Both canonists and secular political theorists of the medieval age insisted that even coercive political structures are often necessary because humans have merited exterior restraints by their lack of self-restraint—dating from Eden. Even the divine Dante, who traced his political theory not from Augustine but from Aristotle and who risked all rather than surrender his own political liberty, believes that coercion of the people is sometimes necessary: *"Ahi gente che dovresti esser devota, / e lasciar seder Cesare in la sella"* ("Ah, people, that ought to be obedient and let Caesar sit in the saddle . . ."). He also holds that some are ordained by their nature (as the noblest) to be set in rule above others. And the theologian John Calvin suggests that Christians must obey the powers that be, remembering that even when human governments are tyrannical, this may well be punishment by God for the faults of the populace.[1] Thus victims deserve their victimization.

Elizabeth Barrett Browning never speaks to the tradition that governments are remedy for sin, although—having read Dante and the English theological writers—she is aware of the concept. For example, in *Of the Laws of Ecclesiastical Polity* the "immortal" Richard Hooker (whom a very young Elizabeth Barrett credits with "show[ing] a milder Heaven") says that laws exist first because of the human inclination to live in societies and second because human will is "little better than a wild beast," that is, "obstinate, rebellious, and averse from all obedience unto the sacred laws of his nature." Thus depraved and bestial, humans require a law of

---

1. Dante, *Purgatorio* 6:90–91, in *The Divine Comedy* (*Purgatorio* 1:60); Dante, *De Monarchia*, in *Latin Works of Dante*, 179, 200; Calvin, *Institutes of the Christian Religion*, 2:689.

a commonweal (the very soul of a politic body) that may allow them to live harmoniously.[2] Barrett Browning does not speculate about the *origin* of law; indeed she also knows the set of political thinkers who replaced the notion of patriarchal theocracy (with the political *king*dom as reflection of God's macrocosm) with the theory of government by contract, either between the governor and the governed or among the governed to cede power to a centralized authority. These thinkers were chiefly Locke, Hobbes, Rousseau, and Paine. The young Barrett was especially drawn to Locke, whom she read avidly in her teens, saying that his "moral greatness, and creating mind" illuminate "An Essay on Mind" (*CWEBB* 1:88.895). In later life, she was less infatuated with Locke. But she also was an avid reader of Milton's political prose, and Milton argues in *The Tenure of Kings and Magistrates* that—after Adam—derivative power is "transferr'd and committed to [magistrates] in trust from the People to the Common good of them all."[3] Her strong advocacy of political liberty parallels Milton's measuring stick of "Christian liberty" and her own consistent advocacy of free will. After wrestling with Calvinism, she rejected foreordination for a belief that one is free to struggle and suffer for the good. Governments must grant individuals their God-given right to self-actualization; governments themselves evolve in whatever form the people devise as appropriate to their needs and their struggle. This is the key: the people must be free to choose their political destiny, a freedom that the poet finds grounded in her theology. She acknowledges that—as Milton would say—"governments must be," and furthermore that they are not inevitably evil, any more than an individual human is predestined to evil or election.

> . . . Government,
> If veritable and lawful, is not given
> By imposition of the foreign hand,
> Nor chosen from a pretty pattern-book
> Of some domestic ideologue who sits
> And coldly chooses empire, where as well

2. "On laying Hooker under my pillow at night," an unpublished manuscript at the Armstrong Browning Library of Baylor University; Hooker, *Of the Laws of Ecclesiastical Polity,* 1.10.2 in *Works of Mr. Richard Hooker,* 1:240.

3. Milton, *Complete Prose Works of John Milton,* 3:202. Barrett Browning's underlined and annotated copy of Milton's prose works is in the Turnbull Collection, Library of New Zealand.

> He might republic. Genuine government
> Is but the expression of a nation . . .
>   (*AL* 8.867–74)

The "genuine" government she supports, however, is based upon permanent, eternal values, and, for her, religion and politics prove to be as inseparable as religion and aesthetics. It is unalterably God's will that individuals be free, but human institutions have all too often enslaved them. She notes, "[I]n every advancement of the world hitherto, the individual has led the masses. Thus, to elicit individuality has been the object of the best political institutions and governments" (*LEBB* 1:468). Repeatedly Barrett Browning invokes her religion in the *issues* of government: tyranny and rebellion, democracy versus various forms of elitism, the individual and the masses. Religion is consistently the basis of her insistence upon liberty and self-determination.

Furthermore, her religion is heretical, Barrett Browning says, in her interpretation of John's Revelation, the prophesied Second Coming of Jesus, the end of existence of the human race on earth, and eternal punishment for the damned. Individuals may suffer consequences of the errors committed of their own free will, but God does not punish in fire and brimstone. In 1853, she notes that her son, Pen, has been spared the teachings of damnation, has never heard the word *hell,* because "I am schismatic in some opinions & believe less in arbitrary punishment & still less in physical brimstone as generally received" (*LMO* 109). In 1855 she says, "I doubt much whether Christ's 'second coming' will be personal. The end of the world is probably the end of a dispensation" (*LEBB* 2:194), a Swedenborgian concept that she may well have accepted from Swedenborg's arcana on the Revelation, *The Apocalypse Revealed* (which begins with the premise that the New Jerusalem is a "New Church" on earth).[4] And in 1861, the year of her death, she says there is no hell, but that "consequences and logical results" (not arbitrary reward or punishment) are God's way of working, that (as Swedenborg has shown her) the scriptural phrases on this matter are simply symbolic (*LEBB* 2:426). If this present world is not merely in the Calvinist sense a stopping-off place on the perilous journey to heaven, then it is a legitimate object of love, work, and passionate concern.

---

4. Swedenborg, *The Apocalypse Revealed; Wherein Are Disclosed the Arcana There Foretold, Which Have Heretofore Remained Concealed,* 31.

And, although Barrett Browning accepts the concept that the soul is immortal and will exist on some other plane, she does not think that this present world will be consumed in flames, either at the end of a millennium or at the time of a great judgment. If the physical world is not mortal, but subject to renewal and reform, why then should not the poet have a hand in dismantling the old dispensation and ushering in the new Jerusalem (that is, in internalizing the Apocalypse), for to Barrett Browning poets are prophets, soothsayers, and seers. This particular poet expects the apocalyptical new age to include a great development of Christianity in opposition to the churches and of humanity in opposition to the nations; human conditions will improve *in spite of* the very organizations that are supposed to ensure and enable human safety and salvation. Human individuals are capable of salvation; thus revival is possible also for human institutions—even the most moribund and corrupt of them.

In correspondence and poetry, Barrett Browning documents having witnessed the squashing of hope for the independent and free republic of united Italy (a disappointment that she describes as an onlooker in *Casa Guidi Windows*); she has also been saddened by continued slavery in America (a nation that she claims to love), the exploitation of women and children everywhere (though she writes chiefly of these particular social evils in Great Britain), and the partisanship and chauvinism of sect, nation, and political faction, producing rifts and discord (while God's desire is unity and harmony). She explains that the "Oneness of God" produces a tendency to become one, a "perpetual sympathy between man & man" (*BC* 3:219). From the windows of Casa Guidi in her beloved Florence she witnessed the dashed promise of a would-be reforming duke and reforming pope (both of whom proved false, she says, against the will of God who is Truth). And from the date of her sojourn in Paris, where she was in residence upon the coup d'état of Napoleon III, and thereafter until the end of her life she defended the political life of the French emperor in the face of charges from most of her democratic allies, more on the basis of his support of the Italian risorgimento, it is to be suspected, than for his having been elected through a free and democratic process. Alethea Hayter, in summarizing the wide range of Barrett Browning's political and social concerns and values says:

> . . . she was an anti-legitimist, but a
> supporter of some parvenu monarchies; a radical

and anti-clerical, but a strong anti-communist;
an opponent of aggressive wars, but not a
pacifist; a believer in plebiscites and
referendums, but skeptical about parliamentary
democratic procedures, an attacker of social
evils and deficiencies, but a critic of
bureaucratic interference; a partisan of
Italian, Greek, and Polish independence, yet
dreading the excesses of nationalist feeling,
and looking forward to a world community.[5]

Barrett Browning was not always consistent in her political thought, but she was consistently an advocate of liberty in all forms, and she believed that the poet of God should—as a divine duty—speak out against oppression. She also admitted her heterodoxy in politics and religion, sometimes even delighted in it, but she believed that the true poet, like the true Christian and true patriot, must commit herself to holy liberty and to mercy, fellowship, classlessness, and justice. Like her poetic predecessor John Milton, Barrett Browning believed that the people make the king or magistrate, not the other way around, and one might logically conclude that she also assumed, then, that the people have the right to depose, or unmake, that king or leader who refuses to see that the people are holy. For example, she regretted Florence's acceptance of the grand duke after he first defected and later returned. Were she in the political shoes of the Florentines, she implied, she would not have done so.

Barrett Browning called herself a democrat, a lover of liberty, a republican (especially in the sense of the bid for an independent Italian republic), a universalist, a political latitudinarian, a leveler, and a supporter of universal manhood suffrage (although she seems not to agree with Victorian feminists Harriet Martineau, Harriet Taylor Mill, and the Brownings' friend Anna Jameson that women should be permitted to vote and hold office), but she at the same time denied communism and socialism because she believed that such systems are based on compulsion of some type, rather than the consent of enlightened individuals (*LEBB* 1:359). But individuals are the salvation of systems, governments, and peoples. Even Christian socialism, she insisted, if implemented would shrivel up human destinies and desecrate human nature, which must experience suffering

5. Hayter, "Windows toward the Future," 32.

for its purification, struggle in its progress, temptation to prove its virtue (*LEBB* 1:467–68).

This chapter will consider Barrett Browning's political stances in the light of her reforming religion, with special attention paid to *Casa Guidi Windows, Poems before Congress,* the overtly political works in *Last Poems,* and the antisocialism of *Aurora Leigh. Casa Guidi Windows* reveals the political tension between the people and their leaders, anticipates the unification and liberation of all Italy, castigates tyranny in all forms, and speculates whether the people are ready for self-determination and whether a political messiah might arise to lead them forth to liberty. Several short works from *Poems before Congress* and *Last Poems* single out for praise the heroes and near messiahs in the Italian struggle. *Aurora Leigh* reveals how, in the poet's judgment, Christian socialism has failed to remedy human ills and human want. Since Barrett Browning subscribed wholeheartedly to the Gospel of Work, she seeks to clarify the rightful works of the political poet in tempestuous times, but also to understand and demonstrate the works of the populace, the social activist, the religious figure, the hero, and the would-be teacher, often by demonstrating the failed works of those potential rulers and leaders who were misguided, weak, or untrue (not merely in the sense of deceitful but also in the lack of commitment to a higher Truth). She depicts tyranny in the form of pope and prince, factory owner and slave owner, politician and capitalist. She invokes the heroic freedom fighters of her own personal mythology: Savonarola, Dante, Michelangelo, and Brutus (although she insists that modern society must not make gods of them but merely bring them violets and libations, then stand upon the shoulders of these giants to reach new heights). She invokes the high priesthood of Jesus in human affairs, applying in the political realm the cry of Peter sinking in stormy waters, "Wake Christ!" And, because she believes that, if not a new paradise, then at least a reformed policy can be brought to earth, *Christians are not meant to wait complacently for the hereafter.* They are to commit themselves to action. Barrett Browning's political charge is to "extinguish hell" and "plant the great Hereafter in this Now" (*CGW* 1.299).

II

Casa Guidi Windows was written in two parts, the first in 1848 when Duke Leopold made a triumphal procession through the streets of Florence and there was great hope—at least in Tuscany—for the Italian risorgimento, the second in 1851 when the Austrians had temporarily squashed the freedom and unity movement. Part 1 is written in the spirit of joyful hope for immediate resolution; part 2 in outward disillusionment, but a less ebullient, more somber hope for eventual restitution of the people's rights and liberty, but with no clear conception of how or when this hope is to be realized, with no great leader in sight and still no evidence of an enlightened people ready to be led into freedom.

Italy was in 1848 by most standards a backward country that had been for generations under the domination of one foreign influence or another (including Austrian rule, Napoleonic invasions, and Spanish encroachment). René Albrecht-Carrié suggests that *internal* reasons for Italy's lack of political sophistication and activism at the midpoint of the nineteenth century were the hindrance of Rome and the papacy (which stood for ancient Empire and the Church, not contemporary nationalism) and the phenomenal fiscal successes of key cities that had seen themselves with nothing to gain and every financial advantage to lose in the case of unification, successes principally in commerce, shipping, and banking, for example, which date from Dante and Petrarch's era. Dennis Mack Smith notes that since 1815 there had been secret pro-Italy societies and glimmers of revolution in the form of protests and demonstrations led by republican agitators, students, anarchists, peasants, and soldiers. And for two decades the fermentation that produced the Italian risorgimento had enjoyed the leadership of a prophet in exile in the form of Giuseppe Mazzini, who after 1831 was a citizen of the world, launching societies and newspapers for Italian unity throughout Europe, especially in London.[6] Mazzini had first written to Robert Browning in 1845, and the Brownings eventually met him in London. While impressed with his single-minded dedication, Barrett Browning considered Mazzini somewhat of a madman and felt sure he would receive for his pains either a bullet in the heart or a knife in the back (*LEBB* 2:78). Much of *Casa Guidi Windows* is a direct address to Mazzini the "extreme theorist"; even more of it a direct address to the Italian people, who wait "Like God: as He, in His serene of might, / So they, in their endurance of long straits" (*CGW* 2.335–36).

6. Albrecht-Carrié, *Italy from Napoleon to Mussolini*, 4–12; Smith, *Italy: A Modern History*, 11–13.

In 1846 there was new hope in the form of a new pope, Pius IX, who had proceeded with certain reforms such as granting freedom of the press and amnesty to political prisoners.[7] After the Brownings' marriage the two settled in Italy, where they found not only a climate more friendly to her precarious health, but also a setting that was to take on mythic proportions in the poetry of both. They chose Florence, home of Dante, Boccaccio, and Petrarch, of Giotto, Michelangelo, and Raphael, and of the political tactician Machiavelli. Not only did Florence enjoy a unique history; it was also the Italian city with the best education, least police intrusion, greatest tolerance of Jews and Protestants, and highest standard of welfare and culture in Italy.[8] On the first anniversary of their wedding, September 12, 1847, from the windows of Casa Guidi, their Florentine residence, the Brownings observed a joyful celebration for Tuscany's Grand Duke Leopold II, who had granted citizens the right to form a civil militia, to "use their civic force / To guard their civic homes" (*CGW* 1.460–61); it was a hopeful sign for individual liberty and a clue that at some point Tuscany might unite with the other states and oust the Austrians who, under Metternich, controlled Tuscany.

But Italian unification was not to be achieved in Barrett Browning's lifetime, although when she died in 1861, it was in sight. In 1848, the year of European revolutions, soldiers from insurgent Naples joined Tuscans, Romans, and the Piedmontese army to save the insurrection of Milan. Charles Albert (Carlo Alberto) of Piedmont declared war against Austria, only to be defeated by the Austrians in the battle of Novara and forced to abdicate to his son, Victor Emanuel. The defeat of the Constitutionalist Army by the Austrians and the Army of the Second French Republic followed shortly, leading to acknowledgment of the risorgimento as a lost cause—at least for the time being. Upon the assassination of the pope's minister late in 1848, Pius IX, who had appeared supportive to the cause of Italian unification but who had found himself in a bind on the issue of separating versus uniting the spiritual and temporal powers, fled in disguise to Sicily. Furthermore, Grand Duke Leopold (later considered somewhat of a buffoon) agreed to a Constituent Assembly in Rome but, realizing that a republican form of government would evolve, fled Tuscany early in 1849 and returned in 1851 wearing an Austrian

7. Julia Markus, "Revaluating *Casa Guidi Windows,*" in *Casa Guidi Windows,* ed. Julia Markus, xv.

8. Smith, *Italy,* 17.

uniform and an Austrian title and accompanied by an Austrian guard and Austrian advisers. He proceeded to suppress the assembly and reintroduce censorship and finally abolished the constitution, an act for which Barrett Browning could not forgive him but, inconsistently, the same act that she later brushed aside when it was cited as objection against Louis Napoleon's establishment of empire in France.[9]

In *Casa Guidi Windows* the nation is feminized as the enchained body of a lovely woman laid "corpse-like on a bier" (*CGW* 1.33), a personified image of the nation that Barrett Browning uses again in "Napoleon III. In Italy" (from *Poems before Congress*). Fair Italy has lain dead

> With a wound in her breast,
> And a flower in her hand,
> And a grave-stone under her head . . .
> (*N* 113–15)

English poet Dora Greenwell uses a modified version of the republic as female in "The White Crusade—Italy 1860" in which Italian Freedom is called forth from the grave by a voice saying "The maiden is not dead," an echo of Jesus' words in raising the daughter of Jarius in Luke 8. In *Casa Guidi Windows*, Italy is the conflation of many women: the weeping mother Niobe, the slain lover Juliet, and the lost Magdalen of a sister. The icon of Italy as both angel and fallen woman is invoked also by Dante Gabriel Rossetti (an admirer of Barrett Browning's work and a poet with artistic and emotional—as well as familial—ties with Italy); in his "Dante at Verona," the historic republic is no "lily-sceptred damsel fair" (a Juliet or Beatrice) but a "shameful shameless prostitute." In *Casa Guidi Windows*, Italy's salvation requires the sacrifice, perhaps even the death, of her sons and lovers. Sandra M. Gilbert has noted that the feminine principle operates not only in the form of the motherland, but also in the persona/narrator (the English woman observing the action from an upper-story window) who toils as a midwife bringing Freedom to birth or as a nurse caring for an ailing body politic.[10] (It is usually Napoleon

---

9. Markus, *Casa Guidi Windows*, xxv–xxvi; Martin, *The Red Shirt and the Cross of Savoy*, 348.

10. Greenwell, in *Poems*, 334.40; D. Rossetti, *The Collected Works of Dante Gabriel Rossetti*, 1:5, 13 (lines are not numbered); Gilbert, "From *Patria* to *Matria*: Elizabeth Barrett Browning's Risorgimento," 200, 194. Actually, Gilbert uses the midwifery metaphor for *Casa Guidi Windows* and the "literary-political Florence Nightingale" for the healing persona in *Poems before Congress*.

who is deliverer, however, and in *Last Poems,* King Victor Emanuel plays midwife to Italy, "delivering the land by the sword" [*CWEBB* 6:52.36]). A poet, however, cannot act alone. Even Giuseppe Verdi's passionate lyrics—riveting and inspiring though they were to the risorgimento— would not replace a soldier/savior. Barrett Browning knows that more is required than " . . . just trilling on an opera-stage / Of 'libertà' to bravos" (*CGW* 2.226–27); Italy requires a hero to unify her and bring her forth to freedom.

But what form of hero will suffice, and what virtues must he demonstrate? And are not the attributes of Christianity essential in his character if he is to effect the apocalypse, to build a nation in which, as the poet says, the eucharistic bread and wine are set on every table?

Alethea Hayter and Helen Cooper agree that Barrett Browning shares Thomas Carlyle's notion of the Hero as King and echoes Carlyle's sixth lecture on history and heroes.[11] But Barrett Browning departs from Carlyle in significant ways, both upon the kind of hero she will single out for praise and upon the issue of the relation of the people *(il popolo)* whom Barrett Browning believes to be "dukedom, empire, and majesty" (*CGW* 1.500) and whom Carlyle does not. Barrett Browning is essentially a democrat, and this stance causes her to differ from the Florentine predecessors Dante and Machiavelli and from her contemporary Carlyle, all of whom advocate a strong ruler but also vest less faith in the holiness of the populace, or on a more mundane level, the worthiness and ability of the people to rule.

Barrett Browning, a "democrat to the bone" (*LEBB* 2:110), believes, in the first place, that the world has advanced beyond monarchy. Her distrust of the archaic system is shared by her female contemporary Harriet Martineau who, for example, instead of rejoicing that there is a woman on the English throne, objects to the pageantry, music, and "blasphemous" religious services of the 1838 coronation, which Martineau attended. To Martineau the young queen has inherited a ceremonial position that has no influence and no political power, a throne and a crown out of which all virtue has gone.[12] In 1838 Barrett herself was drawn in both directions; she admired the young queen for her

---

11. Hayter, *Mrs. Browning,* 128 (Hayter here refers not so much to the idealized hero as to Barrett Browning's alleged worship of Napoleon); Cooper, *Woman and Artist,* 133.
12. Martineau, *Harriet Martineau's Autobiography,* 1:423.

"tender heart" and "natural emotions," yet feared that there is something "hardening" in power and even in the pomp of state etiquette. "How can loyalty & republicanism be brought together," she ponders, " . . . particularly when Miss Martineau is writing, that kings have ceased to be necessary evils . . ." (*BC* 3:261). In "The Young Queen," however, Barrett applauds Victoria for calling upon Divine Providence, which had called her to the "work" of the throne; in "Victoria's Tears" she notes that the queen has wept to wear a crown and remarks: "The tyrant's sceptre cannot move, / As those pure tears have moved!" (*CWEBB* 2:109.33–34). "Crowned and Wedded," first published in 1840, celebrates a second occasion of pageantry in Victoria's reign, her wedding to Prince Albert. The occasional poem is not the ideal opportunity, perhaps, to indict the system of monarchy and certainly not to criticize the queen. Rather, Barrett speaks of (and to) Victoria as "woman" and "beloved," the personal vow to love paralleling the "priestly vow" she has already taken to reign, but, on this occasion, receiving the spotlight. Yet this early work of Barrett, positive and patriotic in tone though it is, includes two concepts consistent in Barrett Browning's political view: the people as holy and the crown as empty. In "Crowned and Wedded" the crowds gathered to honor Victoria and Albert include knights, ministers, highborn ladies, legates, princes, and peers, and finally, the people: "And so, the people at the gates with priestly hands on high / Which bring the first anointing to all legal majesty . . ." (*CWEBB* 3:60.17–18). As in *Casa Guidi Windows*, theirs is the greatest mandate; only they have the God-given right to anoint political authority. And in the final stanza when Barrett Browning asks what blessings shall be prayed for the married couple, she says that "None straitened to a shallow crown will suit our lips today" (*CWEBB* 3:62.60). One might say that the poet is exalting marriage rather than devaluing monarchy, and certainly she is doing just that; her choice of the word *shallow*, however, recalls the *hollow* crown that "rounds the mortal temples" of monarchy in Shakespeare's *Richard II*.[13]

In "Napoleon III. In Italy," the poet also undercuts monarchy as a *system* (while endorsing Napoleon as emperor):

> I was not used, at least,
> Nor can be, now or then,

13. *Richard II* 3.2.160, in *The Riverside Shakespeare*, 865.

> To stroke the ermine beast
> Of any kind of throne
> (*N* 56–59)

Elsewhere Barrett Browning speculates that a queen or king can do little in the modern world except patronize the arts and literature (she or he might as well do something rather than nothing [*BC* 9:186]). When Barrett Browning was questioned about how—since she is an avowed democrat and no royalist—she could have supported Louis Napoleon in France, she answered that he has garnered the support of the democratic French public. "I am no Napoleonist," she says, but adds that seven and one-half million Frenchmen cannot be wrong, and therefore Napoleon, whom they have freely chosen, is a legitimate chief of state (*LEBB* 2:48). In *Aurora Leigh,* she says of Napoleon: "This Head has all the people for a heart; / This purple's lined with the democracy,—" (*AL* 6.72–73). Hayter, who has expended more ink on Barrett Browning's politics than more recent writers have done, insists that she is hardly a democrat, despite her claims. In fact, Barrett Browning remains true to Napoleon (some say, inconsistently) even after he makes himself emperor by a coup d'état four years after his election to the presidency. Certainly her "Napoleon III" hails him as a savior of Italy. In *Last Poems,* she endorses also the rule of Victor Emanuel in Italy because in 1860 he symbolically unites all of Italy as "King of us all." Thus, while never upholding the *institution* of monarchy, she rather endorses the individual ruler who would seem to hold paramount the will of the people, and the right of the populace to choose its leader (*as well as* its system of government). This avowed democrat does not rule out all monarchies. Even in *Casa Guidi Windows,* Barrett Browning suggests that once when people were simpler and more childlike, they may have accepted monarchy, but now kings have ceased to be "necessary" evils:

> . . . Children use the fist
> Until they are of age to use the brain;
> And so we needed Caesars to assist
> Man's justice, and Napoleons to explain
> God's counsel, when a point was nearly missed,
> Until our generations should attain
> Christ's stature nearer.
> (*CGW* 1.685–91)

(She then retracts the near compliment, however, by doubting whether the people of Florence have come so far.)

Barrett Browning's political view is occasionally self-contradictory: one cannot be both democrat and monarchist, leveler and worshiper of the hero. With one major distinction, however, her idea of the power of prerogative could have come right from the pages of Barrett Browning's early mentor John Locke, who advocated modern government as compact, but recognized that in the infancy of governments the monarch often had to use personal discretionary power even when such use impeded liberty. The distinction between Locke and Barrett Browning is precisely in the religious issue: he endorsed prerogative until a state is advanced to rational patterns, she until the people are more Christ-like. It seems a rather naively optimistic view that the human species is advancing nearer Christ's stature, but such seems to have been Barrett Browning's hope for Italian politics. At least she was in famous company in advocating the perfectibility of the people, company that includes William Godwin and Percy Bysshe Shelley, although neither the philosophical anarchist nor the Romantic poet included Christ as a necessary element of the equation.

Casa Guidi Windows holds up for examination history's heroes and villains (especially those in the history of Italy) and theorizes what traits or attributes the political hero should have, whether and how he should lead the people. In spite of her theoretical objections to monarchy, Barrett Browning often confesses herself vulnerable to the temptation to honor the "Great man" (or tenderhearted queen). For example, in a letter to Mitford, she calls herself a "hero-worshipper" (*BC* 7:346) several times, a trait that Carlyle says is inherent in the species: "all men, especially all women, are born worshippers. . . ." And, indeed, in *Casa Guidi Windows,* Barrett Browning honors numerous heroes who would rather risk persecution and martyrdom than succumb to the powers of tyranny. Savonarola was burned as a heretic because he "swore [the church-waters] stank" even before Luther came to spill them (*CGW* 1.270). George Eliot says in *Romola* that destiny had chosen this "sacred rebel" Savonarola to be a great man, undertaking the trial by fire because there was no one to fulfill the destiny if he forsook it.[14] Milton is typically numbered among

14. Carlyle, *Past and Present,* in *Works of Thomas Carlyle,* 10:55; Eliot, *Romola,* in *Writings of George Eliot,* 9:348.

Barrett Browning's heroes and martyrs for freedom because he had the courage of conviction in proclaiming Charles I a tyrant, and made an eloquent defense of the English people's regicide. Although not Italian, Milton deserves inclusion with the Tuscan heroes because he, like Barrett Browning herself, took inspiration from Italy, the beauty and glory of Vallombrosa filling "[t]he cup of Milton's soul so to the brink" that it flowed forth in the description of Adam's paradise (*CGW* 1.1156). Another Florentine, Michelangelo, is included in the litany because he demonstrated his love of freedom and hatred of tyranny under the Medici. Barrett Browning imagines his contempt:

> . . . "I do not need
> A princedom and its quarries, after all;
> For if I write, paint, carve a word, indeed
> . . . .
> The same is kept of God . . .
> (*CGW* 1.127–31)

And God sees that the artist's creation outlasts lordships and monarchies. Brutus (whom Dante, in the *Inferno*, places in the very mouth of Satan because of his treason against Caesar and Rome) is a hero to Barrett Browning for teaching that illegitimate Caesars "swoon as feebly and cross Rubicons / As rashly as any Julius of them all!" (*CGW* 2.89–90). He is a rebuke to her (and by implication, to others) for having put her faith in princes (as she had done in the Grand Duke Leopold). "Tender Dante" is heroic because—though he loved his Florence well—he suffered exile rather than surrender either to papacy or political state his right of political dissent. When the Florentines search for a "holier ground" than the statue of Perseus or Brutus, "Rome's sublimest homicide," they converge on Dante's stone, and Barrett Browning implies that the passionate lover of freedom looks down from heaven in approval.

Among contemporary heroes who have died for freedom and the risorgimento are Charles Albert, Garibaldi's wife, Anita, and the Bandiera brothers. The Bandieri, inspired by Mazzini and passionate idealism, deserted from the Austrian navy and theatrically "invaded" their homeland to liberate it, but were executed in 1844; they now accuse "the sins / Of earth's tormentors before God the just" (*CGW* 1.884–85). Charles Albert, king of Sardinia, promised to risk "his life, his sword, his army and his dynasty for the Italian cause."[15] "[T]he only constitution-granting Italian prince whose good will to the people outlasted the year 1848," he held out against Austria, fought bravely, and finally abdicated to his son, Victor Emanuel, after defeat by the Austrians at Novara (*CWEBB* 3:421–22). He was, Barrett Browning says, "shriven . . . in cannon-smoke" (*CGW* 2.709). Anita Garibaldi rode and fought beside her husband, had been knocked down by a cannonball in Brazil and captured by the enemy, and in the skirmishes for Italian freedom continued to "[o]utfac[e] the whistling shot and hissing waves" (*CGW* 2.679). She died of fever at the front (along with her unborn child).[16] There has been some debate whether Barrett Browning includes the pope and the grand duke among the heroes of contemporary history. She appears to be inconsistent in her judgment about Pope Pius IX, but always considers the grand duke a mediocre statesman (though a "tender-hearted man" [*LHS* 100]), yet reserves hope that he would allow the populace the freedom to achieve solidarity. After all, was he not moved to tears by the adulation of the people? In a letter to her sister Henrietta she calls Pope Pius a "great man" and a "liberator."[17] Nevertheless, she maintains in the "Advertisement" to *Casa Guidi Windows* that she had never been susceptible to pope worship, that she, for one, has escaped the epidemic "falling sickness" for the pope.[18] Perhaps Barrett Browning felt, as did most of the Italian patriots, that it was the pope, not they, who had changed. Certainly she never considered either the pope or the grand duke as having the potential to be included among the litany of "great men" in her personal pantheon. Also, it is unlikely that a pope, schooled in the system of hierarchy, could become a democratic leader to liberate the people. And, indeed, neither Pio Nono nor Leopold was a liberator.

Rather, in the second part of *Casa Guidi Windows,* both prove cowards and tyrants. Barrett Browning reveals the tyrannical perversion of

---

15. Martin, *The Red Shirt and the Cross of Savoy,* 249, 311. Giuseppe Mazzini had written a short account of the Bandieri's heroism; in 1845 he sent Robert Browning a copy, which was shared with Elizabeth Barrett.

16. Ibid., 253–54, 364–65.

17. Markus, appendix to *Casa Guidi Windows,* 68.

18. Markus in her edition of *Casa Guidi Windows* cites several episodes in which Barrett Browning shows reservations and outright distrust of the Pope, but sometimes she claims to admire him and to believe in him.

authority to which monarchy and oligarchy (in church and state) tend. Classical political philosophers had, of course, speculated in great detail about the uses and perversions of power. For example, Plato's scheme for human government is the analogy of precious and mundane metals: gold typifies rulers, silver auxiliaries, iron and bronze the masses—the purest gold being the philosopher king at the helm of the ship of state. Tyranny is only the most perverse form of several perversions (democracy being to Plato among these perversions). To Aristotle, tyranny is a perversion of humans' natural inclination toward an orderly social and political life and an inversion of the good in that it is the rule of the worst over the best. To the Florentine Dante, a devout Aristotelian, the principle of rule of the worst by the best requires a monarchy of nation-states (modeled on the Roman Empire) as necessary for the world; it is the noblest form, the most reflective of God's will and God's divine order of the universe. Most of the political theorists from antiquity acknowledged that the greatest danger of monarchy is that power corrupts. Monarchies may evolve into tyrannies, and Barrett Browning was well aware of this. (She knew her classical sources as well as her Dante and John Locke, who defined tyranny as a monarchy voluntarily entering into a state of war with its subjects.)[19] Thus she might well conclude that this is a legitimate reason to reject monarchy as a political structure of the modern world. Among the many tyrants considered in *Casa Guidi Windows* (past and present) are Caesars and czars, popes and priests, Urbino and the Magnificent, and Pius IX and the grand duke. The pope is a tyrant because he represses inquiry; he

> . . . must resent
> Each man's particular conscience, and repress
> Inquiry, meditation, argument,
> As tyrants faction"
>
> (*CGW* 1.995–98)

He is spiritually dead, a "mummy in the priestly cope" (*CGW* 1.973). False Leopold is a tyrant because he has misled the people into thinking that there might be hope, which he is not prepared to offer. In 1849 Barrett Browning notes that "[The duke] is made of the stuff of princes—faithless and ignoble" (*LHS* 108); his patriot's oath has become the oath of a

---

19. Plato, *Republic* 4.414c; Aristotle, *Politics* 4.2.1289b; Dante, *De Monarchia,* in *Latin Works of Dante,* 149, 179; Locke, *Two Treatises of Government,* 129.

perjurer. In "An August Voice" she accuses bluntly: "He cheated, betrayed, and forsook, / Then called in the foe to protect you" (*CWEBB* 3:343.39–40). The grand duke is dead too in a sense because he has abandoned Tuscany; returning to power as Austria's puppet, he is worse than a lame duck—he is vile as a whited sepulchre: "Resuscitated monarchs disentomb / Grave-reptiles with them, in their new life-throes" (*CGW* 2.332–33). Thus the pope and grand duke, like tyrants everywhere, are putrefying in the metaphorical sense, like Hapsburgs and Bourbons who "fester / Above-ground with worm-eaten souls . . ." (*CWEBB* 6:55.61–62).

In his series of lectures *On Heroes, Hero-Worship and the Heroic in History,* Thomas Carlyle explains that, throughout human history, great men have risen to the occasion when chaotic times demanded a prophet, a soldier, or a king. He believes that the monarchy of the great leader is the most essential and natural form of government. "Without sovereigns, true sovereigns, temporal and spiritual, I see nothing possible but an anarchy."[20]

Carlyle supports what one might call the modern version of Plato's philosopher king. While Plato sees the ideal king as the least interested in power and the most interested in the world of pure ideas, Carlyle, however, will settle for the ablest man in the sense of vision, integrity, and skill.

> Find in any country the Ablest Man that exists there; raise *him* to the supreme place and loyally reverence him: you have a perfect government for that country; no ballot-box, parliamentary eloquence, voting, constitution-building, or other machinery whatsoever can improve it a whit. It is the perfect state; an ideal country.

To Carlyle all "Hustings-speeches, Parliamentary motions, Reform Bills, French Revolutions" are but the means to an end, the end being the attainment of the Ablest, Noblest man as king (call him what you will) and the surrender of the will of the body politic to the leadership of that Great Man, who will then lead the people in goodness. "The Commander over Men; he to whose will our wills are to be subordinated, and loyally surrender themselves, and find their welfare in doing so" is the most important of Great Men—the summary of Great Priest, Prophet, and Teacher.[21]

---

20. Carlyle, *On Heroes, Hero-Worship and the Heroic in History,* in *Works of Thomas Carlyle,* 5:124, 197.
21. Ibid., 197, 196.

Carlyle believed in a golden species of men, an "Aristocracy of Talent" who, refined and purified in the crucible of the times, will lead the nation wisely. Only the wisest has any "divine right" to rule, and, furthermore, the wisest and best of all the wise and good (the hero-king) must rule a nation of heroes, not flunkies. Carlyle saw his own age, however, as promoting flunkeyism, the gospels of Mammonism and Dillettantism, quackery, competition, Utilitarianism, the profit motive, Sansculotism of the most chaotic type. Democracy was to Carlyle the most retrograde of systems, the despair of finding any able heroes to govern, the admission that the nation has reduced itself to the lowest common denominator. Whereas the role of government is supposed to be to guide men to "the good," democracy serves to degrade them to the brutish level: the worship of Mammon, the liberty to die by starvation and want, thralldom to their own brutish appetites.[22] Barrett Browning admired Carlyle, but considered him an impractical and "vague prophet" with impossible requirements of a republic; her view of hero and of populace were different from his (*CWEBB* 6:318).

Carlyle's examples of the hero as king (in lecture 6 and in *Past and Present*) include only generals and autocrats such as Joshua and Moses, or their modern European counterparts Napoleon, Cromwell, and William the Conqueror. (As George Eliot points out, the " 'Carlylean theocracy' features the 'greatest man' as a Joshua who is to smite the wicked [and the stupid] till the going down of the sun.") On the other hand, among Barrett Browning's heroes in *Casa Guidi Windows* only Brutus is a general, only Charles Albert a king, and most are artists. Besides, what Brutus and Charles Albert have in common with the artists Dante, Michelangelo, and Milton and the priest Savonarola is not conquest and rule, but rebellion against tyranny. Here is a direct contrast in Carlyle's hero and Barrett Browning's. Carlyle believed that the Great Man is always a "son of Order, not of Disorder." His heroes seize the reins of government and restore order, as Napoleon did with the French empire, Cromwell in the Interregnum. Carlyle's hero inevitably brings equilibrium out of cataclysm. Barrett Browning focuses upon the hero who would risk chaos and anarchy to bring freedom. This is a very different assumption indeed: Carlyle despises anarchy and worships the heroic order; Barrett Browning hates bondage of any sort and is willing to honor the man who will liberate the

22. Carlyle, *Past and Present,* in ibid., 10:30, 143–45, 167, 209–21.

people. We see *her* heroes in their Promethean aspect, as Lord Byron terms Dante, the "new Promethean of the new man," and they never ascend to Jovian monarchy or tyranny. In fact, among the mythic heroes of the poem, Dante and Charles Albert die in exile, Brutus falls on his own sword rather than be taken by Augustus, Savonarola is burned as a heretic, and Michelangelo and Milton (though not martyrs) suffer for their dedication to liberty (Milton in an English prison after the Restoration of Charles II). Perhaps this aversion to tyranny and identity with the rebel are the reasons that her later single-minded adoration of Napoleon III is so troubling; once draping himself in the mantle of Bonaparte, he becomes (especially in the peace at Villafranca) more like the heroes whom Carlyle touts and less like the freedom-loving radicals enshrined in *Casa Guidi Windows*. In fact, in his own writings Louis Napoleon reveals that he could have been reading Carlyle when he notes that the great men of history (among whom he lists Moses, Caesar, Charlemagne, and his ancestor Napoleon I) have so much "Divinity" in them that they never die entirely.[23]

Not only are assumptions about the leader different in Carlyle's and Barrett Browning's philosophies, but so also is the relationship between the leader and the people. Carlyle believed that the people should follow their natural proclivity for hero-adoration, step aside and allow the great man to lead them. Barrett Browning saw the great man as a man of peace, a teacher and example, but not a dictator or monarch. It should be recalled that Aeschylus's Prometheus gave humans the alphabet and the power to read and write, numbers and the skill of mathematics; Promethean fire is not only political revolution but also knowledge. And the ideal leader is, to Barrett Browning, a great teacher. Further, Barrett Browning's term *il popolo* (the people) reflects the motto of Giuseppe Mazzini *Dio e il popolo,* ("God and the people"): it also reflects her own view that only the people have the holy right to rule the nation, although she admitted that the Tuscans were as yet ill prepared for full exercise of freedom. Wanting in intelligence, courage, and resourcefulness, they had all the more need for a great teacher, for the "instructed are not patriotic, and the patriots are not instructed" (*LEBB* 1:416).

---

23. Eliot, *Thomas Carlyle,* in *Writings of George Eliot,* 22:311; Carlyle, *On Heroes,* in *Works of Thomas Carlyle,* 5:203; Byron, "The Prophecy of Dante," in *Complete Poetical Works of Lord Byron,* 4:14; Napoleon III, *The Political and Historical Works of Louis Napoleon Bonaparte, President of the French Republic,* 1:261 (he explains that this divinity resides in their combination of wisdom as legislator and prowess as general).

It matters not whether the hero be a commoner, a peasant, a rich man, a king, a prince, a priest, or a pope (though a hero from the priesthood is improbable and from the papacy incomprehensible). Barrett Browning's great leader will be a holy teacher/leader, good and great, liberal and affectionate, will reflect God, will be

> . . . but God's like organized
>   In some high soul, crowned capable to lead
> The conscious people, conscious and advised,—
>   For if we lift a people like mere clay,
> It falls the same. We want thee, O unfound
>   And sovran teacher! if thy beard be grey
> Or black, we bid thee rise up from the ground
>   And speak the world God giveth thee to say,
> Inspiring all this people round,
>   Instead of passion, thought, which pioneers
> All generous passion, purifies from sin,
>   And strikes the hour for. Rise up, teacher! here's
> A crowd to make a nation![24]

(CGW 1.761–73)

Essentially the idealized political messiah must be Christ-like in three aspects: he must be a great teacher, he must bring God's holiness ("holy knowledge, holy liberty, / O holy rights of nations!" [*CGW* 2.184–85]), and he must be willing to suffer for others, as Christ has done—all criteria that Napoleon III never exhibits. Dorothy Mermin thinks it significant that *Casa Guidi Windows* refuses to valorize suffering (except for heroic death in battle).[25] Yet if suffering does not make a person great, certainly the great person must be willing to suffer on behalf of *il popolo*. The hero will teach, lead, strike fire into the masses; will teach them to "smite a foe upon the cheek / With Christ's most conquering kiss" (*CGW* 1.703–4). In obeisance to Christ's martyrdom and opposition to the papal chair of Pius IX, Barrett Browning accepted "Christ's cross only," the other authority being false as that of the thief crucified beside Jesus. The image of Christ's martyrdom on earth, however, is replaced by that of the eternal persona of monarchy and holy priesthood:

---

24. Carlyle in *Sartor Resartus* advocates a messiah leader: "Great men are the inspired. . . . Texts of that divine BOOK OF REVELATION, whereof a Chapter is completed from epoch to epoch . . ." (*Works of Thomas Carlyle*, 2:177).
25. Mermin, *Origins of New Poetry*, 165.

> When Christ ascended, entered in, and sate
> (With victor face sublimely overwept)
> At Deity's right hand, to mediate,
> He alone, He for ever.
>
> (*CGW* 2.487–90)

The poet accepts only Christ's authority, only his laws, and only his divine example of love. As she says, she has no "political philosophy" to propose, and a gospel of love probably does not carry much weight in a pragmatic world. Nor did it ever. Nevertheless, it is the political proposal of Barrett Browning here and elsewhere (especially in "Italy and the World"), as it is the proposal of Shelley in *Prometheus Unbound* (love without Christianity) and (ironically) of the Christian socialism of the reformer Romney Leigh that she rejects in *Aurora Leigh* (because Romney too fails as a teacher, but also because he has not himself learned to reform souls but only superficial forms of life—and that imperfectly).

The implication of the Italians' plight is universal in that the poet compares tyranny in world religion and international politics to the suffering in Italy. To Christ their divine priest and king, the churches arrogantly "cramp the souls of men," perpetuating "false doctrine" by "hireling hands" instead of good shepherds (a comment recalling Milton's assertions in *Lycidas*). The nations bring, instead of gold, frankincense, and myrrh, nothing but selfishness and mammonism: no teaching for the poor, no cure for women sobbing in brothels, or for the slave trade, children in poverty, workers in mines. In "Christmas Gifts" (from *Poems before Congress*) the gifts of the season are gold for the haft of a sword, incense to sweeten a crime, and myrrh to embitter a curse (*CWEBB* 3:347.33–36). Deirdre David says that Barrett Browning attributes England's woes to "contemporary spineless liberal politics and to rampant mid-nineteenth century mercantilism." Barrett Browning's contemporary John Ruskin is direct in his castigation of English greed: ill-gotten profits had been converted into foreign loans, he charges, to keep down all noble life in Italy, murder Polish women and children, and provide cartridges and bayonets to India.[26] To Barrett Browning the oppression of the churches against their people, of the monied classes everywhere against the poor, and of governments worldwide against the citizenry parallels the oppression of Austria against Italy. But she anticipates a new order bringing Christianity

---

26. David, *Intellectual Women*, 130–31; Ruskin, "Work," in *The Crown of Wild Olive and Lectures on Art*, 21.

in opposition to the churches and humanity in opposition to the nations; therefore she ends in hope that God will convict humans of their folly and erect a monument like the four-walled new Jerusalem that Aurora and Romney visualize at the conclusion of *Aurora Leigh.*

> We will trust God. The blank interstices
> Men take for ruins, He will build into
> With pillared marbles rare, or knit across
> With generous arches, till the fane's complete.
> (*CGW* 2.776–79)

In a discussion of the electoral reform in her own nation years earlier, Barrett had said that unless "the majority of the nation, called *the people,* should have a proportionate weight & influence in the government of the nation, I confess I do not understand what freedom means" (*BC* 2:311–12). Not every political thinker of the age, however, was enamored of democracy. As noted above, Carlyle believes this freedom that Barrett Browning advocates is dangerous: it means the liberty to die of want. Carlyle's implication that democracy is anarchic recalls the theory of Edmund Burke who recoiled from the French reign of terror as the expected outcome of revolution. Thomas Babington Macaulay has similar reservations: for him the danger of democracy, at least as envisioned by the greatest happiness ideal of the Benthamites, is that the populace would have the power not only of plundering the rich but also of annihilating the capital of the future. Macaulay insists that a government cannot at once protect property and level the masses. The French positivist Auguste Comte (whom Barrett Browning in *Aurora Leigh* calls "absurd") sees the scientific course of government as obviating the arbitrariness of both theology (the divine right of kings) and metaphysics (the sovereignty of the people), the positivist application in governmental systems making obsolete both tyranny and democracy.[27]

While she advocated democracy *in principle,* Barrett Browning—in spite of her love for the people of Tuscany—did not believe that the

---

27. Macaulay, "Mill on Government," in *Macaulay: Prose and Poetry,* 602. Supporting the Reform Bill, however, he remarks that the empowerment of the middle class will bring a closer balance among citizens and promote the end goal of government, the happiness of its people ("Parliamentary Reform I," in ibid., 671); Comte, "Plan of the Scientific Operations Necessary for Reorganizing Society," in *Auguste Comte and Positivism: The Essential Writings,* 50.

Italians were ready for self-rule, at least not at the time she wrote *Casa Guidi Windows*. In 1849 she admits that the Italians are wanting in knowledge, faith and energy, that poor Tuscany "has not brains to govern itself" (*LEBB* 1:423). She charges that what the Florentines comprehend of the Italian League is "to wear silk velvet and each a feather in his hat, to carry flags and cry *vivas,* and keep a grand festa day in the piazzas" (*LEBB* 1:389). In *Casa Guidi Windows* the citizens of Florence prove adept at singing rebel songs, strutting in parades, breaking a few windows, and chalking the walls with "bloody caveats / Against all tyrants" (*CGW* 2.152–53). But for the most part, revolution amounts only to talk. And mere talk proves the talkers lazy and cowardly.

> We met, had free discussion everywhere
>   (Except perhaps i' the Chambers) day and night.
> We proved the poor should be employed, . . . that's fair,—
>   And yet the rich not worked for anywise,—
> Pay certified, yet payers abrogated,—
>   Full work secured, yet liabilities
> To overwork excluded,—not one bated
>   Of all our holidays, that still, at twice
> Or thrice a week, are moderately rated.
>   We proved that Austria was dislodged, or would
> Or should be, and that Tuscany in arms
>   Should, would dislodge her, ending the old feud;
> And yet, to leave our piazzas, shops, and farms,
>   For the simple sake of fighting, was not good—
> We proved that also.
>
> (CGW 2.157–71)

The Tuscans had not, as of yet, learned the poet's Gospel of Work and Gospel of Suffering. Nor even, for that matter, the Gospel of Waiting. They are rebuked in words that echo Jesus' question to his sleeping disciples in Gethsemane: "Couldst thou not watch one hour?" (*CGW* 2.13). Ultimately, Barrett Browning believes the inner soul must be renovated before civic heroism can occur. That is, the Apocalypse must be internalized. The people are enjoined to bring swords, but must first bring souls. The people wait, as God waits, for justice and freedom, with the implication that if God is just, then a leader will be sent and wrongs shall be redressed. Here again her ideal leader is different from Carlyle's examples. She longs for a teacher who will inspire through teaching; Carlyle admits that Cromwell turned despot because he could not lead and inspire the Parliament, that Napoleon founded a dynasty because he believed in the dupability—rather than teachability—of the populace. Neither was a great Teacher. (This is not to say, of course, that Barrett Browning's heroes were wholly successful in this regard. But then Savonarola, Michelangelo, and Dante never attained a post as teacher to the nation.) *Casa Guidi Windows* remains an idealistic poem: not only may a great leader and leader arise, but certainly the people will persevere as well.

> You kill worms sooner with a garden-spade
> Than you kill peoples: peoples will not die;
>   The tail curls stronger when you lop the head:
> They writhe at every wound and multiply
>   And shudder into a heap of life that's made
> Thus vital from God's own vitality.
>
> (*CGW* 2.340–45)

Unfortunately, the people are as yet "simple, blind and rough" (*CGW* 1.599); they exhibit the want of soul conviction and self-confidence, scantness of valor, accursed schisms, fickleness (being willing, apparently, to rejoice whether the grand duke is out or the grand duke is in). They have yet to learn that Metternich "[c]an fix no yoke unless the neck agree" (*CGW* 1.663). This populace hardly seems ready for democracy, Barrett Browning's ideal form of government. But the ideal teacher/leader will know, as Romney learns in *Aurora Leigh,* that the people must be revived from within—the inner person before the outer.

III

The theme of the people as "dukedom, empire and majesty" expressed in *Casa Guidi Windows* is foremost also in "Napoleon III. In Italy" (in *Poems before Congress,* 1860). While the heroes in *Casa Guidi Windows* had been artist patriots from Italian history or the idealized messiah figure prophesied to come, the heroes and heroism celebrated in the final political poems celebrate Italy triumphant, including tributes to the French emperor Louis Napoleon, the Italian political strategist and Piedmont's first minister Camillo Cavour, the flamboyant general Garibaldi, and the Savoynard king Victor Emanuel (whose triumphant entry into Florence in 1860 is celebrated in *Last Poems*). Especially in the "Napoleon" poem does Barrett Browning remind us that the people-as-holy is still her unalterable standard in politics, though it may seem that in practice she has forgotten it. While Barrett Browning has been accused of turning reactionary in her last days and in her last poems (which most critics have judged too polemic and too political), in basic theory she remains essentially the same. In her support of Napoleon's coup d'état, however, she was disloyal to her most basic proliberty stance: the holiness of the people. In worship of the "great man" she forsook her great principle.

In recounting the poet's adulation of Napoleon III, Barrett Browning's biographer Margaret Forster is not entirely fair: never bothering to reveal Barrett Browning's periodic reservations about and criticisms of Napoleon III, Forster maintains that in the poet's deluded eyes, Louis Napoleon could do no wrong.[28] In truth, Barrett Browning—like any avid observer of international politics—was quite capable of changing her mind as events unfolded, judging a political leader always by his most recent decision or action. For example, she praises the pope as a "great man" in 1847, enthusiastically declaring in a letter to her sister Arabella that the pope is a liberator, a devout church reformer, brave, and gentle (*LHS* 46), then claims in 1849 that she and Robert had never been caught "for a moment" in the pope enthusiasm, that "the old serpent, the Pope is wriggling his venom into the heart of all possibilities of free thought & action . . ." (*LEBB* 2:98). She notes that if ever a "good excellent Grand-Duke" deserved benediction, then Tuscany's grand duke does (*LEBB* 1:357); later she realizes that he is a liar and a tyrant and that she had been stupidly wrong to put her faith in princes. However unorthodox and unbalanced he may be, Mazzini is considered early in the Brownings' Florence days a great champion of liberty; in 1860 he has become the unscrupulous "apostle of assassination" (*LMO* 139).

Likewise, Barrett Browning's views on Louis Napoleon were also subject to change. She opposed his initial election to the presidency, believing him "flaccid," ill equipped to lead. But when he was elected by a majority, then he deserved support as the people's president, be he ape or angel. In the face of his overwhelming popularity, however, she later criticized his handling of rebellion in Rome, as well as his repressive action in confiscating newspapers and curtailing freedom of the press. In her

---

28. Forster, *Elizabeth Barrett Browning: The Life and Loves of a Poet*, 264.

reaction to Napoleon's December 1851 coup d'état—a step taken because the constitution allowed no second term and the vote to amend failed of the required majority—Barrett Browning earned the ire both of her liberal contemporaries and of generations of Browning biographers, even those disposed to admire her as a champion of oppressed peoples. In the matter of suppressing the constitution, Napoleon's action (as Robert Browning says in "Prince Hohenstiel-Schwangau": "order gained by law destroyed") preserved and augmented illegitimate power and could be fairly judged as provocation deserving of deposing, impeaching, or recalling—whatever retribution the system allowed.[29] Barrett Browning mistakenly defends him as still a democrat at heart and a French George Washington (the constitution not reflecting the people's desires, she says, with insufficient evidence). She declares that the people of France supported him (again her scant evidence, based in this case upon the pro-Napoleon comments of her French *cuisinière* and concierge). Illogically, she says he is "Translated to the sphere of domination / By democratic passion!" (*N* 54–55). When in the Treaty of Villafranca Napoleon supposedly negotiated away the advantage he had gained in his victory over Austria, however, she was devastated and instructed her son, Pen, to remove his Napoleon badges and medals.[30] In "First News from Villafranca" she reveals the feeling of betrayal: how could the brave, thoughtful Napoleon whom the Italians had vainly trusted have surrendered his gains and counted as nothing the blood of the patriots dead for Italy's salvation. Incredulous, she asks: " . . . peace, do you say? . . . Because we triumph, we succumb?" (*CWEBB* 6:46.13, 15). The peace is only of such type as the quiet between "the rifle's click and the rush of the ball" (*CWEBB* 6:47.39). At the last analysis, Napoleon—though he be "corrupt as seven devils"—has created a free Italy (*CWEBB* 6:54.34); in "Summing up in Italy," Barrett Browning asks:

> . . . Suppose
> Some hell-brood in Eden's sweet greenery,
> Convoked for creating—a rose!
> Would it suit the infernal machinery?
> (*CWEBB* 6:54.37–40)

29. Browning, *The Poems*, 1:953.343.

30. Dorothy Hewlett suggests that she "sorrowfully" asked Pen to remove the French tricolor from the balcony because Florentines had everywhere taken down the busts of their Napoleonic "liberator" overnight (*Elizabeth Barrett Browning: A Life*, 348).

In the poems following Italy's (partial) unification under Victor Emanuel, Barrett Browning has chosen a celebratory, triumphant mood, putting aside recriminations and past criticisms. Not only Napoleon but also military heroes from the great to the lowly are celebrated, both those who have tasted victory and those who have fallen as martyrs to bring about victory. Garibaldi, whom she considered not very bright, is depicted in "Garibaldi" (from *Last Poems*) as valorous, lionhearted, and noble. Stalwart Cavour "bore up his Piedmont ten years" until she could be united with all Italy (*CWEBB* 6:54.47). King Victor Emanuel, "freedom's first soldier" (*CWEBB* 6:48.15), earned from the people the flowers they rained down from roof and terrace, the shouts they raised, and even their souls: "They tore out their hearts for the King" (*CWEBB* 6:50.6). In "Mother and Poet," Laura Savio mourns the deaths of her sons, price of the "birth-pangs of nations" (again employing Barrett Browning's familiar metaphor for Italy as political matriarch) (*CWEBB* 6:75.93). And in "A Forced Recruit" a nameless lad is praised for his sublime sacrifice of his life for his homeland.

"Napoleon III" is certainly a tribute to the French emperor, who

> . . . might have had the world with him,
> But chose to side with suffering men,
> And had the world against him when
> He came to deliver Italy.
>
> (*N* 413–16)

Attribution of Napoleon III as savior of Italy from Austria is echoed in Robert Browning's "Prince Hohenstiel-Schwangau," a work ambivalent about Napoleon's nobility of motivation in some things but on the issue of Italy's independence claiming to have acted for the "absolute right and truth" of God in his charge to

> Come with me and deliver Italy!
> Smite hip and thigh until the oppressor leave
> Free from the Adriatic to the Alps
> The oppressed one!"[31]

But even more than a tribute to Napoleon, "Napoleon III. In Italy" is a tribute to the people. Here Barrett Browning (consciously or not) echoes

31. Browning, *The Poems*, 1:990.1880–83.

the argument for deposition and regicide made by Milton (whose ecclesiastical and political essays she had studied, underlined, and annotated).
It is the people who create the king, not the other way around, Milton
argues in *A Defence of the People of England:* "Our fathers begot us, but
our kings did not, and it is we, rather, who created the king."[32] The people
may, therefore, reject him, retain him, or depose him. Barrett Browning
does not follow this argument through to its conclusion; while Milton
sees the Parliament as the expression of the people's will, she denies that
authority to the French Assembly, permitting Napoleon to go around (or
over) France's very provision for the voice of the people.

In her praise of Napoleon, Barrett Browning does suggest, however,
that he has been created by the people, not by himself. In this her argument
in favor of Napoleon III is the inverse of Milton's against Charles I. She
says that "The people must transcend / All common king-born kings"
(*N* 296–97) and that Napoleon is made alive by democratic blood flowing
in his veins:

> The people's blood runs through him,
>   Dilates from head to foot.
>   Creates him absolute . . .
>   (*N* 301–3)

To the degree that he has the people's heart throbbing in his own breast,
then he can do no wrong. Presumably, if and when he no longer has
that heart beating within him, then he is dead to liberty and the people
and is no longer the rightful emperor. Unfortunately, Barrett Browning's
political ideology never concludes just how the people's will is ascertained
by its champion. Interviewing the concierge will not do.

As far as Barrett Browning is concerned, she has never in her allegiance
to the Italian risorgimento violated the principle of the holiness of the
people. In an essay comparing American and Italian republicanism and
published only months before her death she says:

> I honor Republicanism everywhere as an expression of the people;
> but it seems to me that a theoretical attachment to any form of

---

32. Milton, *Complete Prose Works of John Milton,* 4:327. In Barrett Browning's copy
of *Prose Works of John Milton: Containing His Principal Political and Ecclesiastical Pieces,*
"The Tenure of Kings and Magistrates" is marked and underlined.

government whatever is simply pedantry,—as if one should insist upon everybody's wearing one kind of hat, or adopting one attitude. A genuine government is simply the attitude of that special people. What we require for every man (or state) is life, health, muscular freedom to choose his own attitude. Let us be for the Democracy, and leave the rest. Who cares for the figure at the helm, as long as the people's wind is in the sails? (*CWEBB* 6:361)

Although most of her political works proclaim the tyranny within Italy and forecast Italy's salvation, Barrett Browning also, like her hero the Florentine poet Dante, advocates a form of Christian empire. This vision is developed most fully (yet still unsatisfactorily) in "Italy and the World" (from *Poems before Congress*). Dante, however, sees world empire as Italian empire with its center in Rome and a Christian Italian monarch at the helm, while Barrett Browning has a more nebulous idea of some type of league that will minimize or eradicate nationalism, transcend chauvinistic boundaries, ensure peace, and make all people one, "one confederate brotherhood planting / One flag only" (*CWEBB* 3:350.48–49). Hence, national selfishness and civic vaunting will be inadmissable—indeed, unthinkable—and there will be, as St. Paul writes in another context, neither Jew nor Greek. Barrett Browning everywhere advocates developed Christianity as "civilization perfected"; it is the heavenly Jerusalem that Aurora imagines in the final lines of *Aurora Leigh*, ushering in the new age of renewal and freedom.

IV

As Romney and Aurora, the cousins/counterparts of *Aurora Leigh*, visualize that new Jerusalem of reformed social, economic, and political systems, Romney acknowledges that he has been wrong in his misguided Christian socialism, that Christ—not the French school of socialism—will reform the human condition, that the world needs more activism inspired by love and

> "Fewer programmes, we who have no prescience.
> Fewer systems, we who are held and do not hold.
> Less mapping out of masses to be saved,
> By nations or by sexes. Fourier's void,
> And Comte absurd,—and Cabet puerile.

> Subsist no rules of life outside of life,
> No perfect manners without Christian souls:
> The Christ Himself had been no Lawgiver
> Unless He had given the life, too, with the law."
>   (*AL* 9.865–73)

Aurora Leigh contains Barrett Browning's "highest convictions upon Life and Art" (*CWEBB* 4:1), she says in her dedication, and one of those ideas on life is surely the system whereby governments and social structures seek to heal the inequities, poverty, unemployment, greed, prostitution, chaos, and despair that result from the roots of "Evil's own existence" on earth (*AL* 8.764). The novel-poem was written following a time of intense political ferment and activity, including not only the revolutions in Austria and France but also several important works of political theory, including the *Communist Manifesto* of 1848, as well as numerous socialistic theories and experimental communes in France and England conceived throughout the 1830s and 1840s. In *Aurora Leigh*, Barrett Browning engages in debate the doctrines of theorists such as Charles Fourier and Pierre-Joseph Proudhon (the latter of whom she had read avidly in the preceding two years before writing the poem), as well as the English Christian socialists such as Charles Kingsley, whose *Alton Locke, Tailor and Poet* she parodies for the purpose of undermining his reform theory. She finds the socialists' theory troubling, she says, because they attempt to reform superficial aspects of the economic environment and fail to see that "it takes a high-souled man, / To move the masses, even to a cleaner stye" (*AL* 8.431–32), and it takes an ideal, an internalizing of Apocalypse, to rectify the evils that the human species has inherited from Adam.

Barrett Browning's own England had witnessed, during the opening decades of the nineteenth century, various attempts at socialism. Perhaps the most prominent example was Owenism, based upon the teachings of Robert Owen but having its theoretical foundation in the English political thinkers of the immediate past: William Godwin's call to eliminate private property and annihilate government, Mary Wollstonecraft's plea for the emancipation of woman, Percy Bysshe Shelley's advocacy of liberation from the bondage of marriage, Thomas Spence's tracts on an agrarian communist utopia. The Owenites believed that the three primary sources of social *dis*unityism (to play upon Fourier's term) were religion, private property, and marriage: a slave market in which wives and daughters were themselves property. The anticlerical cry of Owenites was for "more bread and less bibles, more pigs and less parsons," and in turn they were attacked by the established churches as adulterers, infidels, and worse. Owenite communities were very similar to those advocated by Fourier, and an important by-product of the quasi-familial in practice was the liberation of many (though not all) women from the monotonous drudgery of housework. By 1840 Owenism, now established in every major English city, attempted communal living arrangements, approved "moral marriage" and easily obtained divorce, and actually performed the function of religion for its adherents. According to Barbara Taylor, socialism with its doctrine of love and classlessness became an alternate (infidel) church.

> By the late 1830s many Owenites were describing Socialism as the Rational Religion, thereby placing themselves in direct competition with orthodox Christianity. From 1838 on, the meeting halls of the working class became arenas in which the conflicting claims of Christianity and the Social Science met in head-on collision. . . . [For] Owenite feminist "infidels" . . . the struggle for sexual emancipation became inextricably tied to the struggle against patriarchal Christian orthodoxy.[33]

Barrett Browning protests in her letters that she and Robert are no communists, and she comments that with socialism there is always some compulsion, some suppression of individuality. She says, "Nothing can be more hateful to me than this communist idea of quenching individualities in the mass. As if the hope of the world did not always consist in the eliciting of the individual man from the background of the masses, in the evolvement of individual genius, virtue, magnanimity" (*LEBB* 1:363). In a letter to Miss Mitford, she suggests that socialism is an antithesis to freedom: " . . . for I love liberty so intensely that I hate Socialism. I hold it to be the most desecrating & dishonoring to Humanity, of all creeds. I would rather (for *me*) live under the absolutism of Nicholas of Russia, than in a Fourier-machine, with all my individuality sucked out of me by a social air-pump" (*LMRM* 3:302). She claims to believe that the people of France fear socialistic societies as they fear social chaos (*LMO* 62).

33. Taylor, *Eve and the New Jerusalem: Socialism and Feminism in the Nineteenth Century,* 17, 20, 148, 143, 123.

She does not defend capitalism or competition or explain how a more egalitarian society will evolve from her doctrine of liberty, but insists that democracy is preferred to socialism and that love and altruism in all things will minimize, though not eradicate, social evils. As George Eliot says of the Middlemarch doctor Tertius Lydgate, Barrett Browning has warmed herself at the fires of French social theories but has brought away no smell of scorching. One suspects that she would reject socialism out of hand because, to one of Barrett Browning's views and values, it has no soul. And—to her thinking—"The soul's the way. Not even Christ Himself / Can save man else than as He holds man's soul" (*AL* 8.544–45). Though she, like the French socialists and their English disciples, wants to "blow all class-walls level as Jerico's" (*AL* 9.932), she believes the reformation should come not through schemes and statistics but through wholehearted acceptance of Christ's humanitarianism as related in the Gospels.

The political philosopher who seems the principal target for attack in *Aurora Leigh* is socialist Charles Fourier. He reasons that the direction of all creation is the "unityism" that is in God, and that human society is in transition (the Social Organism, like all other organisms, being in a constant state of evolution). In future, the Divine Social Order will evolve, adapting to the nature of Man and conforming to the primary attributes of God. This renovated social order will not only grant universality of justice but also provide for the young, helpless, sick, infirm, and unfortunate, as well as guarantee jobs and economic opportunity for all—women and children included. Furthermore, this social renovation would occur without the system of "Coercion and Constraint" heretofore the basis of every system in centuries of governmental experimentation. Fourier proposes the *phalanstère,* or collective unit of combined households (the model for Romney's phalanstery in *Aurora Leigh*). In Fourier's system, combined living units will also mean nurseries and kitchens, thus reducing the work of females by three-fourths; this system will prove much more economical than current households, and the women thus liberated may choose other careers and pursuits. His proposal to liberate women from hearth and home is endorsed by American feminist Margaret Fuller, with whom the Brownings associated in Italy. Fuller accepts Fourier's communal living arrangements because—while there will always be plenty of mothers to make the nest soft and warm—the wings of other women need not be clipped to prevent migratory flight from the nest and into the professional world. Like Friedrich Engels,

Fourier recognizes that capitalism as currently practiced is oppressive to women just as it is to the proletariat. As a feminist thinker, Fourier says that the noblest nations have always been those with most liberty for women, that he recognizes no liberty (including sexual) unless it is extended to both sexes. In his evolving social order both marriage and theology are soon to be outdated, and society will cease to judge women on the basis of chastity (a proposal already advanced by Mary Wollstonecraft). The wedding ceremony is, after all, a notification that "some libertine or scapegrace will deflower a young innocent," and theology keeps the underclass repressed in that it extols poverty as the path to eternal riches (as political science extols the riches of this world while waiting for the next). To Fourier, modern propagandists who uphold either view are charlatans. Like most of the French socialists, he opposes the "absurd" notion of "free competition." Cabet, Blanc, and Fourier all propose some method of the produce of the society going to each according to needs, Fourier through a "stockholder" system of economy, each contributor (man, woman, and child) sharing the profits and losses.[34]

Barrett Browning had reservations about Fourierism on the grounds that there is some compulsion in any socialistic system, that the spirit of the people resists such restrictions on their freedom, that centralization (which she believes to be the central doctrine of Louis Blanc) circumvents liberty while the opposite extreme (the socialistic commune of Fourier) accomplishes—through different means—that same end. Emerson says as much when he notes that Fourier treats man as a "plastic thing, something that may be put up or down, ripened or retarded, moulded, polished, made into solid, or fluid, or gas, at the will of the leader. . . ." And Robert Browning's Prince Hohenstiel-Schwangau contemptuously dismisses Fourier, along with Comte, as not worth risking the "whiff of [his] cigar."[35]

Barrett Browning must also have disliked the socialists and anarchists whom she had recently studied because their atheism was unsettling and because their radical view on women and marriage would undermine

---

34. Fuller, *Woman in the Nineteenth Century and Kindred Papers Relating to the Sphere, Condition and Duties, of Woman,* 124; Fourier, "Theory of the Foundation of the Human Passions," in *Social Destiny of Man, or Theory of the Four Movements,* 51, 91–97, 137; Fourier, "History of the Four Movements," in *Social Destiny of Man,* 67, 76, 87, 116–17.

35. Emerson, "Fourier and the Socialists," in *Essays and Lectures,* 1207; Browning, *The Poems,* 1:955.438.

the bourgeois family. Proudhon, for example, chastises God as envier of Adam, tormentor of Prometheus, adding, "God is stupidity and cowardice; God is hypocrisy and falsehood; God is tyranny and poverty; God is evil."[36] Proudhon believes the species is destined to live without religion (or at least religion as defined by the dogma of Catholicism and Protestantism) but instead by some authoritative basis for justice.

Still more offensive was that socialists with their avowed agnosticism, "moral marriages" (or common-law marriages), and economic-based communes would destroy Christian marriage and the family, a value endorsed by church and society, and certainly by Barrett Browning herself.[37] Nowhere is there evidence that Barrett Browning, like her friend Margaret Fuller, found Fourier's opposition to traditional marriage to be potentially liberating for the female. It is also significant, I think, that Aurora's Romney is never misled enough in his socialism to practice "nature's chastity" (free love) in his marital life; rather, he proposes traditional marriage to both Aurora and Marian. In Romney's recantation, cited above, he notes that we need "[l]ess mapping out of masses to be saved / By nations or by sexes" (*AL* 9.867–68), a reference in which the poet might well have had in mind the feminist socialism of Fourier or his disciples.

Fourier's brand of liberation must have been especially repugnant to Barrett Browning's sense of morality, which in her Christian world was based on self-discipline and restraint. As Roland Barthes comments, however, pleasure—not restraint—is for Fourier the "everlasting principle of social organization." Pleasure guilt free and commodious in every activity from employment to sex. This aspect of the commune is the most revolting for Nathaniel Hawthorne's fictional reformer Hollingsworth of *The Blithedale Romance,* an examination both of Fourier's theory and of the "knot of dreamers" who constituted Brook Farm. Blithedale is founded upon the principles of equality, the division of labor and of the rewards of labor through the phalanstery, the spirituality of work, and the rejection of Pride for the higher good of unselfish love. Hollingsworth

---

36. Proudhon, "Religion," in *Selected Writings of Pierre-Joseph Proudhon,* 223.

37. Not all the thinkers whom Barrett Browning attacks advocate free love. Comte considers monogamy the greatest gift of the Middle Ages and suggests that modern wives exert influence through their moral superiority ("A General View of Positivism," in *Auguste Comte and Positivism,* 373–78). Proudhon taught the "consolations of love," family virtue with its abegnation of self compensating for the disrespect of mutualist society (Ritter, *The Political Thought of Pierre-Joseph Proudhon,* 143).

accuses Fourier of the "Unpardonable Sin" of choosing the selfish principle as the "master-workman" of his system, of seizing upon and fostering
"whatever vile, petty, sordid, filthy, bestial, and abominable corruptions
have cankered into our nature."[38] Both Barrett Browning and Aurora
Leigh extol delight in one's work (and count themselves fortunate to
have found their life's labor joyful); so do the hypothetical citizens of
Fourier's utopia and the fictional citizens of Hawthorne's (or at least they
temporarily persuade themselves). Both Aurora and Barrett Browning
would, however, certainly reject the open and free sex readily available in
Fourier's "Harmony." But in Fourier's system every passion is "absolute
grapheme of the utopian text," and that includes a wide range of passion,
from elementary sensual desire to the aspiration toward "unityism."[39]
One important scene in *Aurora Leigh* is no doubt a direct response to
the socialist utopia with its dissolution of marriage. At a dinner party a
university student who is a socialist like Romney (whom the student calls
"our ablest man") engages in a debate with Sir Blaise, a traditionalist. The
foreign student ridicules the English as backward on the woman question
and on liberation from the bondage of marriage. (Even Romney—for all
his advocacy of liberation and socialism—lags behind the philosophers,
says the student, for he takes in Lady Waldemar a bride who is a Venus
Meretrix but whom he no doubt has metamorphosed in his mind to the
Blessed Virgin.) Sir Blaise puts the young upstart in his place with a retort
that no doubt voices Barrett Browning's own view:

> If young men of your order run before
> To see such sights as sexual prejudice
> And marriage-law dissolved,—in plainer words,
> A general concubinage expressed
> In a universal pruriency,—the thing
> Is scarce worth running fast for, and you'd gain
> By loitering with your elders."
>
> (*AL* 5.723–29)

Certainly Sir Blaise (like the hosts and guests at the dinner party) comes in
for his share of satire; in his case, he is satirized for narrow allegiance to the
catholic, apostolic, mother-church that draws the line so plain and straight

---

38. Barthes, "Fourier," in *A Barthes Reader*, 340; Hawthorne, *The Blithedale Romance*,
in *The Works of Nathaniel Hawthorne*, 3:53.
39. Barthes, "Fourier," in *A Barthes Reader*, 357.

that everybody outside is, in his view, not Christian but animalistic, a view that Barrett Browning rejects. (As far as she is concerned, the best Christians may well be outside *all* churches.) But she just as obviously agrees with him about the morality of traditional marriage for all classes (as witnessed by her insistence in letters to Miss Mitford that her servant Katherine *must,* since she is pregnant, marry the father of her child—never mind the issues of mutual affinity or compatibility.) The conclusion of *Aurora Leigh* with Aurora and Romney united in romantic love, marital partnership, and ostensible equality provides a very different answer to the woman question from that proposed by Fourier or Owen. Like Sir Blaise, the poet prefers "sexual prejudice" and "marriage-law" to "general concubinage" and "universal pruriency."

Another important issue for socialism is the question of property, of wealth versus poverty. At the beginning of the novel-epic, when a young, recently orphaned Aurora arrives from Italy to live with her austere aunt in England, she finds the landscape also austere—cold, frosty, and foggy. Small patches of individual plotted ground indicate demarcation among neighbors. Aurora notes that "The ground seemed cut up from the fellowship / Of verdure, field from field, as man from man" (*AL* 1.260–61). At the time she does not note that property causes division, inequities, and competition. But Romney does, saying, "And rich men make the poor, who curse the rich, / Who agonise together, rich and poor . . . (*AL* 2.271–72). Barrett Browning has read in Proudhon that property is thievery and thralldom, the mother of tyranny, and source of civic and political inequality.[40] When, as an adult, Aurora lives an independent life making her own way in the world as a writer (rather more like Letitia Landon or Harriet Martineau than Elizabeth Barrett), she ventures into St. Margaret's Court to meet her cousin's intended bride. There she receives the weak jeers of a child sick from an ague fit and the curses of a lascivious woman with rouged cheeks and bedraggled locks. Emptying the contents of her purse on the paving stones, Aurora causes a near riot as, with oaths and blows, the London poor fall to, combatting one another for her sparse charity. From Marian Erle, who she thinks will become her cousin-in-law, Aurora learns that the rural poor are no

40. Proudhon, *Qu'est-ce que la propriété?* in *Œuvres Complètes de P.-J. Proudhon* 5:133, 286. Proudhon's theory of property does not preclude *possession* (that is, acquisitions made possible by talent, industry, and thrift).

more fortunate, their lot no pastoral paradise. (Marian's hard-drinking, wife-beating father trespasses, poaches, tramps, and works at random jobs in farm labor, and her child-beating mother has offered to sell or barter Marian's sexual favors to the local squire.) On the day of Romney and Marian's ill-fated nuptials, the unwashed lame, sick, and poor ("The humours of the peccant social wound" [*AL* 4.544]) remind Aurora of the "dreg-fiends" of slimy hell.

When she dines at the home of her friend Lord Howe, on the other hand, the host expounds his theories of social justice and equality (like Noah safe on the ark), while the elegant Lady Howe exhibits before her guests the grace and serenity of a swan ignoring all the tadpoles of the world swimming around her. Also on the evening of the Howes' party Aurora receives (via a message delivered by her friend Howe) the attentions of a reputable gentleman, John Eglinton, who, Howe boasts, is an excellent landlord of the old school, admittedly slack in new philanthropies, but giving a tenants' dance on his birthday, scolding the tenants if they miss church or keep their children from catechism, and allowing them to gather wood from his estate. Aurora retorts that Eglinton is, like the snail, "[k]nown chiefly for the house upon his back" (*AL* 5.866), and she contemptuously rejects his attentions. Thus is Aurora educated in the evils of capitalism—in the form of demarcated property, urban squalor, decadent values, rural poverty, abused children, rampant prostitution, paternalistic squirearchy, and the luxury of the aristocratic class who can very well afford to talk socialism with their titled cronies and a few artists and representatives of the intelligentsia. Aurora does not advocate "more bread and less bibles" as a cure for the world's evils; yet Aurora's cousin Romney, owner of Leigh Hall and the Leigh lineage, does. He proposes to give his energy and his property in actually doing something about the deprivations and inequalities he sees everywhere (and finds corroborated in his statistics, theories, facts, and diagrams).

Yet another objection to socialism is that it destroys the most idealistic and talented of its own misguided advocates, a point that Barrett Browning was not the first to make. In Hawthorne's *The Blithedale Romance* (published four years before *Aurora Leigh*) the Fuller-like prophetess Zenobia commits suicide, and Hollingsworth is ruined, the narrator Miles Coverdale says, because Philanthropy as a "profession . . . and ruling passion" ruins the heart, "the rich juices of which God never meant to be pressed violently out, and distilled into alcoholic liquor, by an unnatural process."[41] As noted elsewhere, Romney Leigh suffers from a messiah complex. He hears and feels, almost palpably, the world's sufferings and imagines the poor tugging at his skirts. When he tells Aurora that the world gets from her gender no Christs, but only Miriams, he perhaps mocks the "female Messiah" talk on the radical fringe and no doubt implies that he, being of the appropriate gender, is eligible as the new Christ. Romney's decision indicates that he will take the opposite extreme from that of the rich, young ruler who, upon asking Jesus what he should do in order to become a disciple, was told to sell his possessions and give the money to the poor. The ancestral estate, Leigh Hall, will be "christianised from Fourier's own" (*AL* 5.784), and its denizens of all social levels will live and prosper together in peace and harmony. By means of pamphlets, plans, speeches in Parliament, and the sacrifice of his personal wealth, Romney will do his "duty" to his fellow persons in need: the poor, orphans, the homeless, and beaten and bullied wives.

Aunt Leigh cannot comprehend Romney's intent to waste his life on "good-for-nothing" people, and—although Aurora respects Romney's dedication—she gives to his marriage proposal (and invitation to shared socialist labor) a rejection that calls to mind the one that Jane Eyre gives St. John Rivers (as several critics have noted). Aurora will not devote her life to Ragged Schools and Public Baths because, to her, art is the higher calling (and a higher calling too than nursing in military hospitals, as Barrett Browning notes in her reservations about Florence Nightingale's work). Your cause is good for you, Aurora tells Romney, but—as you are married already to your social theories—I will have none of you. Even Lord Howe, educated in the socialism to which Romney ascribes, implies that theory is one thing, practice quite another. Instead of giving up his estate and devoting himself to good works, Howe cynically observes that the world as he knows it might just as well end. To him, converting one's home into a phalanstery is madness and the mad Romney is a modern Hamlet. Naturally, Marian Erle adores Romney as her personal savior, and she never faults his schemes and plans. But we scarcely expect her to criticize her savior, who has given her meaningful work and proposed honorable marriage. Marian is living proof that, for some few individuals, Romney's system succeeds. The other woman in Romney's life, Lady Waldemar, is smitten by the young philanthropist; she reads the French political philosophers and employs her own blue-blooded hands for a

41. Hawthorne, *The Blithedale Romance,* in *The Works of Nathaniel Hawthorne,* 3:243.

time in the work of his phalanstery. Eventually, though, even she learns her lesson, and after the spectacular failure of Romney's great social experiment, she vows to have no socialist within the space of "three crinolines" (*AL* 9.136). In short, Romney's socialist utopia is rejected as foolhardy by everyone who is in a position to know and is candid enough to voice her or his objections (such as the wedding guest who calls Romney "quite lunatic" when he could, like Prince Albert, simply practice moderation on the question of the poor [*AL* 4.662]; Lord Howe; the painter Vincent Carrington; Aurora; Aunt Leigh; and at last Lady Waldemar).

Still another objection to contemporary French political thought was the lack of freedom that resulted from political centralization, which Barrett Browning like Proudhon opposed.[42] Louis Blanc and Cabet, she charged, would suppress all journals except one as a condition of the so-called free state (*LMO* 73). As an advocate of liberty, she would consider this curtailment of the free press as an unforgivable transgression. One of her criticisms of Emperor Louis Napoleon, it should be recalled, was his seizure of three newspapers on what she considered insufficient provocation. She argues that, although families might be tempted to yield to the communal life as proposed by the "theorists in Paris" in order to attain cheaper employment for their livelihood, such systems are at best patriarchal and at worst absolutist. Patriarchy and absolutism may work for societies more or less barbaric but are not appropriate for advanced, informed, and independent peoples. In *Aurora Leigh,* however, they are a disaster for the rabble as well as for the enlightened. Romney erred by bringing in "men and women of disordered lives" (of the barbaric order [*AL* 8.889]), and they smashed not only the waxen masks he made them wear but Leigh Hall as well. Romney's patriarchy was his "tyrannous constraint / In forcing crooked creatures to live straight . . ." (*AL* 8.893–94). As it turns out, Romney is just as paternalistic in his own way as is Sir Eglinton.

Musing upon life and art, Aurora tells herself that what is wanted is a larger metaphysics for both poet and philanthropist, making a more complete poetry and a better social system:

> More fully than the special outside plans,
> Phalansteries, material institutes,

---

42. This opposition to centralization was one of Proudhon's bases for opposition to the unification of Italy, and there Barrett Browning parts company with him (Alan Ritter, *The Political Thought of Pierre-Joseph Proudhon,* 10).

> The civil conscriptions and lay monasteries
> Preferred by modern thinkers, as they thought
> The bread of man indeed made all this life . . .
> (*AL* 6.209–13)

Addressing Romney, Aurora is even more adamant that she is right and Fourier wrong. In rejecting his marriage proposal, she tells him:

> . . . Ah, your Fouriers failed,
> Because not poets enough to understand
> That life develops from within."
> (*AL* 2.483–85)

After her words have proved true, Romney recites them back to her *verbatim* in their final reunion (*AL* 8.434–36), signifying that he has learned the lesson that Barrett Browning had intended for him all along. In a letter to Isa Blagden, Barrett Browning explains:

> Christian Socialists are by no means a new sect, the Moravians representing the theory with as little offence and absurdity as may be. What is it, after all, but an out-of-door extension of the monastic system? The religious principle, more or less apprehended, may bind men together so, absorbing their individualities, and presenting an aim *beyond the world;* but upon merely human and earthly principles no system can stand, I feel persuaded, and I thank God for it. If Fourierism could be realized (which it surely cannot) out of a dream, the destinies of our race would shrivel up under the unnatural heat, and human nature would, in my mind, be desecrated and dishonored—because I do not believe in purification without suffering, in progress without struggle, in virtue without temptation. Least of all do I consider happiness the end of man's life. We look to higher things, have nobler ambitions. (*LEBB* 1:467–68)

In the final two books of *Aurora Leigh,* Aurora and Romney are permitted a full discussion of the flaws of Christian socialism. Romney recognizes that he has vainly considered himself as a modern Christ, has been "absolute in dogma, proud in aim, / And fierce in expectation" (*AL* 8.369–70), and he accepts the destruction of his home and his health (particularly—and symbolically—his sight) by those very persons whom he attempted to help and who burned Leigh Hall to save themselves from their savior. Instead of moving the swine into a cleaner stye as he had vowed to do, he has driven them over the cliff into the sea like the herd into which Jesus cast demons. But now Romney knows that humans cannot live by bread alone, that the inner person must be reformed lest the outer manifestation be only superficial and temporary. He actually believes that this failure was an appropriate punishment from the "great Taskmaster" God, who through the disaster has taught him to attempt lesser things, not greater, for the distressed. Also, he learns that he has erred in his attempt to reform the system all alone, without working through the church and the squires. His pride has been chastened (as has Aurora's for aspiring to become the great poetess of her age). Since Romney's pride is linked with his social system, however, Barrett Browning disposes of both in one swoop. Significantly, though, Aurora's poetry is not abolished. She will continue the practice of art and "work for two," although presumably her art will now become more mature and more true. As for Romney, though the fallen world still cries for help, he will have to work with the "little ones" and forget all grand schemes for social utopias. Socialist utopianism (unless otherworldly like that of the Moravians) will not work because human nature is fallen. Romney at last, despite his literal blindness, sees

> Impossible social questions, since their roots
> Strike deep in Evil's own existence here,
> Which God permits because the question's hard
> To abolish evil nor attaint free-will.
> (*AL* 8.763–66)

Adam's disobedience guaranteed human evil, as it guaranteed human suffering. In Christian thought, Christ as the second Adam brought the possibility of restoration to each individual creature—soul by soul—though not salvation for the masses by scheme and diagram. Romney says that each individual remains an Adam to the general race. He has previously identified himself with the new Adam; now he must accept his kinship with the old Adam. It is his lesson in humility. Christ, however, has ennobled work, endorsed human governments, and enabled those who love God and love their fellows to invest their lives in noble work on behalf of humanity. A chastened Romney must lay aside the theories of socialism, even Christian socialism, for a less grandiose, more elementary social gospel.

Aurora Leigh also undermines Christian socialism in that it is a direct parallel and response to Charles Kingsley's *Alton Locke*. Cora Kaplan has noted that *Aurora Leigh* is a countertext to Kingsley's 1850 novel,

that Barrett Browning even uses the same initials for her poet that
Kingsley does for his, and that the character Romney Leigh might
well be based in part upon Kingsley, whose goal was to "Christianise
socialism, socialise Christianity." Barrett Browning's work is a retort to
Kingsley (a Christian clergyman whom she personally liked and admired,
believing that "he never can speak or write otherwise than according
to a noble nature, I am sure" [*LMO* 85]). The retort works in several
ways: Alton as poet represents his class as Aurora represents her gender, Lord Ellerton is a nobleman and social reformer whom Romney
parallels, and his wife, Lady Eleanor, is a purer Lady Waldemar. Or,
rather, Barrett Browning's Lady Waldemar is a sensualist who attempts
to be taught social activism by Romney as Eleanor learns from Lord
Ellerton, but whose conversion convinces no one (not even herself) for
long. Lady Ellerton's education comes from reading Bentham, Malthus,
Fourier, and Proudhon, among others. When her reforming husband
dies young, she spends her fortune on the poor. Jessica Gerard notes
that in the landed classes of the 1830s through 1850s the traditional
obligation of the lady of the manor to attend upon the poor and sick
was "expanded and more energetically undertaken," partly due to religious revivalism and partly to the ideal of "True Womanhood" that
inspired middle-class woman to activism, but also because the land-
owning class was responding to threats of social protest. For a year
Lady Ellerton sets the example of charity endorsed both by the evangelical revival and by the Christian socialism of Kingsley; she earns
her bread by living and working with a socialistic order of "East End
needlewomen," a significant choice in Kingsley's novel because needlewomen and lace makers had a reputation as women of easy virtue.[43]
Therefore Lady Ellerton is working among the lost as well as the lowly.
In Barrett Browning's ironic mockery, Lady Waldemar reads Proudhon,
Considérant, Louis Blanc, and even half of Fourier (*AL* 3.584–85);
she contributes to Romney's schools, asylums, and hospitals, and tries
her hand at milking, churning, and scrubbing laundry alongside the
lowest women in Romney's phalanstery. But she does not remain for
a year as Eleanor does; rather she "has tarried half a week" (*AL* 5.787).

---

43. Kaplan, introduction to *"Aurora Leigh" and Other Poems,* by Barrett Browning,
30–31; Jessica Gerard, "Lady Bountiful: Women of the Landed Classes and Rural
Philanthropy," 187; Kingsley, *Alton Locke: Poet and Tailor,* 2:284.

Barrett Browning is not only parodying the socialism of Eleanor but also illustrating what Aurora says: that there can be no conversion except from the heart.

Alton Locke is more pedantic and consciously political than is *Aurora Leigh*. Kingsley castigates laissez-faire economics; exposes the exploitation of the "sweat" system in clothing manufacture (the subject also of his essay "Cheap Shirts and Nasty"); condemns capitalism (because the freedom of industry ensures the despotism of capital); rejects Malthusianism because it excuses laissez-faire and the suffering of the underclass; condemns the system that closes Dissenters out of Cambridge; exposes the "good, free, and happy" heresy of Benthamites, economists, and High Churchmen; and condemns the injustices of taxes, poor rates, and underrepresentation of the disenfranchised (which is treason against the kingdom of God and which the Reform Bill had not adequately remedied). From the French political economists Proudhon and Blanc he has learned that the destruction of property is necessary for human salvation (though Alton does try in vain to prevent the *destruction of property* in the Chartist riot and arson that Barrett Browning echoes in the burning of the phalanstery at Leigh Hall). Like Barrett Browning, he believes that the only change that matters is that which comes from within, and that renovation of social systems comes from the practice of Christianity. "He who would honor Christ, let him become a Christ himself," Alton says, an ideal like that animating Barrett Browning's ideal hero in *Casa Guidi Windows*.[44] But in *Aurora Leigh* eventually even the stubborn Romney abandons the views that Eleanor and Alton Locke die for.

Cora Kaplan is sharply critical of Barrett Browning's politics of negativity, noting that in comparison to Fourier, Owen, F. D. Maurice, Charles Kingsley, and others,

> her solutions to class conflict are even less adequate than theirs. Inevitably a theory which identifies the radical practice of art with the achievement of radical social change, or asserts the unity of female experience without examining the forms taken by that experience in different social groups, will emerge with a theory of art and politics unconnected with material reality and deeply élitist.[45]

44. Kingsley, *Alton Locke*, 2:81.
45. Kaplan, introduction to *"Aurora Leigh" and Other Poems,* by Barrett Browning, 12.

It is undeniable that Barrett Browning had no firsthand experience either in the struggling class or in communal living. She also has no practical scheme for remodeling the world; rather, she has a hypothetical Christian ideal in which the rich will be inspired by love to part with their world's goods to feed the poor. (Socialists "trouble" the close bonds "[b]etwixt the generous rich and grateful poor," Romney concludes [*AL* 8.901–2].) To Barrett Browning socialism is also tyrannical, thwarting the soul's salvation and the individual's free will, as well as undermining the soul's relationship to its God, the morality of marriage and sanctity of the family. Furthermore, institutionalized social welfare systems are, she claims, too cumbersome.

> . . . If we give,
> Our cup of water is not tendered till
> We lay down pipes and found a Company
> With Branches.
>
> (*AL* 8.810–13)

Certainly Barrett Browning considers herself no elitist, but a democrat and humanitarian to the very core. Furthermore, she believes that the poet can do much, that "[a]rt's a service" (*AL* 9.915); she has witnessed art changing the world in, for example, the swing of public opinion that had resulted from Harriet Beecher Stowe's *Uncle Tom's Cabin* or in the enlightenment brought about by such works as her own "Cry of the Children" and Hood's "Song of the Shirt." Therefore fictional Aurora will persist in the same kind of work and service as her creator, whose understandings are secondhand and insufficient but whose sympathies are vast.

At first glance it would seem that Romney's and Aurora's bourgeois union at the closure of the book is no better for the world's woes than that of the rich laissez-faire epicurean Lord Howe and his socialite wife. This is not the case, however. Barrett Browning's goal of equality, justice, and the freedom from want is not that different in outcome from the goal of nineteenth-century socialist theorists. The irreconcilable difference between them, however, is in her insistence upon spirituality rather than matter at the core of what constitutes humankind. To her, the error of most reformers is in thinking of the "natural world too insularly, as if / No spiritual counterpart completed it" (*AL* 8.617–18). She and Romney will not give up on the human condition, as both Howe and Lady Waldemar have done. Rather, the politics of feeding bellies must be supplanted by the politics of feeding souls, a great challenge, indeed, because it is an age, Romney says, of boasting do-nothingism in politics and philanthropy (*AL* 8.846–47). Kaplan charges Barrett Browning with elitism, impracticality, and an absence of material reality. Of the second and third charges she undoubtedly stands convicted. She advocates the politics not only of a "radical practice of art" but also of a radical practice of Christianity.

When Aurora and Romney stand face-to-face or shoulder-to-shoulder and envision the New Jerusalem of "new societies / Excluding falsehood" (*AL* 9.948–49), the poet is alluding both to John's Revelation and to the eschatology of British socialism, which employed the metaphor of Apocalypse not so much as expression of literal faith in millenarianism (though some socialists were apparently millenarians) but because—like the poet—they have discovered that sacred vocabulary conveys much more than secular. Like the Owenites, Barrett Browning longs for apocalyptic revisionism in the social and political order. Like Swedenborg, she uses the city Jerusalem as metaphor for the descent of heavenly teaching to the residents of earth, bringing about a new *ecclesia,* a heavenly church.[46] Not only in the overtly political poems does she long for Apocalypse, but also (throughout her professional life) in numerous protests about children in the mines and the ragged schools, about the poor reduced to thievery, children driven to premature graves, and women forced into prostitution (women whom she boldly proclaims as victims rather than victimizers), about slavery and the curse for a great nation torn asunder by the slave question, about the pittance offered by peoples of free nations as relief for their distressed underclass sisters and brothers, about the narrowness and hypocrisy she sees in established religion. That is, "[w]e pray together at the kirk," lifting to God the hands that we have soiled and wearied with evil labors (*CWEBB* 3:88.91). Right or wrong, enlightened or naive, she sees her work as that appropriate to the poet, assisting in the birth of a new order at once more humane and more spiritual, bringing the great hereafter to the here and now.

46. Taylor, *Eve and the New Jerusalem,* 139; Swedenborg, *Heaven and Hell,* 228.

4

Death and Resurrection

Face to face in my chamber, my silent chamber, I
    saw her:
God and she and I only, there I sat down to draw
    her
Soul through the clefts of confession: "Speak, I am
    holding thee fast,
As the angel of resurrection shall do it at the last!"
               —Barrett Browning, "Confessions"

I believe and I declare—Certain am I—from this
life I pass into a better, there where that lady
lives of whom enamoured was my soul.

    —Dante, *La Vita Nuova* (copied by Robert Browning
             into his wife's Bible after her death)

I

Elizabeth Barrett Browning's poems, early to late, reveal a preoccupation with death. Indeed, it is hardly an exaggeration to say that the volumes are strewn with corpses. Mothers mourn infants prematurely dead or sons slain in war, widows literal and fictional are bereft of loved ones, nations grieve their slain youth, maidens die for sisters or lovers or because of unrequited love, patriots and heroes are martyred for causes lost and gained, and Barrett herself is inconsolable following the drowning of her brother Edward Moulton-Barrett, "Bro," who had been her dearest companion from the nursery. In "De Profundis" (written after Bro's death) she almost wishes for death, lamenting that still her life goes on and on, as pointless and empty as it is described by Voices of the Aged that, in *A Drama of Exile*, Adam and Eve hear in prophecy after they have invited Death to inhabit their Eden:

> And this life we would survive,
> Is a gloomy thing and brief,
> Which, consummated in grief,
> Leaveth ashes for all gain.
> (*DE* 1685–88)

As Porter and Clarke note, "Through no motion of hers, the motion of the course of life [was] toward the steadfast doom—death . . ." by the time she published her first important volume in 1838 (*CWEBB* 2:viii). The preoccupation with death is a central recurring motif among female poets of the nineteenth century—from Felicia Hemans whom Barrett Browning admired (with reservations) to Christina Rossetti who was an ardent admirer of Barrett Browning—but the morbidity is both personal and pervasive in the Barrett poems of 1844, possibly because she had witnessed death of a loved one and assumed she was in the process of witnessing her own gradual dying. William Irvine and Park Honan, in their biography of Robert Browning, suggest that in the crisis of faith following Bro's death, Elizabeth Barrett had to choose whether to count the crushing blow of God's hand as more than just a catastrophic and senseless loss. Negotiating her way with God, she interpreted it as "preeminently a transaction between her and the Almighty."[1] Either God is not merciful or the death was in some way her fault. She chose the latter, clinging to her idealism about God and absorbing the lesson that thereafter she was to expect nothing from life. Or, to quote Tasso, as she does in "Essay on Mind," *"Brama assai, poco spera, e nulla chiede"* ("Desire much, hope little, and demand nothing") (*CWEBB* 1:55). Given this bereavement and appointment with death, Robert Browning's love came as a complete surprise, and for a long time she doubted whether such a blessing could be her lot. To his repeated marriage proposal, she initially responded that she would be a burden if they should wed because she was

---

1. Irvine and Honan, *The Book, the Ring, and the Poet: A Biography of Robert Browning,* 169.

a sick woman, and she implied that she was likely to die before long. In "Insufficiency," she asks: "Say, what can I do for thee? weary thee, grieve thee?" (*CWEBB* 3:226.6). In the opening sonnet from *Sonnets from the Portuguese*, she is amazed to find that the "mystic Shape" dragging her backward by the hair is not really Death, but Love. She has long expected otherwise. Looking back upon that moribund existence in Wimpole Street, she describes it as a "thoroughly morbid & desolate state . . . which I look back on now with the sort of horrors which one would look to one's graveclothes, if one had been clothed in them by mistake during a trance" (*LEBB* 1:288).

Yet if death or the premonition of death is, for Elizabeth Barrett, a constant companion, so too is the hope of resurrection, the premonition of immortality. At the young age of fourteen, she notes:

> [M]an is naturally enamoured of immortality, and tho the brazen trump of fame echoes his deeds when he sleeps[,] tho the cold sod is closed oer his corrupted form yet he shrinks from that deathlike that awful stillness, the dreadful attribute of the grave—Nothing can more plainly denote the souls eternity than the instinctive thirst for immortality which universally throbs in the heart of man— Would that benevolent Being whose kind spirit finds pleasure in the happiness of his Creatures have implanted in their bosoms such a feeling in vain? (*BC* 1:348)

Comforting Mary Russell Mitford who expects shortly to lose her father in death, she advises, "Let him go my beloved friend, meekly & without a struggle, whenever the Divine Will shall call him . . . do not try to hold him back from the blessedness of the spiritual world . . . Only a thin veil separates, perhaps, the two states of being—of those in the body & those who have left it" (*BC* 6:211).

Though she expected to die young, by the time Barrett Browning reached midlife, love—even more than work—had become her motivation for living. Loving Robert Browning, she confides that materialism is a "miserable creed," that she hopes to "look over the grave with you, *past* the grave, . . . & hope to be worthier of you *there* at least" (*BC* 12:310). Later, she takes no pleasure in anticipating departure from a world that has Robert and their child, Pen, in it, she says after a dangerous miscarriage (her fourth), and she embraces life hungrily. In middle age she says, "I cant look on the earth-side of death . . I flinch from corpses & graves, & never meet a common funeral without a sort of horror. When I look death-wards, I look OVER death—& upwards . . or I cant look that way at all" (*LMRM* 3:401).

But we need no ghost come from the dead to tell us this. Even persons casually aware of Barrett Browning's biography or some highly sentimentalized version of the Brownings' courtship and elopement are aware of the invalidism, the reclusiveness, the bouts of dangerous illness, even the premonitions and symptoms. The more fascinating question for a study of Barrett Browning's poetry is the motif of death transformed into the resurrection and the life—a central tenet of her faith and her art. In *Aurora Leigh* she suggests that her belief in resurrection is central not only to her Christian hope but also in application to every aspect of human life.

> . . . Earth (shut up
> By Adam, like a fakir in a box
> Left too long buried) remained stiff and dry,
> A mere dumb corpse, till Christ the Lord came down,
> Unlocked the doors, forced open the blank eyes,
> And used His kingly chrism to straighten out
> The leathery tongue turned back into the throat;
> Since when, she lives, remembers, palpitates
> In every limb, aspires in every breath,
> Embraces infinite relations.
>
> (*AL* 5.103–12)

The possibility of "infinite relations" is optimistic and intriguing. Barrett Browning's adaptation of the resurrection motif in Christian doctrine and Swedenborgian prophecy applies both to her own salvation and to other earthly resurrections (personal, political, aesthetic) that mirror the transcendental one of the triumphant soul. This faith in social and political resurrections constitutes perhaps a naive theology (as well as naive politics) in the evidence of war, pestilence, slavery, poverty, and injustice that in her poetic works she seeks to remedy.

For Elizabeth Barrett death is not the ending. Writings attributed to the apostle Paul (often cited in her letters) endorsed her ideas of immortality, and for years she considered writing a poem on the Resurrection. In fact, a few months after the death of her brother Sam (and a few days before the drowning of the beloved Bro) she notes, "Lazarus w^d. make a fine poem—w^dnt. he?—I lie here, weaving a great many schemes—I am seldom at a loss for a thread" (*BC* 4:292). Elizabeth Barrett Browning does eventually write a Lazarus poem (apart from "The Weeping Savior" in which Christ weeps at the tomb of his friend in Bethany, and the poet pleads that the Savior look upon the "corruption" and "funeral darkness" of all humans, weeping for us as well) (*CWEBB* 2:115.6, 10). But the Lazarus motif is less obvious in *Aurora Leigh;* hence the Resurrection theme has been generally overlooked in the criticism. In Barrett Browning's modern epic-novel, however, the principal characters' deaths and triumphant resurrections serve as testimony of her Pauline and Swedenborgian spiritual beliefs about the immortal soul and its destiny.

This chapter will deal with the rebirth theme in art, politics, and human life, the degree to which rebirth is attributed to the death and Resurrection of Christ, and Barrett Browning's belief in the immortal soul—its resurrection, its nature, its judgment, its eternal abode.

II

Any work that purports to study Elizabeth Barrett Browning's Christian devotion and the effect of religion upon her poetic work must also take into account the mesmerism, spiritualism, and Swedenborgianism that interested her (especially late in life), the séances that became a source of tension between herself and Robert (apparently because Robert felt there was much charlatanism among the spirit rappers and writers). She had a conviction that the souls of the dead were separated from her by but a thin veil and that she might through a medium encounter the unseen world.

Barrett Browning's most intense speculation into spiritualism came in the last decade of her life, between her mid-forties and mid-fifties. Simone de Beauvoir derisively suggests that the menopause accounts for intensified spirituality in women, that this particular crisis in female life makes one especially susceptible not only to a rational form of faith, but more particularly to excessive emotionalism and religious quackery:

> she is a preordained prey for religious sects, spiritualists, prophets, faith healers, for any and every charlatan. This is because she not only has lost all critical sense in losing touch with the factual world, but has also become eager for a final truth: she must have the remedy, the formula, the key that, all of a sudden, will save her while saving the universe.

De Beauvoir goes on to explain that the crisis of menopause rudely cuts woman's life in two; thus she seeks the illusion of a resurrection into a new life in which she attains the secrets of the beyond. Margaret Fuller, Barrett Browning's contemporary and a more dedicated feminist than the poet, confirms that mysticism—the "brooding soul"—does have particular appeal for women, and she cautions that because the spiritual tendency is strong, women are vulnerable to both priestly deceit and self-delusion, adding that this would not be the case if women's intellects were developed.[2]

According to Rosemary Radford Ruether, there are indeed gender differences in the perception of the "eschatology of immortality," the understanding and anticipation of the soul's destiny. Citing the work of Anne Wilson Schaef, a psychotherapist, Ruether notes that men who contemplate and hope for immortality are typically concerned with self-perpetuation, while women think about immortality in the context of relationship, seeing loved ones who have died.[3] That seems to be the case for Elizabeth Barrett Browning, who longs for a reunion with her brother Edward and experiences one transcendent encounter in which—by means of automatic handwriting—she believes her mother's spirit has been summoned. When her father died unreconciled to her, she tells her sister Henrietta that in dealing with her grief, "It has been a great help to me that of late years I have apprehended more of the ways of life in [the spirit] world" (*LHS* 272). But there was to be one more painful loss before her own death; Henrietta died of cancer just months prior to Barrett Browning's own death, and the poet deeply grieved. Of death she says that

> what we call *death,* does not change the personality or the individuality even, & that even on this earth there is union & access . . .
> I catch out at a forsaken garment & get bewildered between the Seen & Unseen. Only the Divine stands steadily with one foot on the sea & one on the land—and we placed suddenly between the natural & the spiritual, seem to slip & lose our Beloveds . . whom we do not lose, as Christ lives. (*LMO* 167)

2. de Beauvoir, *The Second Sex,* 580–81; Fuller, *Woman in the Nineteenth Century,* 102–5.
3. Ruether, *Sexism and God-Talk,* 235.

Just months before her death, she said that she wished to live only so long as she was growing in soul, no longer. Yet this resigned acceptance of death is not consistent throughout her work: she has worried too that—as she puts it in *Aurora Leigh*—death "quite unfellows us," and like those at the biblical tower of Babel, we can neither speak nor understand a common tongue (*AL* 5.552–55). In her immersion into spiritualism, Barrett Browning seeks not so much a particular message as she seeks a common tongue, a renewed relationship with those whom she has loved most deeply. And as for this need having intensified as she passes midlife, it is pertinent to recall that she has always considered herself somewhat of a mystic, although she quite naturally thinks more fervently of death, immortality, and reunion with departed family as she feels her life slipping away.

Barrett Browning affirms that neither the presence of ghosts nor their absence will affect the fundamental tenets of faith that she has evolved through her life. Her theology, she maintains, comes from her own reading and study of the Bible and theology (particularly the former), from her own meditation and contemplation—together with reasoned judgments about Scripture and theology. God forbid, she says, that she should build her system of theology out of the spirit oracles (*LEBB* 2:104). In 1844, two years prior to her marriage to Browning (and well before the onset of menopause) Elizabeth Barrett reports the progress of Harriet Martineau's supposed cure from cancer by means of her mesmerist trances, adding, "For my own part, I have long been a believer [in magnetism], *in spite of papa*" (*LEBB* 1:197).

Indeed, Martineau's supposedly miraculous cure was the subject of considerable speculation and skepticism. To Harriet Martineau, however, there was no connection between healing mesmerism and the unseen eternal world of angels—Swedenborgian or otherwise. She was mesmerized by her maid as alternative treatment for disease and illness, and she claimed that mesmerism cured the cancer. Martineau believed in neither a personal God nor the eternal soul; to her the only absolute truth was a loose form of Necessarianism (that no action fails to produce effects, and no effect can be lost), a more rational doctrine than either the dogma of free will or predestination. There being no God, and the Christian Messiah being merely Osiris (Christology being the "Worship of Sorrow"), there is also no heaven and no hell. Death is merely passing into nothingness. Anyone attempting to converse with Martineau's own spirit after her death, will get a visit from "but the ghosts of their own thoughts."[4]

According to Katherine H. Porter, both Charles Dickens and Alfred, Lord Tennyson mesmerized patients, the latter his wife, Emily, during childbirth. Less has been made of the gullibility of Dickens and Tennyson than of Martineau and Barrett Browning, probably because the latter were female (and hence, biographers of a more skeptical century believe, more vulnerable to quackery) but, more important, because they chose to make public their involvement with mesmerism.[5] As noted in the case of Martineau, not all mesmerists were spiritualists. Henrietta Barrett, Elizabeth's sister, was repeatedly mesmerized, but was no believer in communicants from the unseen world. A few months after discussing Martineau's strange cure, Barrett Browning revealed her own ambivalence about mesmerism by suggesting that yes, probably the medium shakes the flood gates that the Divine Creator has placed between the "unprepared soul & the unseen world," adding that for herself the idea of submitting one's privacy and will to another person is abhorrent (*BC* 9:266). She was predictably appalled, then, when a Parisian mesmerist asked for a lock of her hair.

Among the Victorians the craze of spiritualism was by no means a phenomenon that captivated only menopausal females. Stanley Weintraub says that after 1852 (with the visit of the first American medium) spirit rappings were recorded all around England, and Julia Markus agrees: "By the spring of 1855, séances and spiritual rappings ran rampant in the well-to-do stately homes in England." Barrett Browning heard that in America there were fifteen thousand mediums and four hundred thousand converts (*LEBB* 2:102). Dante Gabriel Rossetti repeatedly tried to reach the shade of the dead Elizabeth Siddal, his longtime model and finally his wife, in séances conducted principally at the home of fellow artist James Whistler. The Utopian socialist Robert Owen became a spiritualist at the end of his life, and Sarianna Browning, Robert's sister, wrote to Elizabeth about the table rapping in a séance that she attended. The royalty of Europe reportedly consulted the spirits as well: Queen Victoria, for example, was supposed to have attempted communication with the ghost of Prince Albert. In France their majesties received the American

4. Martineau, *Harriet Martineau's Autobiography,* 1:424, 516.
5. Porter, *Through a Glass Darkly: Spiritualism in the Browning Circle,* 15–16, 121–23.

spiritualist D. D. Home at the Tuileries.[6] According to rumor repeated by Barrett Browning, "Louis Napoleon gets oracles from the 'raps,'—and it is said that the Czar does the same . . . & the King of Holland is allowing the subject to absorb him" (*LMRM* 3:393). We cannot be sure where Barrett Browning learned all the tidbits of gossip about the royals and the spiritualists; she subscribed to spiritualist publications and exchanged news and notes with her friends who were among either the converted or the curious: Frederick Tennyson (brother of the poet), American sculptor Hiram Powers, Edward Lytton (who published under the name Owen Meredith), art collector and critic James Jarves, archaeologist Seymour Kirkup, Count Cottrell and his wife, Sylvia (who supposedly held the spirit of her dead infant on her knees for a quarter-hour in a séance), Lady Elgin, the Storys (American friends of the Brownings whose child Joe, Pen's playmate, died in Rome and who apparently attended séances thereafter but never joined the ranks of true believers), and American novelist Harriet Beecher Stowe, who like Barrett Browning wished to communicate with the spirit of a beloved family member, in Stowe's case her son.

In "Mr Sludge, 'the Medium,'" Robert Browning's satire on spiritualism and more particularly on D. D. Home (or *Hume,* as Barrett Browning spells it), he exposes what he believes to be chicanery and fraud of spiritualism, along with the naïveté and foolishness of persons taken in by their own gullibility or desperation. His American medium, Sludge, confesses to his gulled client Hiram H. Horsefall, "Cheat's my name." Sludge has produced the raps under the table, controlled his own hand in supposed automatic writing, and deceived his clients, chiefly, it seems, the ladies. In spite of all, Sludge claims to be doing worthwhile deeds, for after all people do believe in life after death, and spiritualism (as de Beauvoir would say) is not at odds with their religion. Sludge says:

> . . . With my *phenomena*
> I laid the atheist sprawling on his back,
> Propped up Saint Paul, or, at least, Swedenborg!"[7]

---

6. Weintraub, *Four Rossettis: A Victorian Biography,* 148–52 (Weintraub reports that Whistler and William Rossetti too were fascinated by spiritualism, although Christina Rossetti, fearing for her faith, rejected it [113, 148]); Markus, *Dared and Done: The Marriage of Elizabeth Barrett and Robert Browning,* 219; Miller, "Spiritualism: The Victorian Cult," 27; Porter, *Through a Glass Darkly,* 5. (Weintraub reports the séances of Rossetti, Miller the spiritualism of Owen, and Porter on the European royalty.)

7. Browning, *The Poems,* 1:832.430, 838.665–67.

Perhaps one reason that Barrett Browning was so attracted to Swedenborg is his assurances about death and resurrection. Swedenborg confirmed for her the resurrection of the spiritual body, which she maintained that she had believed already and which she interpreted as St. Paul's message about resurrection: that God gives terrestrial bodies and celestial ones, the former abandoned in death for the latter. In *Aurora Leigh,* Romney refers to those who

> . . . fain would enter, when their time shall come,
> With quite another body than Saint Paul
> Has promised—husk and chaff, the whole barleycorn
> Or where's the resurrection?"
>
> (*AL* 8.652–55)

This echoes Paul's discussion on the terrestrial body in 1 Corinthians: "And that which thou sowest, thou sowest not that body that shall be, but bare grain, it may chance of wheat or of some other grain: But God giveth it a body as it hath pleased him, and to every seed his own body" (1 Cor. 15:37–38). Elsewhere Barrett Browning says that the body of flesh is "mere husk" that drops off at death, allowing the spiritual body to emerge immediately, a doctrine she considers consistent with both St. Paul and Swedenborg (*LEBB* 2:177).

For one long preoccupied with death, feeling it her everyday companion, no doubt there was a lurking terror of the unknown and of extinction. The New Testament promise of "many mansions" and "streets paved with gold" could be taken as metaphorical language to describe some kind of ecstatic or blissful existence. But it is vague. Swedenborg's doctrines offer comfort in that death is merely a crossing in which the soul is translated into a different state. Heaven signifies spiritual love, which Barrett Browning had worked her whole life to perfect, while Hell signifies love of self (selfhood), which she had striven her whole life to overcome. The awakening into the spirit world and out of the body is resurrection; when the heart stops beating, the spirit leaves the suffering or decaying physical body to exist in perfect human form. (In Swedenborg's eternity, even God and angels are anthropomorphic.) The resurrected are permitted to engage in every memory, sense, thought, and affection in which they engaged while living. Naturally they are also spared the pain of physical existence, the greatest pain being the loss of beloved ones in death. Souls are permitted conjugal union with deceased husbands or wives if the marriage were of true spiritual love and not merely sensual (which is to Swedenborg merely a form of adultery).[8] For Barrett Browning that meant that in the eternal life she would possess her intellect, and her love of the beautiful, as well as a married state perfected by the inflow of love, truth, and delight emanating from God.

Swedenborg was widely read and appreciated in Barrett Browning's century. His most celebrated influence in poetry had been upon William Blake, an influence duly noted in Blake's theory of correspondences, rejection of Selfhood as Satan, emanations of female from male and sexual cojoining of female with male, and in the prophetic visions that in some ways are similar to those of Swedenborg. Yet among Barrett Browning's contemporaries, persons with personalities and beliefs as diverse as Hiram Powers and Robert Lytton, Emerson and Coleridge, and Fuller and Carlyle were reading and discussing Swedenborg. True, the readers found different reasons for pursuing Swedenborg's tomes: Fuller, for example, because his idea of woman was "sufficiently large and noble" to interpose no obstacle to her progress, Emerson because of the Platonism and the logically based system of correspondences that Swedenborg boldly proclaimed.[9] The Brownings, husband and wife, no doubt discussed him too. Among her contemporaries, however, Barrett Browning's work was more obviously illuminated with Swedenborgian thought than most, and that thought is manifest chiefly in her vision of Apocalypse, her views of death and resurrection.

For Barrett Browning, Death has a luminous side when we know how to look for it. It is not an end, but merely an event, a juncture, in life. Death is but an interruption in life's activities, Barrett Browning says in an 1859 letter to John Ruskin, and for every step she has taken, every pen stroke she has made, there is a connection, a result, in the hereafter (*LEBB* 2:299). St. Paul has taught Barrett Browning about the resurrection of the body, and Swedenborg makes the veil separating life and death more nearly transparent, allowing her to imagine the correspondences beyond the veil.

---

8. Swedenborg, *Heaven and Hell*, 29–38, 474, 345; Swedenborg, *Angelic Wisdom*, 179–202; Swedenborg, *Heaven and Hell*, 400.

9. Fuller, *Woman in the Nineteenth Century*, 122–23. Emerson *dislikes* some aspects of Swedenborg too: that he is humorless and emotionless, with no poetry or transcendence in his soul, and especially because he centers his thought in the Christian religion. Nothing has "the liberality of universal wisdom, but we are always in a church" ("Swedenborg; or, the Mystic," in *Essays and Lectures*, 683).

III

Reclining on her sofa of death at 50 Wimpole Street with the curtains drawn so close that her room was permitted little more light than a tomb, Elizabeth Barrett lived intimately with death. Cessation of life and the embracing of death are recurring motifs in her works. She says, "Death loosens my sinews and creeps in my veins" (*CWEBB* 3:116.161), "Death's forecome shroud is tangled round my feet" (*CWEBB* 3:220.3), and "Fast this Life of mine was dying, / Blind already and calm as death" (*CWEBB* 3:219.1–2). In *Sonnets from the Portuguese*, however, love brings the moribund poet into resurrected life: "Love, as strong as Death, retrieves as well" (*SP* 27.14). If Elizabeth Barrett's lifelong poetic obsession had been her destined face-to-face with her God, then the arrival of Robert Browning abruptly reversed that destiny, or impeded its certain advent. Now her face was averted from the ascent to God, and she found herself—to her amazement—face-to-face with her beloved, who breathed life upon her, and for whose sake she "yield[s] the grave" (*SP* 23.13). Where formerly there was a single soul facing God alone, there are now two souls side by side, "[l]ife to life" (*SP* 24.5), "[f]ace to face" (*SP* 22.2), the wings of their two souls brushing like the tips of angels' wings. Looking to God, she has found Robert Browning; expecting death, she had been overtaken by love; anticipating as her only possible joy the hope of resurrection beyond the grave, she finds herself "safe, and strong, and glad" (*SP* 27.9) in this present life. To love one's beloved face-to-face implies equality, but a closer reading of the sonnets causes one to ask whether the beloved is not her deliverer and deity, as he is king and conqueror. Either romantic love supplants love for God (and therefore is the greater resurrection), or romantic love is a figure for divine love.

Before the advent of the suitor, God has not chosen to grant the speaker life, but rather death. Or at the very least the sonnets emphasize God's role in the persona's immanent death to contrast the beloved's role in her new life. The suitor is God's resurrection angel sounding the trumpet summoning her to life: "New angel mine, unhoped for in the world!" (*SP* 42.14) and the "guardian angel" who has "drawn me back to life & hope again when I had done with both" (*LMRM* 3:191).[10] The speaker says:

10. As she writes to Robert Browning in their courtship, he is also the angel who opened the prison doors in Acts 5:19, and the one who stirred the curative waters of Bethesda in John 5:4 (*BC* 11:147, 177).

> . . . God's own grace
> Could scarcely lift above the world forlorn
> My heavy heart"
>
> (*SP* 25.7–9)

Jerome Mazzaro notes that these lines are an allusion to the stone rolled at the door of Christ's tomb.[11] God's inability or unwillingness to remove her pain is expressed elsewhere in the sonnets, for example, when she says that God has

> . . . laid the curse
> So darkly on my eyelids, as to amerce
> My sight from seeing thee . . .
>
> (*SP* 2.4–6)

God has taken her heart "[a]nd drowned it in life's surge" (*CWEBB* 3:221.26). But her lover is not repelled by "nor sin nor woe, / Nor God's infliction, nor death's neighbourhood" (*SP* 39.9–10); only he has the angel's strength to roll the stone away from the tomb, the faith and love to see behind the mask of suffering and into the lover's soul. What "God's own grace" has not been sufficient to accomplish, his love has done, his "divine sufficiencies" (*SP* 31.12) and "strong divineness" raising her from death into new life. As resurrection angel (in a sonnet series brushed with angel wings), he has "betwixt [the] languid ringlets, blown / A life breath" (*SP* 27.3–4); his is the calming hand to be laid upon her racing heart (*SP* 34.13). (As will be noted in Chapter 5, this God-like/Jove-like laying on of the hand generates artistic and spiritual birth or rebirth in *Aurora Leigh;* it is also the metaphor that Elizabeth Barrett had used to refer to God's calling her back to life after the death of Bro.) The suitor is the earthly angel whom she sees when looking upward to the white throne of God. She says, "I who looked for only God, found *thee!*" (*SP* 27.8) and "exchange / My near sweet view of Heaven, for earth with thee" (*SP* 23.13–14). What is the resurrected lover to do but become, as she says, "acolyte" to such a divine being (*SP* 30.4)?

---

11. Mazzaro, "Mapping Sublimity: Elizabeth Barrett Browning's *Sonnets from the Portuguese,*" 174. Mazzaro suggests that the suitor is Christ-like; actually he is more often the resurrection angel who in *Aurora Leigh* moves (or fails to move) the stone from the tomb (*AL* 6.1274).

The sonnet sequence is permeated with biblical rhetoric (even beyond the Pauline "depth, breadth, and height" in the frequently quoted Sonnet 43.2). Rhetoric that in fact suggests Resurrection and Apocalypse. For example, the poet describes her renovated life as being "caught up into love" (*SP* 7.6), a parallel to the ecstatic "caught up unto God" in John's Revelation (Rev. 12:5) or Jesus' Resurrection "carried up into heaven" (Luke 24:51). Further, she appropriates Jesus' own rhetoric for his divine relationship with God to explain the rapture of her love for the beloved. In Sonnet X, the lover notes:

> . . . And when I say at need
> *I love thee* . . . mark! . . . *I love thee*—in thy sight
> I Stand transfigured, glorified aright,
> With conscience of the new rays that proceed
> Out of thy face toward mine.
>
> (*SP* 10.5–9)

Jesus is "transfigured" when, before the favored disciples, he is pronounced "beloved Son"; in John's Gospel he is to be "glorified" by the Father because, in his incarnated life and works, he has glorified the Father on earth: "And now, O Father, glorify thou me with thine own self with the glory which I had before the world was" (John 17:5). In Sonnet X the beloved is the glorifier; the speaker the glorified. *Her* role parallels that of the Son; *his* looks, like rays from the Father, make her truly alive. This is not merely a passive role (as Christ's is not passive, since he glorifies his Father through his works). It does, however, assign the more God-like power to the beloved who is the greater, possessing the power to glorify, transfigure, resurrect the speaker by the power and fervency of his love.

To appreciate that the salvational role is played by the beloved, it is perhaps instructive to contrast *Sonnets from the Portuguese* with an earlier love lyric, "Catarina to Camoens" (published in the *Poems* of 1844). Like Geraldine in "Lady Geraldine's Courtship" (also in the 1844 volume) both Catarina and the narrator of the sonnets love a poet/prophet (though in the later work he is also prince and king). "Catarina to Camoens" is infused with coldness (that is, the grave, the sun's rays cold) and with the repeated sensation of falling. Catarina is not destined to be "Love-transformed," but will be transformed by death into a spirit watching down from heaven upon Camoens, a muse inspiring his song to other maidens about the "[s]weetest eyes were ever seen" (*CWEBB* 3:125.39–40). In *Sonnets from the Portuguese*, however, the lover's face—opposite

of the sun's cold rays in "Catarina to Camoens"—ignites flames of light
that leap brightly ("[a]nd love is fire" [*SP* 10.5]). The beloved's animating
breath, his kiss, and his love enable the lover to rise instead of fall. Catarina
sinks into death; the speaker in the sonnets "thought to sink," but is
caught up into love (*SP* 7.5–6). Then she is transfigured, of course, but
also transformed from the position of passive muse that Catarina fulfills in
her death. Rather, she arises to become the adoring poet/speaker inspired
by the beloved. Thus the resurrection angel becomes her muse, and she is
the singer/prophet/namer whose role in traditional sonnet sequences the
male lover plays (as Camoens does). The lover's affirmation of life and her
resurrection into love are also the affirmation of the woman as poet, her
right to speak about love and rebirth. In "Confessions," a female lover
pleads guilty to loving too much, and *Sonnets from the Portuguese* is a
confession as well. Yet in the speaker's address to her beloved, she is now
safe, strong, and sure, the power of love's resurrection having empowered
her to take the lead in affirming to her beloved their joined lives:

> When our two souls stand up erect and strong,
> Face to face, silent, drawing nigh and nigher,
> Until the lengthening wings break into fire
> At either curvèd point,—what bitter wrong
> Can earth do to us, that we should not long
> Be here contented?
>
> (*SP* 22.1–6)

Thus the poet is resurrected for life, for love, and for art. While the
speaker adores the beloved as the resurrection angel, God is the source
of resurrection, inasmuch as the deity commissions angels to act on his
behalf. Avoiding blasphemy, the lover recognizes God as giver of death
and resurrection, of spiritual riches and poverty: "God only, who made
us rich, can make us poor" (*SP* 24.14). The overwhelming impact of the
sonnets, nevertheless, is that the earthly lover—not the heavenly father—
has resurrected the female poet by his animating love.

IV

"How scant the gardens if the graves were fewer!" (*CGW* 1.422) Thus
the English poet consoles the Italian nation for the loss of her sons and
her hopes. As noted in Chapter 3, the nation of Italy in *Casa Guidi*

Windows lies as a corpse, and her weak and faithless leaders in church and state are corruption and decay; they rot in sepulchres. Throughout the poem, however, the poet plants the seeds of resurrection's hope in her rhetoric, seeds that she does not harvest until the 1860 *Poems before Congress,* when hope for Italy is again alive in her heart. In fact, with the exception of Rome and Venetia, all Italy was by 1861 united, and the independent nation-state began to achieve recognition from the major European governments. Italy, says Flavia Alaya, enters its "new national being as mother and child at once, delivered out of her [Italy's] own flesh and baptized in her own blood." Thus, a new state is born or, more specifically, a slain and dismembered nation is reconstituted and resurrected into new life. Especially in the neglected poem "Italy and the World," which Hayter calls a "resonant blast to open the graves and prisons of Italy," the eschatology of resurrection is applied in the realm of human politics.[12] Thus in Barrett Browning's resurrection paradigm, dead Italy is both resurrected and reborn, Napoleon is the archangel blowing the trumpet that signals the Last Judgment, and by logical extension, God is a participant in animating the dead corpus with political new life (indirectly, as God is in resurrecting the lover in *Sonnets from the Portuguese*). Therefore, to assist in restoration of dying Italy is to do God's work; to turn an indifferent back on her is—Barrett Browning suggests— to ignore Jesus' admonitions to serve widows and orphans, victims and the oppressed.

Honoring Italy's fallen sons as seeds from which new life will spring, Barrett Browning says in *Casa Guidi Windows:*

> . . . In the name of Italy,
> Meanwhile, her patriot Dead have benison.
>   They only have done well; and, what they did
> Being perfect, it shall triumph. Let them slumber
> . . . .
> These Dead be seeds of life, and shall encumber
>   The sad heart of the land until it loose
> The clammy clods and let out the Spring-growth
>   In beatific green through every bruise.
> (CGW 2.656–66)

12. Alaya, "The Ring, the Rescue, and the *Risorgimento:* Reunifying the Brownings' Italy," 16; Hayter, *Mrs. Browning,* 130.

Part 1 of *Casa Guidi Windows* honors the dead heroes and patriots of Italy's past, including those recently fallen in freedom's struggle, and acknowledges that those alive—including the poet/soothsayer—will soon die too; part 2 prophesies springtime, with life throbbing in Piedmont, and new springs of life "gushing everywhere" (*CGW* 2.762). The poet herself is an augur, studying the flights of doves to cast a particular prophecy for Italy's liberation and unification, and presumably for peace. Not that the second part ends with the same lively spirit of the first; indeed, now the seer's augury is chastened and quiet. Barrett Browning closes part 2, however, with the image of a newborn son, her own, to adumbrate the hopeful future as surely as all those graves of the heroic dead celebrate a noble past.

In an apocalyptic image in a letter to her sister, Barrett Browning reports that the people have a fervent love for Napoleon, and "Italy stretches her arms to him as to the very angel of the resurrection" (*LHS* 314). In "Napoleon III" the resurrection theme operates in several ways: the second Napoleon accepts the regalia from the "open grave" of the first Napoleon, signifying the rebirth of a dynasty; mother Italy awakens and arises at the shout of *her* sons (paralleling the hope represented by the poet's own son in *Casa Guidi Windows* and the third Napoleon as "son" of the first).

In "Napoleon III" Barrett Browning also proclaims in a more direct way than in *Casa Guidi Windows* the link of every living man with his dead predecessor and counterpart, an invisible link of soul with soul, hands clasped across the chasm of death and each living soul quickened into life by his companion spirit from the other side. Thus the seeds of new life arise from the corpses of the dead; thus also the Swedenborgian notion of correspondence between sensual and spiritual is applied in the patriotic cause that the poet espouses.

> Every live man there
> Allied to a dead man below,
> And the deadest with blood to spare
> To quicken a living hand . . .
> (*N* 193–96)

On an obvious level the living men take hope from their predecessors who had been tortured and flogged, taxed and bayonetted, starved and exiled, but the poet expresses a more mystical and more intimate bond as though the spirits of dead patriots animated the living troops as the host of angels animate the dead mariners in Coleridge's rhyme. Thus her Swedenborgian theology—specifically the theory of correspondence between the natural and celestial worlds—animates her vision of national politics.

As noted in Chapter 3, Barrett Browning believes the prophesied Apocalypse of Revelation to be the end of an era—not the end of earth's existence. In this interpretation Judgment Day is every day upon us. And in fact in "Italy and the World" the poet cries in her "poet-passion" (*IW* 96) that the Day of Judgment (and justice) has at last come. The graves are opened, the trumpet sounds, calling

> Beautiful Italy, calm, unhurried,
>   Rise heroic and renovated,
>   Rise to the final restitution.
>   (*IW* 33–35)

"Italy and the World" indicts England with her heptarchy patriotism, outdated and wrongheaded as Indian suttee and heathen suicide. England has failed to hear the resurrection trumpet calling her to action. Or rather, she is deaf to the cockcrow of France announcing this Resurrection New Day; she has sheathed her sword, let her weapons rust, and in insular passivity has failed to assist Italy's resurrection. According to Barrett Browning, the English (as well as others) have turned aside with the aphorism that the hour and day of resurrection passes human foreknowledge; therefore it is best for nations to let well enough alone, rather than risking short-term war and bloodshed to usher in a new world of long-term peace, justice, and harmony. Europe has callously accepted that "Churchyard thistles are wholesome food" (*IW* 14) for asses to graze upon; therefore, Europe will wait for God's own good time, and the poet implies that in so doing Europe has failed to do God's work.

The poet/prophet cites Jesus' statement that in his regenerated coming kingdom, "[m]any *that are* first shall be last; and the last *shall be* first" (Matt. 19:30); she paraphrases Jesus' words in apocalyptic eschatology, suggesting that in the resurrected new-world order the last—formerly the first—might well be the British. "Italy and the World," in fact, prophesies a coming order in which all nations and peoples shall be like rags and remnants stitched into Christ's "broad garment" (*IW* 43). (Here Barrett Browning conveniently ignores Christ's metaphor that old cloth patched into a new garment makes the rent worse; rather, in her vision, the colors and patterns—even "national selfishness" and "civic vaunting" [*IW* 45]—can be pieced together into one unified whole.) She also reinterprets St. Paul's prophecy that there shall be "neither Jew nor Greek," usually interpreted to mean that the Christian faith is destined to cross all national, racial, and ethnic boundaries (Gal. 3:28). To Elizabeth Barrett Browning "no more Jew nor Greek" means "no more England nor France" (*IW* 46–47), the resurrected political order being

> But one confederate brotherhood planting
> One flag only, to mark the advance,
> Onward and upward, of all humanity."
> (*IW* 48–50)

It is, ultimately, not war and strife but Love that will effect lasting political resurrection: "And to love best shall still be, to reign unsurpassed" (*IW* 140).

V

As Christian poet, Elizabeth Barrett Browning explores in *Aurora Leigh* the doctrine of resurrection, especially its prefiguration as new life on earth—to "raise men's bodies still by raising souls" (*AL* 9.853). As female poet, she also exposes the sexual victimization of woman, specifically prostitution and rape. To Marian Erle, the central victim, rape is considered a "death," and Marian, though worthy of salvation, never experiences the resurrection available to all other worthy characters depicted as once dead. Aurora, the questing woman poet, is twice "dead" and twice resurrected—first to art and then to love. Her cousin and counterpart, the Christian socialist Romney Leigh, is—like Aurora's father—a Lazarus figure. He is reborn through love to become Aurora's worthy mate in art and life. But "[s]weet holy Marian" (*AL* 6.782), though mirror of the Virgin Mary, ironically remains dead, her condition raising important questions about the spiritual devastation of rape and the efficacy of resurrection doctrine. In her blatant attention to a taboo topic and her unorthodox application of Christian doctrine, Barrett Browning illustrates the death from which there is no resurrection—not even in God. For those wishing to find comfort in traditional eschatology, this lapse in Christian exegesis is problematic.

While Aurora is merely an orphan, Marian is "worse than orphaned" (*AL* 3.945); she has two parents who abuse her. When her mother attempts to sell her to the squire, Marian runs away, is injured and taken up unconscious by a passer-by who thinks her literally dead (as she thinks herself "dead and safe" [*AL* 3.1087]) and deposits her in a clean, white hospital, "strange as death" Marian thinks when she awakens in a white strait bed, "with others strait and white, / Like graves dug side by side at measured lengths" (*AL* 3.1107–8). Her summons to resurrection from sickness and despair comes from the lips of Romney Leigh, who calls her out of her world, giving her meaningful work and the invitation to be his bride. Romney is here a Christ figure saving her from the first death.

Marian's second death is sexual murder. Leaving him a note that he would "find me sooner in my grave" (*AL* 4.964) than in this life, she abandons Romney at the altar because the Lamia-woman Lady Waldemar, wanting Romney herself, has convinced naive Marian that such as she would never do for the aristocratic gentleman. Delivered into treacherous hands, Marian is raped, "murdered" she says, and becomes an "embodied ghost" (*AL* 5.1100). Catching a glimpse of this ghostly Marian in a Parisian flower market, Aurora imagines a "dead face" as of one who has drowned. In lodgings "[s]carce larger than a grave" (*AL* 6.552) she discovers Marian and her illegitimate infant and takes them into her protection. Later Romney offers to marry Marian and love her child, but she will not permit the husk of her social self to be resurrected into salvation as a wife.

> I told your cousin, sir, that I was dead;
> And now, she thinks I'll get up from my grave,
> And wear my chin-cloth for a wedding-veil,
> And glide along the churchyard like a bride
> While all the dead keep whispering through the withes,
> "You would be better in your place with us,
> "You pitiful *corruption!*"[13]
>
> (*AL* 9.391–97; italics mine)

In Barrett Browning's view, the world itself is corrupt, a huge corpse, or occasionally a vast cemetery. Lucifer in *A Drama of Exile* has "sow[n]

---

13. More than twenty expressions of Marian's (e.g. *grave, dead, murdered, drowned,* and so on) confirm that she is "dead."

it thick enough with graves" greener than the knowledge tree (*DE* 70). In *Aurora Leigh* the protagonist says that our very dreams often "grind us flat, / The heaviest gravestone on this burying earth" (*AL* 7.502–3). Her cousin Romney's rhetoric abounds with images of wounds, gashes, dismemberment, bleeding, and death; city streets are "graves," and squalor is the earthworm feeding on denizens of slums. To the messianic Romney, the world is "one great famishing carnivorous mouth" (*AL* 8.396), the opening, yawning chasm suggesting not only overwhelming human want, but also hell and the grave. Aurora says we are "sepulchred alive in this close world" (*AL* 5.1040). And describing society's dregs she remarks:

> . . . You'd suppose
> A finished generation, dead of plague,
> Swept outward from their graves into the sun,
> The moil of death upon them . . .
> . . . .
> They clogged the streets, they oozed into the church
> In a dark slow stream, like blood.
>
> (*AL* 4.547–54)

The poet knows the world in entirety will never be resurrected until the Apocalypse; we cannot regain Eden, for social evils "[s]trike deep in Evil's own existence here" (*AL* 8.764). God permits evil because, to eradicate it, God must eradicate free will (*AL* 8.766); therefore God limits God's power in order to empower humans unto Godly work. The Christ who liberates the "stiff and dry . . . mere dumb corpse of Earth" (shut in the coffin by Adam, Aurora says [*AL* 5.105–6]) also ennobles work; Romney says, "After Adam, work was curse . . . after Christ, work turns to privilege" (*AL* 8.717–19).

Individual souls, however, are resurrected: reborn through God's love to do God's work. First Aurora, whose name suggests resurrection. Orphaned and living with her cold English aunt, she weakens and sickens, overhearing visitors predict that surely she will die. Reading the living words of dead poets, though, she discovers that poets are God's only truth-tellers, prophets who instruct humankind "[f]rom just a shadow on a charnel-wall" (*AL* 1.865) to say "This is soul, / This is life" (*AL* 1.874–75). Thus, like a princess in a fairy tale, she awakens, realizing:

> I did not die. But slowly, as one in swoon,
> To whom life creeps back in the form of death,

. . . .
I woke, rose up . . . where was I? in the world;
For uses therefore I must count worth while"
(AL 1.559–66)

Aurora says this first rebirth is Life itself, though one may be fooled into thinking it is resurrection by Art or by Nature. Rather, one so resurrected by the dynamic life seeds planted within by God may well attribute the resurrection to art or nature, but these are rather God's handiwork. Aurora's own first resurrection takes the form of rebirth into art and poetry, taking her part "[w]ith God's Dead, who afford to walk in white / Yet spread His glory . . ." (*AL* 2.102–3). Declaring her calling, the aspiring poet twines around her brow a laureate's wreath of ivy, the kind that grows on graves, signifying her poetic commitment to her dead poetic precursors and her dead muses (especially her "stone-dead" father). Romney, having no faith in her woman's art, accuses her of playing beside deathbeds, or—perhaps worse—singing happy pastorals of green meads and trees (*AL* 2.1201) while all around is death. But Aurora believes that were she to marry Romney, that would be her artistic death, for he would sacrifice her to his cause, cutting her body into coins for his paupers. As she creates poetry, she feels—like the summer foliage flaming out in green—her heart's life throbbing in her living verse.[14]

But art and fame are not perpetually life sustaining, and Aurora again experiences a kind of death. Symptoms are dissatisfaction with her work, loneliness (because Death has "unfellow[ed]" her of loved ones [*AL* 5.552]), jealousy, restlessness, irritability, and pique. To regain spiritual health Aurora rushes back to Italy, place of her birth and of her parents' graves. But en route she meets Marian in Paris, saves the outcast and her illegitimate infant, and makes a home for them in Italy. In Italy she is herself almost a Dido, though she does not yet know it is love or Romney (or indeed, resurrection) that she seeks. She says:

And many a Tuscan eve I wandered down
The cypress alley like a restless ghost

---

14. Marjorie Stone notes that such a "physical and poetic rebirth" occurred in 1842–1843 for Barrett as well, as evidenced by her optimism about her health and her desire to furnish herself a "leaf-green" room (*BC* 7:113) like the one she was later to furnish Aurora in *AL* 1.568 (*Elizabeth Barrett Browning*, 23).

> That tries its feeble ineffectual breath
> Upon its own charred funeral-brands put out
> Too soon, where black and stiff stood up the trees
> Against the broad vermilion of the skies.
>   (*AL* 7.1160–65)

Aurora's road to rebirth is her own act of charity to Marian and her child; resurrection comes, however, in loving Romney, accepting that she has loved him always. As she says when they are finally united, "Art is much, but Love is more / . . . Art symbolizes heaven, but Love is God" (*AL* 9.656–58).

As for Romney Leigh, he is austere, shy, reserved, and serious, living by diagrams and social theories. But his "mad" socialist schemes to save humankind fail, his home is burned to the ground by those whom he has tried to save, he is blinded and injured, and his health is ruined. When he finds Aurora and Marian in Italy, Romney's great plans are now dead, and so is he. He has had no more feeling or sight than a man "ten feet under" in the grave (*AL* 9.572). His mistake has been in doing charity by the work of his own hands, rather than through inspiration by God. In Swedenborgian terms, his charity has been *proprium* (ownhood, or selfhood). But Romney is made alive once more by the power of love—God's and Aurora's. With Aurora as his partner, Romney becomes also a poet/artist; his voice rising "as some chief musician's song / Amid the old Jewish temple's Selah-pause" (*AL* 9.844–45). In his previous life Romney could see only the worms under his boot; in his resurrected life he envisions Apocalypse, that "new, near Day / Which should be builded out of heaven to God" (*AL* 9.956–57). Now both the man and the woman can create eternal art, and she can work beside not beneath him, with "all true workers and true lovers born" (*AL* 9.928).

Other resurrections are those of Aurora's father and Romney's friend, the painter Vincent Carrington. The elder Leigh, an "austere English-man," had the proclivity to be as niggardly and narrow as his caged-bird sister, but having spent a "dry lifetime" in England, he went to Italy, fell in love upon sight with a beautiful Italian girl (Aurora's mother) whom he saw in a religious procession, and "received his sacramental gift / With eucharistic meanings; for he loved" (*AL* 1.90–91). Loving, he threw off "old conventions, broken loose / From chin-bands of the soul, like Lazarus" (*AL* 1.177–78), living so long as his bride lived, but existing in somnambulism once she has died. Kind, gentle Carrington, when he makes his muse his wife, conquers a "mad" obsession, changes his artistic style (from classical topics to contemporary ones as Barrett Browning has done in *Aurora Leigh*), and allows Kate Ward's "whole sweet face" to look upon his artist's soul and beget itself in living art (*AL* 7.592–94). Aurora recognizes that in loving he has ascended "from sorrow to his heaven of love" (*AL* 7.972).

Those denied resurrection remain dead because of either perverted love or the inability to love. The icy aunt, to whom Aurora comes after her parents' literal death, is a "soured" Anglican who resented her brother's marriage, despised his Italian bride, and now rigidly eradicates all vivacity in her orphan niece. Her God is not love, but propriety and duty. Aurora's judgment is that she lives "[a] harmless life, she called a virtuous life, / A quiet life, which was not life at all . . ." (*AL* 1.288–89). Lady Waldemar is "an atheist" because a sensualist (incapable of loving the soul of Romney and therefore unworthy of God). Longing for Romney to love her in return, she becomes a spiritual suicide, a ghost "sighing like Dido's" for Aeneas (*AL* 3.473). And like Dives, the rich man in Jesus' parable, she is separated from the blessed by a great gulf, and, deprived of heaven (God's love and Romney's), she curses Aurora (*AL* 9.169–72).

Only the case of Marian Erle troubles our sense of how things ought to be in terms of Barrett Browning's implicit resurrection doctrine, and Marian's insistence upon her unresurrected state seems to deny closure in a work where all other loose ends are neatly tied. Nineteenth-century readers loved Marian; one wrote: "In Marian's peerless mother-heart / The perfect woman stands recorded." Most recent criticism, however, uses Marian's story to uncover Aurora's soul and psyche. Helen Cooper says that Marian is the agent of Aurora's transformation into subjectivity. Virginia Steinmetz and Dolores Rosenblum agree that the Marian plot has to do with Aurora's ambivalence on motherhood—and thereby womanhood and sexuality. Steinmetz sees Marian as Madonna-muse, saying that possession of Marian is management of mother-want for the motherless Aurora, a necessary process for Aurora to acknowledge her own sexuality. Rosenblum argues that the dead face of Marian allows Aurora to enact a symbolic resurrection of both mother and mothered child in herself, that Marian's story is the myth of her own origins. Further, she reads the Marian Erle plot on two levels: as narrative character with a social destiny and mythic character with a cosmic destiny. While Marian has died a cultural death, Rosenblum notes, she is restored to life by her sacred child, a "mythic, miraculous" rebirth, a little world opening out into infinity.[15]

Amanda Anderson and Angela Leighton are more interested in the issue of sister-muse than mother-muse. Anderson interprets the Marian Erle plot as Barrett Browning's conscious absorbing of the rhetoric of fallenness in Victorian literature and culture. To Anderson, Aurora generates a "dialectical interplay between aesthetic and intersubjective experience" through reconceptualizing the relation between herself as woman artist and Marian as fallen woman. She argues that Barrett Browning both authenticates Marian's voice for telling her own story (Marian's having earned the right through suffering) and empowers her sister, Aurora, to redress the reifying distortions of contemporary depictions of fallen woman (Aurora's having earned the right through her care of Marian, her informed rereading of the text of Marian's life). Leighton notes that Aurora's obsession about the deadness of Marian is Barrett Browning's quest for a female poetics, saying that Marian alone answers Aurora's desperate call and returns from the dead to make her desert place bearable.[16] But the fixation on her death is Marian's more emphatically than Aurora's, although Aurora certainly accepts Marian's trope in her own rhetoric, such as, for example, when she charges Lady Waldemar with setting Marian's love "to digging its own grave / Within her green hope's pretty garden-ground" (*AL* 7.312–13). Furthermore, the dead is never made alive again—sisterly love notwithstanding. To Marian, Marian remains dead, in spite of Aurora's and Romney's later insistence upon her resurrected state. Her "Marian's dead" and "I'm dead, I say" and "I was murdered" and her insistence that she is now corpse, ghost, and carrion contrast the "Live, Aurora" and "I lived" of the protagonist.

In explanation of Marian's decision to remain celibate, Gardner Taplin notes, "A girl in a Victorian novel who gives birth to a baby without sanction of Church or civil authority is not permitted to marry and

15. H. Buxton Forman, in *The Poets' Enchiridion: A Hitherto Unpublished Poem,* by Barrett Browning, 53; Cooper, *Woman and Artist,* 178; Steinmetz, "Images of 'Mother-Want' in Elizabeth Barrett Browning's *Aurora Leigh,*" 360; Rosenblum, "Face to Face," 333; Rosenblum, *"Casa Guidi Windows* and *Aurora Leigh:* The Genesis of Elizabeth Barrett Browning's Visionary Aesthetic," 66.

16. Anderson, *Tainted Souls and Painted Faces: The Rhetoric of Fallenness in Victorian Culture,* 177, 190; Leighton, *Elizabeth Barrett Browning,* 153–56.

enjoy the pleasures of a home with husband and children." Granted, such is tradition, and granted too that Barrett Browning goes only so far in flouting Victorian tastes and morality. But to say as much leaves still too much unsaid and does nothing to answer the problem presented by Marian's perpetual deadness as contrasted to Aurora and Romney's newly resurrected life together. Barrett Browning could just as easily have described Marian's state as soul transcendent beyond the needs of human conjugal love. She could easily have written some "Behold, I am alive again" dialogue for Marian to counter all the death, dying, and burial metaphors that Marian utters. Cora Kaplan believes that rather than telling us about subjectivity and the self, rather than sticking to the novelistic formula of further punishing the victim, Barrett Browning is revealing her class bias. Kaplan considers the poet an elitist who, in relegating the "fallen" Marian to a nunlike existence of celibacy, chastity, and good works, denies her the passionate consummation within marriage that Barrett Browning reserves for the well born. Marian "must be denied the self-generated sexuality which is permitted to upper-class women in *Aurora Leigh* but which taints all working-class women except Marian."[17]

Not about sisterhood, motherhood, or class, the *rape* of Marian Erle is about rape. In her commentary upon rape, death, and resurrection, Barrett Browning consciously writes within and against a literary motif of sexual betrayal and death dating from Samuel Richardson's *Clarissa,* which is to Barrett Browning "a book apart, a poem apart—a beatitude in a fiend's mouth!" (*BC* 5:254). Victim of the consummate rake (and rapist) Lovelace, who hates the sex in general and Clarissa's innocence in particular, Clarissa wills her own death. In dying, she drives the nails into Lovelace's coffin, undermining his creed of egomania and sexual conquest. The degrees of her descent into death mark her ascent above and beyond her seducer. In "thankful rapture" she attains "an heavenly crown . . . such assurances of it as I have, thro' the all-satisfying merits of my blessed Redeemer."[18]

In *The Scarlet Letter,* Nathaniel Hawthorne delineates the resurrection of the seducer, not the seduced (if indeed we can assume that the reverend divine Dimmesdale undertook the seduction). The fallen woman Hester

17. Taplin, *"Aurora Leigh:* A Rehearing," 22; Kaplan, introduction to *"Aurora Leigh" and Other Poems,* by Barrett Browning, 25.
18. Richardson, *Clarissa or, The History of a Young Lady,* 8:4.

Prynne wears her scarlet *A* like a badge; she lives serenely, her indomitable demeanor marked by "moral quietude." Both she and Dimmesdale believe that the child, Pearl (Hester's pearl of great price), was born into the world to "keep [her] here in life." "Heaven . . . had frowned upon her, and she had not died," but Arthur is "d[ying] daily a living death." Recognizing his life is "all falsehood!—all emptiness!—all death!" he resolves to claim Hester and Pearl and quit his life of hypocrisy, and he then describes *his* resurrection: "to have risen up all made anew, and with new powers to glorify Him that hath been merciful!"[19]

Like Clarissa Harlowe, Ruth Hilton (in Elizabeth Gaskell's *Ruth*) experiences a premonition of eternal resurrection at the moment of physical death. A moral innocent, Ruth is initially happy with her seducer, but when Bellingham abandons her as a ruined maid, she contemplates suicide, followed by resurrection: "Surely life was a horrible dream, and God would mercifully awaken her from it." But she is as innocent of the doctrine of God and mortal sin as of the knowledge of sex and society's strictures. Ruth is essentially a child, and Gaskell does not speak in terms of her sin and salvation, or her spiritual death and resurrection; rather, Ruth suffers in order to learn "that it is more blessed to love than to be beloved."[20] Barrett Browning approved of *Ruth* (published only three years before *Aurora Leigh*), believing that her case illustrated a "moral frightfully wanted in English society" (*LEBB* 2:141). In 1853 Gaskell wrote Barrett Browning a personal letter, and Barrett Browning commented in a letter to Mrs. Ogilvy that *Ruth* has "considerable power & beauty, & deals in a bold true Christian spirit with a detestable state of Christian society. I would rather have written that book than two 'uncle Toms' inclusive of the flourish of trumpets" (*LMO* 107). Like ruined Hester and ruined Marian, the seduced Ruth afterward lives an exemplary (that is, celibate) life, devoting herself to rearing a fatherless child and doing charitable works, as humbly inured to Eccleston's ostracism as Hester is immune to Boston's. Is this, then, the moral frightfully wanted in English society?

Aware of the novelistic tradition, the poet modifies it, knowing readers will note the modifications. Hester steadfastly refuses to abandon life, Ruth is naive about spiritual life and death, and Clarissa is gradually

19. Hawthorne, *The Scarlet Letter,* in *The Works of Nathaniel Hawthorne,* 1:226, 113, 194, 171, 192, 202.
20. Gaskell, *Ruth,* 94, 248.

resurrected or translated into eternity. Among these parallel cases, only Marian insists that she is dead *in life* and will remain so.[21]

Elizabeth Hardwick in *Seduction and Betrayal* sees seduction as psychological rather than moral drama. Women like Clarissa and Hester— and in later works Hardy's Tess and Tolstoy's Maslova—are "given the overwhelming beauty of endurance, the capacity for high or lowly suffering, for violent feeling absorbed, finally tranquilized, for the radiance of humility, for silence, secrecy, impressive acceptance."[22] They turn their heroism into an accusation of the rapist/seducer. Marian's courage, endurance, and suffering rank with that of her predecessors and successors, but since neither we nor she knows the identity of the assailant, we cannot see her integrity undermining his egoism, nihilism, or sensualism, as the case may be. Therefore, we are thrown back upon the issue of the act and the victim, not the victimizer: "man's violence . . . made me what I am" (*AL* 6.1226–27), Marian says, but Barrett Browning is not interested in the name or face of the man who has done it.

Marian's case focuses upon the violence of the act (which she recalls as drowning, choking in hell-foam, going deep into the pit from where her cries cannot be heard even by God) and upon its horrendous aftermath:

> To go down with one's soul into the grave,
> To go down half-dead, half-alive, I say,
> And wake up with corruption . . .
> (AL 6.1199–1201)

Marian recognizes the several ways in which the rape victim is dead: in self-esteem, as merchandise in the marriage market, as sexually responsive woman. She says the best miracle God could perform is to resurrect the maternal instinct within her, that otherwise the stone upon her sepulchre is too heavy and angels "too weak" to roll it away (*AL* 6.1274), as the resurrection angel/lover had done for the dying speaker in *Sonnets from the Portuguese.*[23]

---

21. In George Eliot's *Adam Bede,* however, the ruined maid Hetty Sorrel does remain dead, the ministrations of the "angel" Dinah Morris notwithstanding. Hetty's gallows confession to infanticide "saves" her physical life; nevertheless, she is unfit for marriage, so Eliot writes her out of the plot by means of transportation and death.

22. Hardwick, *Seduction and Betrayal: Women and Literature,* 180, 185.

23. Isobel Armstrong comments that Marian has attributes not only of Mary but also of Christ: "The suffering female Christ awakes to a vision of physical and moral

The death, defilement, and decay expressed by Barrett Browning in the words of Marian Erle reveal subtle theological implications, as well as not-so-subtle misogyny. That is, in both theology and tradition, woman has been associated with filth and death, and the slain and "corrupted" Marian conveys this message, perhaps more than even her creator realizes. A look at the theological tradition, together with contemporary feminist thought, sheds light on the subtext about woman and death.

Andrea Dworkin in *Intercourse* says that sexual violation is for the male an entry into death, defilement, and corruption, the vagina filthy and the womb a grave: "Men use the penis to deliver death to women who are, literally, in their genitals, dirt to the men." This is certainly what happens to Robert Browning's Pompilia of *The Ring and the Book,* who is raped by her spiteful and wicked husband, Guido, who has "imperiled" his own soul by "polluting" hers, then sealed his eternal death by stabbing her to death (the only kind of violation that can, by the way, make Pompilia alive again—and that only in the sense of her resurrected soul).[24] When the dead voices from their graves refer to Marian as "you pitiful corruption!" (*AL* 9.397) or when Marian describes herself "cheek to cheek" with stinking corruption (*AL* 6.1197), we recall St. Paul's teaching that we are "sown in corruption . . . raised in incorruption" (1 Cor. 15:42).[25] The state of "corruption" suggests the sensual body, the sexual act, the womb, the grave; it is the same Greek term that the same writer uses in reference to the corruption that Eve brought into the world. To "put on incorruption," says the writer of the letter to Corinth, is to come forth from the bondage of Eve (who was beguiled ["corrupted"] by Satan [2 Cor. 11:3]), to "swallow up" Death in victory, to transmute body into spirit (1 Cor. 15:54).

Marina Warner points out that in the myth of the Fall, sex and death (concupiscence and putrefaction) are seen as twin evils caused by

corruption, an untransformed world . . ." (*Victorian Poetry: Poetry, Poetics and Politics,* 369). I differ with Armstrong in that I see Marian as reflecting death more than life: if Christ, without Resurrection; if Virgin, without Assumption.

24. Dworkin, *Intercourse,* 188–89; Browning, *The Ring and the Book,* 7.786.

25. The Greek term is, in modern biblical translation, "to perish," but Paul would have considered the dead as corrupt, following the Mosaic edict, "He that toucheth the dead body of any man shall be unclean seven days" (Num. 19:11). The word *corruption* that Barrett Browning found in her King James Bible carries the sense of repugnance more closely than the revised *perishable.*

the woman Eve; therefore the daughters of Eve bear in their physical persons and bodily fluids the reminder of filth, decay, and corruption. For example, St. John Chrysostom (whom Barrett Browning knew intimately) warns that all women are corruption: "For the groundwork of this corporeal beauty is nothing else but phlegm, and blood, and humor, and bile, and the fluid of masticated food . . . if you consider what is stored up behind those beautiful eyes . . . you will affirm that the well-shaped body is nothing else than a whited sepulchre; the parts within are full of so much uncleanness." In reading Chrysostom's homilies on Corinthians, which she reports having done (*BC* 2:232, 290), the young Barrett would have encountered a similar description of the beautiful woman, together with the injunction to think of "it" as filth, as diseased and old. Even the meditations of Jeremy Taylor, which the young Elizabeth Barrett studied from childhood, taught her that the womb is defiled: "Remember what thou wert before thou wert begotten. Nothing. What wert thou in the first regions of thy dwelling, before thy birth? Uncleanness. What wert thou for many years after? Weakness. What in all thy life? A great sinner." Rosemary Ruether corroborates that in clerical misogyny of medieval times and beyond, woman's very body is described with violent disgust, for example as a tombstone that reveals a rotting corpse. She says that *Mundus,* or world (or nature), formerly described as a haughty male demonic figure, had by the thirteenth century been replaced with a female figure, *Frau Welt,* or dame nature, who from the front is alluring but from the rear is covered with foul, reptilian creatures of hell and the grave,[26] the very image that literary audiences would recall as Errour and Duessa in Edmund Spenser's *The Faerie Queene.*

Interestingly, Barrett Browning elsewhere twice uses corruption as analogue for woman, once in "The Virgin Mary to the Child Jesus" in the 1838 *Poems* and again in "Where's Agnes?" in *Last Poems.* In the early poem, the Virgin does not dwell on her *personal* corruption; she only mentions corruption as the trait of mortality that she shares with all sinners. As a Protestant, Barrett does not extol Mary as holy Mother of God, but only feeble and flawed like the rest of humanity, although "blessedest"; her Mary renounces any claim to extraordinary holiness

---

26. Warner, *Alone of All Her Sex: The Myth and the Cult of the Virgin Mary,* 78; Chrysostom, "To the Fallen Theodore," in *Select Library,* ed. Schaff, 9:103–4; Chrysostom, Homily 7 on 2 Cor. in ibid., 12:316; Taylor, *Rule and Exercises,* 1:114; Ruether, *Sexism and God-Talk,* 81.

("not holiest, not noblest" [*CWEBB* 2:75.89]). In Barrett's "Virgin Mary" the speaker is merely a creature born to death in the body and immortality of the spirit—just as we all are. Amazed that she, an ordinary girl, has been chosen, she says, "So, seeing my corruption, can I see / This Incorruptible now born of me . . ." (*CWEBB* 2:76.106–7). Mary is neither traumatized by nor preoccupied with *personal* (or gender) corruption as her namesake Marian is. Certainly she does not repeatedly assert that she is dead, nor does she request, as Marian does, "but dig a hole / And bury her in silence" (*AL* 6.895–96).

In Barrett Browning's late poem "Where's Agnes?" though, the fallen Agnes is, more like Marian, both dead and corrupted, although it is the narrator—not Agnes—who struggles to accept the result of Agnes's shameful sexual fall, incredulous that one so angelic that she "scarcely trod the earth" has "[t]urned mere dirt" (*CWEBB* 6:37.86–87). The persona first questions:

> But dead that other way,
> Corrupted thus and lost?
> That sort of worm in the clay?
>   (*CWEBB* 6:35.16–18)

She then accepts the responsibility for Agnes's death and decay, concluding:

>   . . . No, not she:
> Rather I! or whence this damp
> Cold corruption's misery?"
>   (*CWEBB* 6:38.101–3)

In the case of Agnes, as in that of Marian, "corruption" carries the connotations of sex, defilement, and death.[27]

The case of Marian is quite different from either the Virgin or Agnes, although like the Virgin Mary she is spiritually unsoiled and like Agnes she will bear the world's contempt. Barrett Browning apologized to Sarianna

---

27. The sexual fall of "Agnes" represents the deceit of Sophia Eckley, who deceived Barrett Browning about her communication with the spirit world. Barrett Browning's letters reveal that, like the persona, she blames herself for what has occurred. Robert Browning called the work "Where's Sophie?" (Markus, *Dared and Done,* 294–96).

Browning for Marian's suffering in the poem, explaining that Marian had to be dragged through the uttermost debasement of circumstances to arrive at the sentiment of personal dignity (*LEBB* 2:242). Marian expresses this dignity and independence in affirming that

> . . . a woman, poor or rich,
> Despised or honoured, is a human soul,
> And what the soul is, that she is herself . . .
>
> (*AL* 9.328–30)

The enlightened Marian thus knows herself to be capable of rearing her child without taking in marriage the hand of a man whom she does not (and cannot) love. More important, she understands that she is "clean and sweet from devil's dirt" (*AL* 9.345), that in the eyes of God and angels (as in the eyes of Romney and Aurora) there is no guilt on her own soul. This epiphany is not without its satisfaction; the problem is that the resurrection motif everywhere apparent in the work excludes Marian, who is in many ways, especially in her Christian purity and humility, the most deserving.

Barrett Browning had not the benefit of twentieth-century feminist theology, and she would not believe with Dworkin that every sexual act is death and corruption, but she asserted that every rape is. She did know Chrysostom and surely must have sensed that in Christian theology women's bodies and spirits carry a specific curse and specific implications of corruption and decay. By expressing revulsion in Pauline terminology, she illustrated that rape makes the victim feel as defiled and disgusting as the rapist sees her. (Marian is "clean as Marian Erle" but would not be as Marian Leigh [*AL* 9.399–400]; her soul is not "dirtied," but her body is.) In its analysis of rape, *Aurora Leigh* reveals the limits of society and religion, victim and God—and of the poet herself. Barrett Browning understood that all mortals, specifically all women, are born in corruption because they are born to bear in corruption (and because they have inherited Eve's particular corruption).

Being forbidden passionate though chaste sexual (that is, marital) love, Marian is further denied the full expression of God's love. A troubling aspect of *Aurora Leigh* is that, to Barrett Browning, a human stands incomplete and an imperfect witness of God's love unless that person loves passionately and purely her or his counterpart, as do Aurora's

parents, Carrington and Kate, and Aurora and Romney.[28] Margaret
Reynolds notes that Barrett Browning, like other women poets of her
age, "internalizes the ideology of the woman's sphere where, as a *woman*
she can be fully *human* only with the fulfillment of romantic love and a
sexual relation." Reynolds is only half right; Barrett Browning's ideology is
that any *human* can be fully *spiritual* only with the fulfillment of romantic
love. (As for contentment in the human sphere, Barrett Browning in her
letters repeatedly contends that marriage is more essential for men than
for women.) Nevertheless, this ideology is at least as troubling as the one
Reynolds suggests. The cousins Romney and Aurora are like two sides
of the same leaf (*AL* 8.330), a cleft sphere, a sword and its sheath (*AL*
9.834), each requiring the other for completion. Such a view, in fact,
seems to be the Victorian ideal. In Tennyson's *The Princess* the Prince
and Ida agree that

> . . . either sex alone
> Is half itself, and in true marriage lies
> Nor equal, nor unequal: each fulfils
> Defect in each . . .

In *Of Queens' Gardens,* Ruskin says, "Each . . . completes the other, and
is completed by the other. They are nothing alike, and the happiness
and perfection of both depends on each asking and receiving from the
other what the other only can give."[29] This love experienced through
sexual union is more akin to Aristophanes' ideal in Plato's *Symposium*
(reforming the complete human circle of wholeness) than it is like the
celibate ideal of the letter to the Corinthians (best to remain single, but
better to marry than to burn [1 Cor. 7:9]). Yet it seems to be a basic
assumption of *Aurora Leigh.*

In the closing lines of the epic, Romney compares the spiritual love with
the sexual in terms of the Swedenborgian doctrine of correspondences:

> "And next," he smiled, "the love of wedded souls,
> Which still presents that mystery's counterpart.

28. As a young woman Elizabeth Barrett was highly skeptical about marriage, vowing
that she would never marry.
29. Reynolds, "Critical Introduction," *Aurora Leigh,* 37; Tennyson, *The Princess,*
7.283–86, in *The Poems of Tennyson,* 839; Ruskin, *Of Queens' Gardens,* in *Sesame and
Lilies,* 137.

Sweet shadow-rose, upon the water of life,
Of such a mystic substance, Sharon gave
A name to! human, vital, fructuous rose,
Whose calyx holds the multitude of leaves,
Loves filial, loves fraternal, neighbor-loves
And civic—all fair petals, all good scents,
All reddened, sweetened from one central Heart!"
                                                (*AL* 9.882–90)

Shortly after her marriage Barrett Browning began contemplating Blake, Swedenborg, and the doctrine of conjugal love (*LMRM* 3:231). In Swedenborg, Blake's teacher as he was to become Barrett Browning's, marriage is preferred to celibacy because it was ordained from the beginning, because it is the condition in which humans are actualized in both the natural and the spiritual realm, and, especially, because in the system of correspondence, Christ is the bridegroom, the church is bride. Thus conjugal love *corresponds* to the marriage of love and wisdom, good and truth. This is one aspect of Swedenborg's thought that Ralph Waldo Emerson finds most troubling, saying that heaven ought not be considered "the pairing of two, but the communion of all souls."[30] Swedenborg's endorsement of marriage over celibacy is easy for Barrett Browning to accept, however, because she has been fortunate enough to find herself in a marriage of love and contentment, one in which her intellect and her spirit are accepted, respected, and nourished. She *wants* to believe in a resurrection to conjugal union, both in this world and in the next. She feels sure, she says, that marriage is not part of the "old cerements" the soul leaves behind with its husk of a physical body (*LEBB* 2:426). Therefore in the afterlife Aurora will be with Romney (as Elizabeth will be with Robert), but Marian will be alone.

Thus on both the natural and the spiritual plane Romney loves Aurora and Aurora loves Romney; Marian does not now love Romney, only worships him. Or so she says, in rejecting his proposal. She does not love because she *cannot* love. "Once killed, this ghost of Marian loves no more . . ." (*AL* 9.388). Naturally there is more to it than that: Marian, like Barrett Browning, realizes that Romney and Aurora were made for one another. Thus Marian's decision is in part an act of wholly unselfish

---

30. Swedenborg, *The Delights of Wisdom Pertaining to Conjugial Love,* 156, 21, 57; Emerson, "Swedenborg; or, the Mystic," in *Essays and Lectures,* 680.

caritas. Nevertheless, Marian cannot and will not experience God's love on the same plane that Aurora and Romney will. Attempts to parallel her continued celibacy to that of the Virgin Mary, and thereby to declare her a greater holiness than the married couple Aurora and Romney would be to read into the poem a Mariolatry that Barrett Browning would never accept, as well as acceptance of the sanctification of celibacy over marriage, which she also rejects.

VI

Contrasting the brutal violation of Marian is the rape that Aurora desires, and receives, from the arch ravisher, Zeus. This metaphorical violation, life-giving rape as contrasted to murdering rape, impregnates the poet with the "hot fire-seeds of creation" (*AL* 3.252). When a male uses the metaphor of rape as John Donne does in the Holy Sonnet "Batter my heart, three-personed God," the trope is shocking enough, but with the female poet it is incredibly bold, foregrounding female artistic desire against the background of rape fantasy (supposed of the female in such commentary as "She asked for it," "She enjoyed it"). And, while the metaphor is bold and unusual in Victorian women's poetry, it has roots in fervent mystical religious experience of both women and men, for whom divine revelation was often expressed as explicitly sexual/genital in character, notes Susan Dowell. Ursula King says that bridal or nuptial language was used by mystics of both genders to describe the soul's intimacy with God, but women's language was especially ecstatic in tone—"an all-consuming love affair with God." (Teresa of Avila, for example, spoke of the "ravished understanding" of God and of the "rape of love.")[31] Thus, Barrett Browning's metaphor is not without precedent, although it was certainly not part and parcel of nineteenth-century Protestantism.

Aurora fantasizes herself as three mythological rape victims: Ganymede, Danae, and Io. At the time of her first resurrection (into her androgynous

---

31. Dowell, "A Jealous God? Towards a Feminist Model of Monogamy," 206–28; King, *Women and Spirituality: Voices of Protest and Promise,* 105. Denis de Rougemont notes the influence of the Song of Songs on ecstatic religious devotion, but adds that St. Teresa's particular ecstasy arose from her doting upon the chivalric romance (*Love in the Western World,* 161).

or perhaps masculine stage as young poet) she is the abducted lad
Ganymede:

> ... poetry, my life,
> My eagle, with both grappling feet still hot
> From Zeus's thunder, thou hast ravished me
> Away from all the shepherds, sheep, and dogs,
> And set me in the Olympian roar and round
> Of luminous faces for a cup-bearer,
> To keep the mouths of all the godheads moist
> For everlasting laughters ... [32]
>
> (*AL* 1.918–25)

To Aurora, separate studies of Danae that Carrington has executed
represent two versions of the "recipient artist-soul" (*AL* 3.139) like herself,
one of them:

> A tiptoe Danae, overbold and hot,
> Both arms a-flame to meet her wishing Jove
> Halfway, and burn him faster down ...
>
> (*AL* 3.122–24)

When Zeus lays his calming hand on his outcast victim Io (and God
lays his hand on Aurora), that is to "genuine artists'" prophetic message and
divine progeny. The touch of Zeus's hand, as prophesied in Aeschylus's
Prometheus Bound and recalled in his *The Suppliant Maidens*, impreg-
nated Io with her son, Epaphus (Caress), and thus Aurora seeks divine
touch and heavenly possession.[33] The Danae myth is that Zeus appeared
to imprisoned Danae in the form of a shower of gold coins, raping
and impregnating her. When Marian describes her rape and resulting
pregnancy, she says that God dropped a "coin of prince" within her flesh
to recompense her for her loss (*AL* 6.681), the allusion suggesting the immaculate conception of Mary and the rape of Danae, and recalling Hester

---

32. About the seduction (or rape), Ovid says only that Jove loved Ganymede and
Juno was jealous of the boy who served Jove's nectar (*Metamorphoses* 10), Hyginus that
the Trojan lad is Zeus's lover (*Poetica Astronomica* 2.16, in *The Myths of Hyginus*, 203),
but in Lucian's *Dialogues of the Gods*, Zeus describes favors the lad will receive in the
Olympian's bed (*Lucian* 8:287–91).

33. Aeschylus, *The Suppliant Maidens*, in *The Complete Greek Tragedies*, 2:10.47,
19.312.

Prynne's conception, her "Pearl of great price," which is itself an allusion to Jesus' parable of the kingdom of God as a "Pearl of great price" (Matt. 13:46). Aurora's pearl of price, however, is her creative work; she says that when an artist thus possessed, ravished, or "touched" by God witnesses for God's work, we ought not to say that he *produced* this, but rather, " 'Tis insight and he saw this' " (*AL* 7.854). Barrett Browning speaks for the woman poet's part in entreating the divine inspiration in words, as Mary received in immaculate conception the Word (as Io also conceived a divine child and as did Marian, though the boy's conception is diabolical, not divine). Words and thoughts—the inspiration—will burn through Aurora, leaving her spent and enervated like Danae. And rape by God, as it were, produces the resurrection of "Complete, consummate, *undivided* work" (*AL* 7.839; italics mine), the same imagery and concept employed to represent the perfection of Aurora and Romney's sexual union and their united work in art and politics: complete, reunited, resurrected, whole. That this is the case forces another uncomfortable recognition about Marian's story. Her purity, the "immaculate conception," her devotion to her son of promise, her self-effacement and humility all mark her parallel to the Virgin Mary and to Io. But Marian, enthroned by her innocence and worthiness, is effaced by her creator, Barrett Browning, and assigned a lesser role, an outcome that is troubling not so much from the plot or genre (or class) expectation as from the philosophical and theological implications. Yet it suits Barrett Browning's aesthetic gospel to make God's receptacle the poet Aurora (personally identified with Barrett Browning in that she is striving, ambitious, sarcastic, witty, intellectual, and gifted in ways that Marian never can be). It is not so much, as Kaplan charges, class bias as it poetry bias. Barrett Browning's friend Mrs. Ogilvy remarks that in matters of poetry the Brownings certainly are not democrats but believe that they—as poets—are the privileged class, empowered to interpret poetic truth for the "common herd" (*LMO* xxviii). Said in these words, it sounds like arrogance. At the very least it is the belief that the poet is sanctified by God for a special calling, receiving the power of inspiration (the "laying on of hands") just as surely as the apostles received the power of tongues in the fires of Pentecost, or as surely as Io is calmed by the laying on of the hand of Zeus.

Furthermore, Aurora as receptacle of wisdom and word in the poetic sense as Mary was receptacle of Christ the Word and Wisdom, becomes a passive object through whom the divine acts rather than an active human agent creating poetic work on her own. In *Aurora Leigh* licit possession by God and human lover resurrects woman into aesthetic and spiritual life; illicit violation by man slays her. It is at once a troubling theology and a troubling doctrine of female aesthetics.

If the young Elizabeth Barrett was obsessed with premonitions of death, the mature poet Elizabeth Barrett Browning was at the height of her career a prophet of resurrection. When the languishing Barrett believed she had been marked by God for death, she acquiesced; when she was quickened body and soul by romantic love, she accepted the lover as a godly (or angelic) call to resurrected life in the body. Prior to her immersion in Swedenborg (around 1851 but beginning in 1848) she seems to have taken her doctrine on resurrection directly from the apostle Paul, whose rhetoric, she says, depicts a perpetual struggle between flesh and spirit (death and life) common to all Christians (*BC* 6:193). In the writings attributed to Paul the body is proclaimed dead because of sin, but the spirit alive because of righteousness: "But if the Spirit of him that raised up Jesus from the dead dwell in you, he that raised up Christ from the dead shall also quicken your mortal bodies by his Spirit that dwelleth in you" (Rom. 8:11). Her mortal body decaying, Barrett hoped only for life beyond the grave; she was ready to drink "[t]he cup of dole / God gave for baptism" (*SP* 7.7–8). Fatalistically she accepted that death—having entered the world through sin and having become the common lot of humankind—was inevitable sooner or later, and in her own case very soon. Therefore, if in a trancelike state she had for years drifted toward physical death, she nevertheless looked forward to Paul's promise of a spiritual resurrection in heaven, and she interpreted Paul as teaching that at the moment of death, the body of flesh drops away as a mere husk and the spiritual body emerges at once in glorious resurrection (*LEBB* 2:177).

After her temporal resurrection to romantic love, however, Barrett Browning was also miraculously alive for spiritual service through art. Further, the figure for a resurrected life (spirit triumphant over flesh) became a dominant recurring motif of her work, and resurrection ideology permeated every major work from *Sonnets from the Portuguese* onward: resurrection to art, to love, to Italy's national freedom and unification, to amended social and political systems, to a triumphant apocalypse of world peace and harmony.

In her discovery of Swedenborg, Barrett Browning was not forced to renounce St. Paul, but merely to augment him. (She says Swedenborg fills in the chinks of her life; no doubt some of those chinks related to questions about the nature of the resurrected body and the conditions of eternal bliss.) Love had given her new life and hope. She now desired assurance of another hope that she had not found confirmed in the apostle Paul, the hope to love her beloved eternally. (For example, she closes the most famous of her love sonnets with the desire, "if God choose, / I shall but love thee better after death" [*SP* 43.13–14].) Swedenborg fills in the gaps of faith by promising a heaven not only of a "living body in resurrection" but also of conjugal love that will not leave behind its beloved as the resurrected body abandons the death shroud (*LEBB* 2:426). From Swedenborg, Barrett Browning also learns the doctrine of correspondences: that every step of the foot or stroke of the pen in this life has connection with the hereafter (*LEBB* 2:299). Therefore the poet writes not merely for her time but for eternity. Also in Swedenborgian thought, the separation between life and death is but a thin veil, and therefore the souls of deceased friends hover around us. Thus death then loses its sting and the grave its victory. Death becomes a mere incident (elsewhere "accident"), perhaps scarcely greater, Barrett Browning says, than the occurrence of puberty. And after death one goes on living and loving eternally, she affirms: "I believe in an active, *human* life, beyond death as before it, an uninterrupted human life. I believe in no waiting in the grave, and in no vague effluence of spirit in a formless vapour" (*LEBB* 2:177).

To read the Elizabeth Barrett Browning canon without perceiving it as resurrection doctrine is to consume grain and chaff without tasting the "kernel of sweetness" at its core. But to understand Barrett Browning's reading of the resurrection teachings of St. Paul and Swedenborg is to perceive spiritual "truths" that the poet perceived as the center of the texts. As the ashes of life are ignited by the spark of love in *Sonnets from the Portuguese,* Barrett Browning (like Aurora Leigh) prays to be animated and enflamed with God's divine gift of prophecy to "raise men's bodies still by raising souls."

5

Prophetess of Divine Love
and Wisdom

Spiritual goods and truths are of wisdom,
and heavenly goods and truths are of love

— Emanuel Swedenborg, *The Apocalypse Revealed*

Can Wisdom be put in a silver rod?
Or Love in a golden bowl?

— William Blake, "The Book of Thel"

God is in the truth, and He is called also love.

— Barrett Browning, Correspondence

I

At a social gathering of aristocracy and literati, the fictional Lord Howe says of Elizabeth Barrett Browning's fictional poet Aurora Leigh:

> . . . "What, talking poetry
> So near the image of the unfavoring Muse?
> That's you, Miss Leigh: I've watched you half an hour
> Precisely as I watched the statue called
> A Pallas in the Vatican;—you mind
> The face, sir Blaise?—intensely calm and sad,

> As wisdom cut it off from fellowship,—
> But *that* spoke louder.
>
> (*AL* 5.795–802)

Later, when Aurora has rebuffed the romantic interest of his acquaintance for whom he has been commissioned to act as intermediary, the same Lord Howe acknowledges that it is most difficult for the poet to live purely for art.

> In this uneven, unfostering England here,
> Where ledger-strokes and sword-strokes count indeed,
> But soul-strokes merely tell upon the flesh
> They strike from,—it is hard to stand for art,
> Unless some golden tripod from the sea
> Be fished up, by Apollo's divine chance,
> To throne such feet as yours, my prophetess,
> At Delphi.
>
> (*AL* 5.936–43)

Prophetess of Delphi, Pallas of the Vatican, unfavoring Muse, azure-eyed Athena, Miriam with her timbrel, Cassandra at the gate, Io-turned-Isis, Godiva of silent, eloquent witness, humble Magdalene who proclaims the Resurrection, Eve schooled by sin to demonstrate heavenly grace and teach God's Gospel of Work. The allusions to woman as prophet, as teacher, as wisdom figure recur throughout the canon of Elizabeth Barrett Browning. The allusions to the prophetess/priestess/goddess and the aspirations to wisdom often refer to Barrett Browning's characters such as Aurora Leigh instead of directly to herself; in her correspondence, however, she facetiously compares *herself* to Io, Godiva, Cassandra, a Pythia, and a prophetess, though she usually comes off a poor second in the comparison (*BC* 10:53; *BC* 11:46, 85, 130; *BC* 12:167). Nonetheless she willingly and knowingly spins a web of myth about herself as wisdom figure. Generations of readers have also labeled her as prophetess, a trait noted in Barrett Browning criticism. Alethea Hayter, for example, comments: "It is extraordinary how often both her admirers and her detractors compared her with the priestess of Delphi and other prophetesses—she was Deborah, Minerva, Alruna, the Sibyl, the Pythoness, the anointed priestess; delirious, shrieking, possessed and contorted, or clamorously earnest and inspired with a sacred passion, according to whether she was being blamed or praised, but always the Pythoness." Biographer Gardner

Taplin accuses Barrett Browning of "put[ting] on the robes of a high priestess and solemnly explain[ing] the mysteries of her calling" (when she speaks of the work of a poet with "reverence and sincerity" in her preface to the 1844 volume).[1] Both Hayter and Taplin are correct. There is no denying that Barrett Browning dramatizes herself as Lady Wisdom, writing the script and playing the role of beloved sister and daughter, sainted wife and mother, devout Christian, erudite scholar, suffering invalid, inspired poet, and prophetess for God. She thus places herself as poet/priestess/prophet in the tradition of woman as wisdom that has its classical source in the goddess Athena and its Judeo-Christian source in Gnosticism and the Jewish-Hellenistic Wisdom/Sophia, and enjoys a surprising reappearance in Victorian art and literature. Naturally to Barrett Browning all poets are God's prophets and priests, witnesses of the beautiful and true; nevertheless she believes herself uniquely qualified for the Pythian tripod of Delphi.

Once she has positioned herself as spokesperson for God, or rather in fact as the image is evolving, Barrett Browning uses her pedestal to speak out on social issues (in "philanthropic poetry" as reviewers of her day were inclined to call it). Among her issues are child labor, prostitution, illegitimacy, slavery, injustice, poverty, and oppression. And, as noted in a previous chapter, she often formulates her views on both national and international politics by means of her faith. She charges the English empire to uphold God's mandates. Finally in her finest work, *Aurora Leigh,* she feels inspired to teach the Swedenborgian gospel of "Divine Wisdom and Divine Love," of "spiritual and heavenly good."

II

The iconography of woman-as-wisdom was a staple of Barrett Browning's century, employed in art, literature, and political rhetoric. According to Barbara Taylor, in the late eighteenth and early nineteenth centuries there was also a recurring heresy in the millenarian sects of England that prophesied the advent of a female Messiah. As Bride of Christ or Savior of man, women like Ann Lee, Mary Evans, and Joanna Southcott had preached the female-as-savior doctrine; the St. Simonian Gospel also

---

1. Hayter, *Mrs. Browning,* 194; Taplin, *Life of Elizabeth Barrett Browning,* 124.

celebrated the figure of the Mother messiah; the Communist Church evoked Shelley's feminist messiah of *The Revolt of Islam* in its plea for a Christ-androgyne; Florence Nightingale (and others) speculated whether the next Christ might be female. Rosemary Ruether has noted the Christ-as-Mariology figure in nineteenth-century Protestantism, a phenomenon that may well have resulted from conflating woman-as-wisdom with Christ as Word/Wisdom.[2] In addition to the woman-as-messiah heresy, Jesus was in the nineteenth century interpreted as androgynous, as several feminist theologians have noted. Thus Jesus as Word and Wisdom and woman as Sophia/Wisdom are not so unrelated as they seem.

The American feminist Margaret Fuller, whom the Brownings knew socially at the close of her life in Italy, remarks in *Woman in the Nineteenth Century* that the image of the female has from ancient times represented knowledge, insight, and wisdom: the Egyptian Isis who was divine wisdom, the great and holy women who as heroines, prophetesses, and judges in Old Testament Israel were "greeted with solemn rapture," Athena the Greek and Minerva the Roman deities of wisdom, the Sibylline priestesses who told the oracle of the highest God, and Cassandra in her prophetic power. John Ruskin in *Of Queens' Gardens* makes the same point: that Isis became Athena, who represents to his own age "whatever you hold most precious in art, in literature, or in types of national virtue."[3]

The Victorian Wisdom figure represents every kind of virtue: religious, domestic, philosophical, patriotic. In Ruskin's *Queen of the Air*, he notes that Athena is the mythological deity particularly significant *to the nation* because she is "guide of moral passion," directress of human resolution and labor, *to the arts* because, as the Muses teach artists to make their art beautiful, she teaches them to make it "right" (right in the sense of prudent, subtle, moral). Statues and other images of the wisdom goddess proliferated in Victorian England, a trend no doubt enhanced in that the reigning monarch enjoyed an image of good, stable, pious, and domestic "womanly" female. Marina Warner explains that the importance of Athena/Minerva in Victorian England had to do not only with the "coincidence of the Athenian code and Victorian domestic Ideals" of patriarchy, nationalism, legitimacy of authority, and moral Christian

2. Taylor, *Eve and the New Jerusalem,* 161–82; Nightingale, *"Cassandra" and Other Selections,* 230; Ruether, *New Woman, New Earth,* 24.
3. Fuller, *Woman in the Nineteenth Century,* 51, 47, 55, 115; Ruskin, *Of Queens' Gardens,* in *Sesame and Lilies,* 133.

soundness; she also interprets the many nineteenth-century Amazon-like statues and other images of Nike, Victory, Lady Justice, Fortitude, and Britannia as iconographical exemplification of this value, a connection between civic pride and intellectual virtue that Fuller suggests when she notes that "even Victory wore a female form."[4]

Wisdom is prominent too in Victorian literature, as in, for example, the early works of Robert Browning and Alfred, Lord Tennyson. In Browning's *Paracelsus* the protagonist, considering himself singled out for wisdom, exults:

> Think, think! the wide East, where all Wisdom sprung;
> The bright South, where she dwelt; the hopeful North;
> All are passed o'er—it lights on me.

In Tennyson's "The Poet" the personified Freedom is also Wisdom:

> And in her raiment's hem was traced in flame
> WISDOM, a name to shake
> All evil dreams of power—a sacred name.

Wisdom also appears in various female guises in the novels of Dickens, Martineau, Kingsley, George Eliot, and Charlotte Brontë. Alexander Welsh says that the Spirit of the Comforter from the fourth Gospel comes close to fulfilling the needs of Victorian domestic religion. That is, Wisdom or the Spirit of Truth that is to guide man to all things is presented in Victorian icon as female. Welsh further notes that Wisdom, the Paraclete, the Mother of God—though they seem remote from the sweet domestic figure of Victorian imagination—have their origin in the Wisdom-as-female tradition, which Welsh believes inspired positivism (through Comte's love for Clothilde de Vaux) and is recognized in Mill's elevation of Harriet Taylor in his *Autobiography* and Robert Browning's of his wife in *The Ring and the Book*.[5] Thus Elizabeth Barrett Browning was not alone in invoking a female figure for wisdom. Nor is she alone in being considered a "prophetess" for God (Christina Rossetti becoming her successor in

---

4. Ruskin, *The Queen of the Air: Being a Study of the Greek Myths of Cloud and Storm*, 61, 117–18, 123; Warner, *Monuments and Maidens*, 125–26; Fuller, *Woman in the Nineteenth Century*, 55.

5. Browning, *The Poems*, 1:46.370–72; Tennyson, *Poems of Tennyson*, 223.45–47; Welsh, *City of Dickens*, 175–79.

this role). More elaborately than most, however, she was self-created as modern-day Minerva, and she deliberately used the creation to invoke God's blessing on her political, aesthetic, and philosophical doctrine.

III

Facetiously yet seriously (smiling at her pretensions but deliberate about her aims), Elizabeth Barrett set out from an early age to win a reputation for genius, and she was remarkably successful. Her biographer Dorothy Hewlett says that "within this child's veins ran the strange ichor of genius." Like a young Milton, Barrett disciplined herself to read the Bible in Greek and Hebrew, the classics in Greek and Latin. Thus she learned early that Wisdom is a female icon, for in the classical tradition Athena is the goddess of wisdom, and in Old Testament literature Wisdom is the daughter of God present with the male divinity from the foundation of the world. The child Elizabeth Barrett favored the poets Homer, Dante, Milton, Pope, and Byron; at seven she studied the English theologian Hooker, at eight *Paradise Lost,* and at nine Pope, and twice she attempted translations of Dante's *Commedia* (*BC* 1:350).[6]

Among these early favorite writers (excepting Byron) she repeatedly encountered Sophia/Athena/Minerva. In Dante's *Convivio,* Wisdom is daughter of the Emperor of the Universe, "sage and courteous in her greatness" and "mother of all origins whatever . . . with her God began the universe." And in *The Purgatorio,* Beatrice is Wisdom eclipsed only by the Love of Christ, appearing to Dante with the wreath of wise Minerva encircling her brow and leading him to perfect vision (in *The Paradiso*). In Christian euhemeristic tradition, classical Minerva was transformed into divine Wisdom, as Barrett learned from Sir Francis Bacon (whom she addresses in an "Essay on Mind" written while she was yet in her teens). In the works of the English theologian Hooker, Wisdom's role is both ecclesiastical and political, intuitive and empirical. "Some things she openeth by the sacred books of Scripture; some things by the glorious works of Nature: with some things she inspireth them from above by spiritual influence; in some things she leadeth and traineth them only by

---

6. Hewlett, *A Life,* 12. Her personal copy of Dante's *Commedia* is in the Armstrong Browning Library of Baylor University. The Dante translations were not entirely the work of early youth; the second was in 1845.

worldly experience and practice."[7] Milton's "Eternal Wisdom" of *Paradise Lost* is the sister of the muse Urania, who with her "didst play / In presence of th' Almighty Father" (*PL* 7.10–11). Although Raphael insists that Wisdom will not depart from Adam unless he abandons her, Adam himself is convinced that in discourse with lovely Eve, "Wisdom . . . [l]oses discount'nanc 't, and like folly shows" (*PL* 8.552–53). Eve's sin in eating of knowledge is to gain access to Wisdom "though secret she retire" (*PL* 9.810).

In her reading and her imagination young Elizabeth Barrett set out to *become* a Minerva. Of herself, she says she was "one of those hapless monsters yclepped precocious children" (*BC* 8:54), later telling Robert Browning how she "went out one day with [her] pinafore full of little sticks (& a match from the housemaids cupboard) to sacrifice to the blue eyed Minerva," her favorite goddess (*BC* 11:319). It is telling that when in childhood she wrote birthday odes to family members, she invoked Minerva; in her sister Henrietta's ode for Ba's eighteenth birthday, however, she suggests that Minerva scorns herself but loves her older sister, whom the family called the "Poet Laureate of Hope End" (*BC* 1:191). Already in childhood young Elizabeth was Athena incarnate.

It comes as no surprise, then, that the muse of her first published poem, "The Battle of Marathon," is blue-eyed Athena/wise Minerva, nor that in her preface the precocious child of fourteen proclaims that it is wisdom—not folly—on her part to take as her models Homer, Pope, and Milton: "There is no humility, but rather folly, in taking inferiority for a model, and there is no vanity, but rather wisdom, in following humbly the footsteps of perfection . . ." (*CWEBB* 1:9). "The Battle of Marathon" pits Persia against Athens, tyranny versus freedom, "Asia's tyrant king" Darius (*CWEBB* 1:17.221) versus Athens's sage commander "[r]enowned for wisdom" (*CWEBB* 1:30.265). But also the poem is about intellect versus sensuality: Athena of the brain versus the Persians' goddess Cytherea (Aphrodite) of the loins. For a young poet who has vowed never to marry, it is an easy choice on whose side to cast her lot. In addition to Homer, Pope was Barrett's main inspiration for "The Battle of Marathon"; she had begun studying his *Iliad* at age nine and records

7. Dante, *Convivio of Dante,* 134, 221; *Purgatorio* 30.68, in *The Divine Comedy* (*Purgatorio* 1:330); *Paradiso* 5.4–5, in *The Divine Comedy* (*Paradiso* 1:48); Bacon, *Wisdom of the Ancients,* in *The Moral and Historical Works of Lord Bacon,* 255; Hooker, *Laws of Ecclesiastical Polity,* 2.2.1 in *Works of Mr. Richard Hooker,* 1:290.

her great disappointment to discover that her own heroic couplets of war and valor prove inferior to those of her mentor. In Pope's translation of *The Odyssey* divine Minerva—the "martial maid," "blue-ey'd Virgin," and "Virgin seed of Jove"—is also "heav'n-born," rather more like the Jewish wisdom figure Sophia than like Hesiod's brain-birthed warrior.[8] Not only does Athena/Minerva set the stage for Odysseus's successful return against overwhelming odds, but she also teaches the lessons of truthfulness, justice, wise counsel, and peace negotiation. In Barrett's "The Battle of Marathon" warrior and priest learn similar lessons: Clombrotus prays to Zeus for heavenly wisdom; Miltiades, commander of the Greeks, asks wisdom from Pallas Athena; Aristide's "great mind with Minerva glows" (*CWEBB* 1:34.778); Cleon is Minerva's priest "advanced in wisdom" (*CWEBB* 1:37.861); the Athenians sacrifice twelve white heifers to wise Minerva. Small wonder that the Greeks defeat the Persians at Marathon; they espouse the same values as the poet.

Another major work in the Barrett juvenilia is "An Essay on Mind," a speculative treatise on wisdom, genius, and knowledge written, like "The Battle of Marathon," in a style recalling Pope. "An Essay on Mind" is a work of limited success, but then it is not to be expected that poets—even precocious ones—should reach the height of achievement at "seventeen or eighteen" (the age at which Barrett claims to have written the work [*BC* 7:354]). In the "Essay" Mind is, not surprisingly, of the female gender (as are Genius and Truth), and the young poet seeks to reveal not so much the "nature of her (i.e. Mind's) substance" as her effects, noting that "our enlightened Locke" had vainly tried and failed in explaining the former. Predictably, Barrett modestly professes herself unfit to "search her secret chambers" or "enter into her (Mind's) temples" as Bacon and Newton, Locke and Burke, Liebnitz and Longinus, and Milton and Pope have done (*CWEBB* 1:59). In cataloging the effects of Mind, Barrett protests that too much of human knowledge and speculation have been narrow and compartmentalized: that History is inclined to the Procrustean, that Science is vulnerable to arrogance, Philosophy to prejudice. But Poetry is elevated as sacred calling (and poetic fire is—like Vesta's—pure and bright). In a Platonic (and Christian) universe there exists

---

8. Pope, translation of *The Odyssey*, 1.85, 13.426, 1.227, 24.629, 1.138, in *The Poems of Alexander Pope*, 9:35, 10:26, 9:43, 10:377, 9:39.

> Some kindred home for Mind—some holy place,
> Where spirits look on spirits, "face to face,"—
> Where souls may see, as they themselves are seen,
> And voiceless intercourse may pass between . . .
> (*CWEBB* 1:81.661–64)

Although "ungrateful Plato" banished the poets from his utopia, the Poet is the only one who can "[p]ourtray the shadows of the things of light" and "waft the pictures of perfection home" (*CWEBB* 1:88.911, 913). Until Mind attains this heavenly realm of seeing as we are seen, knowing as we are known (as St. Paul says [1 Cor. 13:12]), soul is not liberated from body nor thought from words. When the pilgrim seeking "wisdom's music" lays aside his staff at the end of life's little day, however, his wearied sight is gladdened

> With all that Mind's serener skies impart;
> Where Wisdom suns the day no shades destroy,
> And Learning ends in Truth, as hope in joy . . .
> (*CWEBB* 1:99.1246–48)

David G. Riede says that while it is not surprising that a Christian poet would see truth as available only in heaven ("disembodied spirits basking in God's truth"), the poem demonstrates an impasse in that poetry is celebrated in the romantic tradition, but at the same time nature and the language of poetry are subjected to Christian distrust. Riede notes that as a result the poet seeking transcendent truth is held down by human fallen language.[9] Nevertheless, "An Essay on Mind" is an incredibly bold discourse with philosophers, historians, and poets—classical and modern—as well as a bold pursuit of Wisdom. In making apology for its "pertness & pedantry" Barrett later seems mystified that such a work should emerge from the pen of an author who was not herself of the pert or pedantic character (*BC* 7:354). But perhaps the poet doth protest too much. It is likely the case that she was embarrassed by the barely concealed titanic strainings of her youth (never mind that the "Essay" warns poet and reader of the doomed flights of Icarus and Phaeton) and as a woman wished to disclaim the girl's presumption.

---

9. Riede, "Elizabeth Barrett: The Poet as Angel," 126–27.

From childhood imitations of Pope, the young Barrett wrote her way into early adulthood by learning from Byron, Wordsworth, Coleridge, Tennyson, the "godlike Milton," "the sublime Dante, the reasoning Pope" (*CWEBB* 1:93.1048, 1:56). She cultivated acquaintance with distinguished men whom she respected (as the fictional Dorothea does Casaubon in Eliot's *Middlemarch*) until she grew beyond them. Both Sir Uvedale Price and Hugh Stuart Boyd encouraged her poetic endeavors and did her the honor of arguing poetic or theological issues with her almost as one would with a peer. Boyd nurtured her precocious bent in classics, introduced to her the Greek Christian fathers, and debated issues such as predestination with her; he referred to her by such endearments as "Porsonia" (after the classical scholar he admired) and "true prophetess," a compliment of which she takes note in her diary.[10]

In 1833 Elizabeth Barrett published her first translation of *Prometheus Bound,* in 1838 *The Seraphim,* a bold undertaking that began to establish her reputation for mysticism, erudition, and "philosophizing." *The Seraphim, and Other Poems* was followed in 1842 by a scholarly account of Greek Christian poets, and two years later by *A Drama of Exile,* in which she undertook to remedy Milton's oversights in *Paradise Lost,* especially by reclaiming Eve. As noted in Chapter 1, in *The Seraphim* a weeping Mary (representing the poet herself) kneels at the foot of Jesus. If Barrett Browning conflates Mary of Bethany with Mary Magdalene as was common, the kneeling Mary represents wisdom and contemplation as well as humility. In *A Drama of Exile,* Eve, "schooled by sin," becomes the wisdom figure, teaching Godly grace, human humility, and the doctrine of good works (as noted in Chapter 2). By 1844 it was known among her admirers that, although the learned Elizabeth Barrett was afflicted with serious illness, she continued to praise God, not revile him. The invalid poet became, in the public's eye, a paragon of saintliness, and wisdom as well.

Further, she created female versions of herself as speakers for wisdom. For example, Geraldine of "Lady Geraldine's Courtship" (a "romance of the age" from the 1844 *Poems*) is prophetess for social equality, the willful and independent woman who chooses a husband for love, not for aristocratic rank. Geraldine has political and economic clout, represented by halls, woodlands, castles, and manors; because of social position in the world she can "threaten and command." She is a born general or

10. Barrett Browning, *Diary of EBB,* 70, 1.

manager, "princely" and powerful like Brontë's Shirley Keeldar of *Shirley* or Tennyson's Ida of *The Princess*. Suitors vie for her love and socialites for an invitation to her estate. In her androgyny and independence, Geraldine is a predecessor for Aurora Leigh. Just as the demarcation between male/female roles and values is blurred in *Aurora Leigh,* so gender reversals and androgyny play a role in "Lady Geraldine's Courtship." Geraldine and the poet Bertram are, by turns, bold and tentative, taciturn and talkative, leader and follower, student and teacher, though he mistakenly assumes that she has need of his lecture on class snobbery. Both characters (the aspiring poet and the assertive woman) represent aspects of Barrett herself.

In Bertram's idealized characterization of Geraldine she is a version of the lady Wisdom: an angel clad in wings, a goddess, a priestess in virginal white vesture, a female messiah (blessing the little children on her estate), and a muse; her smile is divine, and her voice of holy sweetness turns common words to grace. When Bertram mistakenly concludes that she disdains him because he is not of the aristocracy, however, *he* is drawn up to a "Pythian height" (here the figure of the female prophetess of Apollo used androgynously for the male prophet). He indicts Geraldine that she and her kind are "more infidels to Adam" than "infidels to God," that is, guilty of ranking some sons of Adam before others (*CWEBB* 2:301.291, 292). Here Bertram's leveling rhetoric anticipates that of Romney Leigh who says that the "tyrannous sword" piercing Christ's heart also rent class from class (*AL* 4.122–24). As Glennis Stephenson notes, however, the Lady Geraldine has consistently been unimpressed with outer show, impressed only with spiritual worth. Nonetheless, Bertram (though not the reader) misapprehends her scorn for social climbers. Upon roundly condemning Geraldine's prejudice, Bertram falls into a swoon, then recovers to find her appearing as a vision at his window like a female Porphyoro emerging from Madeline's visions of love inspired on St. Agnes's Eve. This "Vision of a lady" at the open casement also recalls the lady in the window in Dante's *La Vita Nuova.*[11] The wisdom of Geraldine and Bertram is, briefly, equality for all people regardless of birth and the arrogance of an age that almost worships its technology,

---

11. Stephenson, "The Vision Speaks: Love in Elizabeth Barrett Browning's 'Lady Geraldine's Courtship,' " 21–22. Dante's lady, like Wisdom/Sophia in the Hebrew myth, was born in Heaven and speaks for God (*The Vita Nuova and Canzoniere of Dante Alighieri,* Canzone 19).

"Little thinking if we work OUR SOULS as nobly as our iron" (*CWEBB* 2:295.203).

Yet another wisdom figure from the 1844 poems is the "lady riding slow / Upon a palfrey white as snow" in "A Vision of Poets" (*CWEBB* 2:312.34–35). Here the wisdom figure performs for the questing poet a function similar to that which Virgil and Beatrice serve for Dante; that is, she leads him out of the "dark wood" into wisdom and truth (*CWEBB* 2:327.440). Marjorie Stone points out that, like Spenser's Una, the lady is identified with the moon and that she recalls also Dante's Beatrice of the *Commedia* and Keats's Moneta in "The Fall of Hyperion." It is pertinent to add that in Spenser's *The Faerie Queene,* Una is "wisedome heavenly rare" (as well as "heavenly grace")[12] and, as previously noted, Beatrice is most decidedly Dante's wisdom personified.

Having come forth to crown all poets "to their worth," Barrett's regal lady—"holy, pale, and high"—exposes her poet to the world's cruelty and despair, then teaches him that right avenges wrong, finally leading him to an altar where he encounters the souls of departed poets of God (Homer to Coleridge), a conclave that Tricia Lootens calls "an eerier architectural canon whose monuments simultaneously celebrate Romantic genius, Pythian inspiration, and the agonies of Christian sanctity."[13] Here the lady sums up the loneliness and suffering that are the true poet's lot:

> *World's use* is cold, *World's love* is vain,
> *World's cruelty* is bitter bane,
> But pain is not the fruit of pain.
> (*CWEBB* 2:326.436–38)

She then places her poet in the capable hands of God's sapient angel, who catechizes the world's great departed poets. Dolores DeLuise and Michael Timko, who see "A Vision of Poets" as a work that "sexualizes and feminizes the nature of the poet's work," contend that Barrett is changing her stance that the poet-genius is male to the view that she may be female as well. They note that the chief angel teaches the poets (all male except Sappho) that a "Christ-like, woman-like suffering accompanies the

---

12. Stone, *Elizabeth Barrett Browning,* 88–89; *The Faerie Queene* 1.6.31.1 in *The Works of Edmund Spenser,* 1:77, and 1.6.18.5 in ibid., 1:74.
13. Lootens, *Lost Saints,* 122.

poet's crown."[14] When the poet-pilgrim vows to "ask no wages, seek no fame" but "God's banner," then angel, organ, and incense celebrate his newfound wisdom, the lady kisses him, and the vision of her image melts with the dawn (*CWEBB* 2:336.703, 705). Finally, at the close of "A Vision of Poets," the persona (presumably female like the poet) traces the poet-pilgrim's footsteps, following in his path to poetic wisdom and humility, and concluding that all great poetry is about the grace of knowledge perceived through suffering and perfected by death. The wisdom of the lady, and of the poet, therefore weds religion to poetry, a union that Barrett repeatedly and insistently endorses.

When Richard H. Horne published *A New Spirit of the Age* in 1844, he credited Barrett with mastery of "more knowledge and accomplishments than are usually within the power of those of either sex who possess every adventitious opportunity, as well as health and industry." Horne goes on to build the aura of sanctified prophet about his *New Spirit* collaborator, by calling her an "inspired priestess . . . whose individuality is cast upward in the divine afflatus, and dissolved and carried off in the recipient breath of angelic ministrants."[15] His rather grandiose depiction was apparently influential, augmenting Barrett's fame as idealized woman, combining the fervency of St. Teresa and the long-suffering of a martyr. She was heralded by critics as the prophetess of the age: *Blackwood's Edinburgh Magazine* "disposed to bend in reverence before the deep-hearted and highly accomplished woman" (*BC* 9:350), *Tait's Edinburgh Magazine* noted her "outpourings of a pure and noble spirit, disciplined by study . . . and . . . sorrow" (*BC* 9:364), *The League* proclaimed her a prophetess (*BC* 9:378) and *The Atlas* a priestess (*BC* 9:327). *The American Review* called her an Athenian sibyl (*BC* 10:335), and *The Southern Literary Messenger* praised her work as coming "*invitâ Minervâ*" (*BC* 10:383). This is not to imply that the poems of 1844 received unmitigated praise, for they did not, but rather to note that—in spite of their apprised flaws— they earned for Barrett herself accolades for divine prophecy. She took note of the flattery, and afterward in her letters she facetiously refers to herself as Io and Cassandra, prophetess and sibyl, though no doubt her view of Christian humility would prevent her calling herself a saint,

---

14. DeLuise with Timko, "Becoming the Poet: The Feminine Poet-Speaker in the Work of Elizabeth Barrett Browning," in *Virginal Sexuality and Textuality in Victorian Literature,* ed. Lloyd Davis, 90.

15. Horne, *A New Spirit of the Age,* 2:134, 140.

even in jest. In 1847 when Robert ran into "Father Prout" (the Reverend Francis Mahony) in Florence, he invited the priest to his home, but Mahony was in too much haste to meet Robert's "unveiled prophetess," Barrett Browning says in a letter to her sister Henrietta (*LHS* 61).

Daniel Karlin suggests that Elizabeth Barrett cultivates the "mystery" of her suffering and isolation in the poems as well as in her persona. (After all, she lived a recluse and revealed to Horne and others only what she wanted known about herself; her poems served as letters to the greater world.)[16] In addition to the mystery of the sickroom, though, she also embroidered into her own personal myth traits of wise scholar and prophet. Certainly if she is called to serve God (as all humans are), and if her particular gift is that of poetry, then it follows that she must use her inspiration as prophetess in God's service. As she says, if the poetic wing takes flight, then it inevitably rises to God. Creating poetry was, for Elizabeth Barrett Browning, always an act of worship.

In repeated allusions to Godiva, Io, Cassandra, and prophetesses in general, Barrett Browning builds upon the concept that little Elizabeth Barrett had in mind when she stole the matches to ignite her sacrifice to Athena. Lady Godiva becomes, for example, a personal symbol for courageous outspokenness. In Tennyson's "Godiva" published in 1842, Godiva "rode forth, clothed on with chastity," her act demonstrating courage and humanitarianism more than wisdom or faith. According to Leigh Hunt's essay on Godiva (which Barrett knew), however, Godiva rides naked "like an angelic spirit" through the streets of Coventry after her husband, tyrannical Leofric, offered to decrease the exorbitant taxes if she would demonstrate for the people's frailties in this unprecedented fashion. Hunt focuses not upon Godiva's courage so much as her wisdom, her mind "capable of piercing through the clouds of custom, of ignorance, and even of self-interest," and adding that, "It was reserved for a woman to anticipate ages of liberal opinion and to surpass them in the daring virtue of setting a principle above a custom." When Harriet Martineau confided to Barrett in 1844 that she has published in the *Athenaeum* an account of her healing by mesmerism, she adds, "I cannot tell you how the thought of *Godiva* has sustained & inspired me. Her century was not the only time, nor Coventry the only place, for the exercise of her spirit" (*BC* 9:268). Barrett is so taken with the comment that

16. Karlin, *The Courtship of Robert Browning and Elizabeth Barrett*, 257.

she repeats it in several letters, drawing the parallel between "Godiva's sacrifice for the redemption of her fellow citizens" and the stay-at-home British woman who takes more pride in mental and bodily weakness than in moral strength (*BC* 9:292). It is telling that she chooses the term *redemption,* which is laden with the theological implication of the Incarnation, Crucifixion, and Resurrection. In the section on Tennyson for *A New Spirit of the Age,* which she wrote with Horne, the lesson for the woman is applied to the poet in that "few are the poets who could equally well have dealt with the dangerous loneliness of the story of 'Godiva.'"[17] Barrett Browning's Aurora Leigh is a Godiva living the life of "dangerous loneliness," and no doubt Barrett considered her own life as lonely in its own way (at least until she met Robert). Certainly she considered herself as—like Godiva—a bold prophetess speaking out against the evils of the times, and speaking for the redemption of her fellow citizens. And not just citizens of Coventry, but citizens of the earth.

A similar wisdom allusion is the "divine yet rejected wisdom of Cassandra," loved by Apollo whom she tricked into giving her the power of divination. In *Trojan Women* she is consecrated a virgin of Apollo; as vatic bard she composes and chants the dirge for the fallen Trojans. In Aeschylus's *Agamemnon,* Cassandra as choisest flower of the spoil of Troy is taken by the Greek commander as his concubine. Cassandra prophesies his slaughter and her own at the hand of Agamemnon's wife, Clytemnestra, and her lover, but lives to proclaim, "Apollo . . . has stripped me here of my prophetic robes," and to comment on human affairs:

> When they are fortunate,
> one may liken them to a shadow;
> and if they are unfortunate
> A wet sponge with one dash blots out the picture.[18]

(Barrett Browning's prophetess Aurora alludes to this line in *Aurora Leigh.*) Barrett Browning, like Margaret Fuller and Florence Nightingale (who chose the prophetess's name for her autobiography), was fascinated by the Cassandra myth. In "Wine of Cyprus" she ranks Cassandra alongside Prometheus as great Aeschylean creations recalled by the wine, Cassandra

---

17. Tennyson, *Poems of Tennyson,* 734.65; Hunt, "Godiva," in *The Indicator, and the Companion; A Miscellany for the Fields and the Fire-side,* 4; Horne, *New Spirit,* 2:28.
18. Aeschylus, *Agamemnon,* in *The Complete Greek Tragedies,* 1:85.1269, 1326–29.

with her "wild eyes the vision shone in, / And wide nostrils scenting fate" (*CWEBB* 3:139.139–40). In her correspondence she calls herself a Cassandra, claiming that she too can smell the murder in the bathroom; and when Aurora cries out that Phoebus Apollo ("soul within my soul") has shot down all her works with his silver arrows (*AL* 5.414), she could well be alluding to Cassandra's invocation to Apollo in *Agamemnon,* his unheeded message a "burning arrow through the brain." Francis Bacon interprets the Trojan princess/prophetess as moral exemplar to those who do not listen to Apollo, god of harmony, but Barrett Browning emphasizes the prophecy of the female, not the harmony of her master.[19] Barrett Browning becomes Cassandra combined with Old Testament prophet when she smells the destruction wrought by political systems (chiefly the British empire) to exploit peoples.

Thus Barrett Browning is fascinated by Wisdom in various female guises: from myth (Athena, Cassandra, Godiva), from the bards (Homer, Dante, Pope), from biblical stories refashioned (Eve and Mary Magdalene), and from her own creation (Geraldine and the poet's guide in "A Vision of Poets"). Appropriating these versions of Wisdom for her own private mythology authenticates her voice as Victorian sage and as prophetess for God.

IV

Barrett Browning unabashedly employs her reputation for wisdom on behalf of society's weakest victims. Lending her authority as sage, saint, and pure woman, she is permitted to speak with impunity (unless, of course, her works appear "too pungently rendered to admit of a patriotic respect to the English sense of things" [*CWEBB* 3:314], as they did in "A Curse for a Nation," which some assumed to be directed against her *own* nation). Thus the poet becomes reformer, but it would be a mistake to assume that she developed a social conscience only when she had gained attention as virtuous woman and virtual saint. Rather, like the Minerva complex, her social conscience evolved as she matured. As Deirdre David says, "she creates herself as a ministering healer to an infected world."[20]

19. Bacon, *Wisdom of the Ancients,* in *Moral and Historical Works of Bacon,* 203.
20. David, *Intellectual Women,* 117.

About 1819, for example, the child Elizabeth Barrett demonstrates a precocious social conscience in "On Poverty," in which she entreats "Charity" to "soften the sufferings of the tortured poor."[21] In the volume *Poems, 1833*, "The Appeal" calls upon England to awaken to a universe where Sin and Death hold the ascendancy and where Britain through her empire can exercise power for good. Holding "the Spirit's sheathless sword," she can—if she will—spread the liberating word of Christianity to those in "woe and night" (*CWEBB* 1:159.49, 46). These early works, though lacking in subtlety and sophistication, foreshadow two important strands in Barrett Browning's social indictments: the horror of human suffering and the nation's obligation to relieve it, strands apparent in mature works such as "The Runaway Slave at Pilgrim's Point." Her social protests are connected, always, with her religion, which kept foremost in her mind the conviction that she was her neighbor's keeper. As her fictional Aurora puts it, "Where we disavow / Being a keeper to our brother, we're his Cain" (*AL* 4.467–68).

In her endeavor for social causes Barrett Browning joins the ranks of a diverse and international group of female writers who protest social evils, women such as Harriet Beecher Stowe, Harriet Martineau, Flora Tristan, and Harriet Taylor Mill. Ellen Moers in *Literary Women* uses the term *epic age* from Virginia Woolf's *A Room of One's Own* and invests it with a new meaning in her discussion of these social reformers. To Woolf the epic age of *Jane Eyre* meant smoldering acidity and rancor of women's writing; to Moers the epic quality comes from their "car[ing] less for the growing than for the changing of minds."[22] Among the writers of the new industrial age who make their statements about the injustices of such pursuits as manufacture and agriculture, foundries and factories (and their exploitation of human labor) are Elizabeth Gaskell, George Eliot, Charlotte Brontë, Caroline Bowles, Caroline Norton, Frances Trollope, Charlotte Elizabeth Browne (Mrs. Tonna), Geraldine Jewsbury, and of course Barrett Browning. As she says in "A Curse for a Nation," women know "[h]ow the heart melts and the tears run down" (*CWEBB* 3:355.40).

As for Barrett Browning, her social conscience is usually manifest in the words of a female prophet, a Victorian Wisdom. In the Old Testament prophets typically declared that Israel had broken the covenant with

21. Barrett Browning, *Hitherto Unpublished Poems*, 1:95.
22. Moers, *Literary Women*, 14–26.

Jehovah and warned that, unless the people repent, an angry God would exact suffering. The form is mirrored by St. John in *Revelation* and by various Victorian social prophets. The rhetorical device of an inspired prophet's rebuking a recalcitrant public is apparent in Victorian "sage discourse" or "oracular prose" (as John Holloway terms it when calling to attention the "prophetic utterances" of Victorians from the essayists Carlyle, Arnold, and Newman to the novelists Eliot and Hardy). George P. Landow (who like Holloway limits his application of the term to prose writers) goes on to characterize the traits of sage discourse as different from wisdom literature, which embodies the accepted, received wisdom of an entire society while the pronouncements of a Victorian sage—like the biblical prophet—counter the norms of contemporary society. Landow notes that typically the sage points to an evil sign of the times, interprets the phenomenon as a symptom of falling away from the paths of God (or nature), warns of disaster, and offers a vision of future bliss if the erring people or nation return to its God or its values.[23]

Like sage writing, Barrett Browning's poems of social protest also admonish of injustices offensive to God (and high-minded mortals) and threaten that suffering will fall upon the evildoer. Her threats and curses are usually delivered, Marjorie Stone says, "more daringly and resoundingly" and with "more finesse and feeling" than those of any other Victorian poet.[24] Though she protests in "A Curse for A Nation" that men, not women, should be chosen to deliver curses, she learns that "[a] curse from the depths of womanhood / Is very salt, and bitter, and good" (*CWEBB* 3:356.47–48). And if the woman is a poet/prophet, her words carry extra weight, especially if she is Minerva in one of her many incarnations.

"The Cry of the Children" (from Barrett's 1844 volume) sounds somewhat Blakean. Blake's chimney sweeps are "lock'd up in coffins of black"; for Barrett Browning's children the coffin is a blessing, the alternative being "Death in life" as slaves and martyrs in England's mines and factories (*CWEBB* 3:55.54). Barrett Browning was not, however, the

23. Holloway, *The Victorian Sage: Studies in Argument*, 3; Landow, *Elegant Jeremiahs: The Sage from Carlyle to Mailer*, 22–23; Landow, "Aggressive (Re) interpretations of the Female Sage: Florence Nightingale's *Cassandra*," in *Victorian Sages and Cultural Discourse: Renegotiating Gender and Power*, ed. Thaïs Morgan, 33–34.
24. Stone, "Cursing as One of the Fine Arts: Elizabeth Barrett Browning's Political Poems," 155.

only female poet to abhor in verse the enslavement of children. Eliza Cook, responding to R. H. Horne's *Report of the Commissioners on the Employment of Children* (the same document that inspired "The Cry of the Children"), says in "Our Father" that the rich English hypocritically pray to God from their bright, clean houses, while they neglect the basic necessities of the nation's despairing little working slaves. And Caroline Norton, in *A Voice from the Factories,* insists that freedom is a lie, "Merchant England" a tyrant, and the British senators who deny the sufferings in factories are prostitutes, selling their rhetoric to "justify this great and glaring wrong." Indeed, conditions in England's factories were horrific to outside observers, such as the French socialist reformer Flora Tristan. Visiting the English factories where pale, consumptive workers ("wizened, sickly and emaciated . . . thin and frail") toiled up to fourteen hours a day in improperly ventilated rooms in which song, laughter, and conversation were prohibited, Tristan concluded that English factory system to be the "greatest human misfortune"—worse even than slavery.[25] The mines were, if possible, even worse than factories with their combined evils of darkness, drudgery, and incredible danger for little slaves forced to toil underground in the "country of the free" (*CWEBB* 3:53.12). Using the resounding echoes of machinery grinding, reeling, spinning, moaning, turning, burning, and droning, Barrett demonstrates the wearing away of a child's life and spirit. In the rebuke, "how long, O cruel nation, / Will you stand, to move the world, on a child's heart" (*CWEBB* 3:58.153–54), she echoes the rhetoric of Old Testament prophecy such as that of Jeremiah: "How long wilt thou go . . . O thou backsliding daughter" (that is, the nation Israel) (Jer. 31:22). In admonishing England about the unmitigated greed and cruelty of her "gold-heaper[s]" (*CWEBB* 3:59.157), she further performs the office of prophet, delivering, in the final lines, not her own curse or God's, but that of a child, and a "child's sob in the silence curses deeper / Than the strong man in his wrath" (*CWEBB* 3:59.159–60).

In "The Cry of the Human" (also from the 1844 volume) ruthless profit is again the villain: a "plague of gold" and "curse of gold." As in "Lady Geraldine's Courtship" the poet indicts the social inequities of

---

25. Blake, "The Chimney Sweeper," in *The Complete Poetry and Prose of William Blake,* 10.12; Norton, *A Voice from the Factories,* 16.72, in *Victorian Women Poets: An Anthology,* ed. Leighton and Reynolds, 144; Tristan, *The London Journal of Flora Tristan 1842,* 69–70.

haves and have-nots, together with the hypocrisy of the exploiter, who advocates a laissez-faire economic policy in order that he may build for England a stable economy (and enrich himself at the expense of the poor on whom he stands to move the world).

> The rich preach "rights" and "future days,"
>   And hear no angel scoffing,
> The poor die mute, with starving gaze
>   On corn-ships in the offing.
>   (*CWEBB* 3:86.50–53)

In this work, however, the prophet speaks not a curse, but rather the plea that opens each stanza: "Be pitiful, O God!"—despite England's ill desserts for pity.

In "The Runaway Slave at Pilgrim's Point" Barrett Browning returns to the Promethean iconography that had fascinated her in her youth.[26] Published in the same volume with her second translation of Aeschylus's *Prometheus Bound* (in *Poems, 1850*), "Runaway Slave," however, creates a female Prometheus, something Barrett Browning had not attempted before. Slavery's dehumanization of the female person had been noted by Harriet Martineau, who commented that slavery is degrading to *all* women, but especially to female slaves, the object being "to rear as many [young fecund women] as possible, like stock, for the southern market." And Harriet Beecher Stowe's Cassy and Emmeline, sexual slaves of Simon Legree in *Uncle Tom's Cabin*, are, Stowe says, based upon the "public and shameless sale" of beautiful young women (chiefly of racially mixed blood) whose "particular attractions of form and features . . . connoisseurs prize so highly." Barrett Browning, like Martineau and Stowe, is impelled to indict the slave system for its particular cruelty to women. Julia Markus suggests that Barrett Browning believed she herself had African blood through her grandfather Charles Moulton and that "Runaway Slave at Pilgrim's Point" (a "peculiar poem to write on one's honeymoon") is—in part—about her *own* psychological slavery prior to her marriage. Whether or not Barrett Browning suspected African blood among her Jamaican ancestors, it is telling that she selects for the female slave's narrative the Promethean symbolism with which she had early identified and which to

---

26. It should be recalled that Prometheus brings enlightenment (the power of knowledge) to human beings.

her represents creativity, courage, and rebellion, but also love. Adapting both the Promethean defiance and the Promethean "free-souled reverent love" (which is in Jesus), she makes a memorable statement *in the voice* of the black slave who becomes, like Barrett Browning herself (or like Geraldine or Aurora), a prophet.[27]

In slaying the white baby conceived by the master's rape, the runaway slave of the poem rebels against the cruelty of white patriarchy (the white God, white angels, the slave master, and by extension the slave system). Her punishment—tied and hanging "like a gourd in the sun" at the whipping post—calls to mind Prometheus with the wedge in his heart, manacles on his wrist, and eagle wounding his side.[28]

Because human agency is required to effect freedom and justice, however, no god answers the woman's cries. God is similarly deaf in "The Cry of the Children": although the exploited children cry to God, "He is speechless as a stone" (*CWEBB* 3:57.126), his image reflected in the master exploiter is that of the indifferent "white God" in "Runaway Slave." Barrett Browning's God never swoops down to alleviate the suffering induced by humankind, but rather allows humans to take responsibility for social justice or injustice. As her Prometheus "[s]howed us looks of invocation / Turned to ocean and the sun" (*CWEBB* 3:139.144–45), Barrett Browning's slave invokes also the "sky and sea" (*RSPP* lines 7, 63, 85, 197), the father God (rather like Blake's Urizen) "[c]oldly [sitting] behind the sun" (*RSPP* line 89). But like the children exploited in England's factories and mines, she encounters silent endorsement of the slave/master system in that God is merely master among masters.[29] Finding the white God indifferent, the slave boldly compares herself to Jesus on the cross, warning that the captors cannot make a Christ of her, that the wounded wing of this black eagle will smite them too, falling from the cross to crush their seed (*RSPP* line 245), a curse that reverses

27. Martineau, *Society in America*, 2:118; Stowe, *Uncle Tom's Cabin; or, Life among the Lowly,* 491; Markus, *Dared and Done,* 106, 92, 93.

28. Mermin notes the Prometheanism of Barrett Browning's "The Runaway Slave" and "The Greek Slave," her sonnet about Hiram Powers's statue of a female slave at auction. Mermin argues that the Olympian culture provoking rebellion is both the false liberty of Pilgrim fathers and the misogynist version of classicism promulgated by Powers and others (*Origins of a New Poetry,* 160).

29. In referring to her family's involvement in the West Indian slave trade, Barrett writes that her own great grandfather "flogged his slaves like a divinity" (*BC* 13:24).

the prophecy usually interpreted to mean that Jesus as divine seed will bruise the head of Satan (Gen. 3:15).

Not only is the curse Promethean, but it also recalls the Old Testament prophecies against Israel for having broken the covenant; in Barrett Browning's poem the pilgrim sons have broken the freedom promise of their white pilgrim fathers, who on bended knee thanked God for liberty. Kneeling at the same spot and in the presence of the "pilgrim-souls" (*RSPP* line 8) of the dead founders, the slave lifts her black hand "to curse this land" that they had blessed (*RSPP* line 20). She bears no curse on *her* soul; it was the "fine white angels" (*RSPP* line 157), not herself, that liberated the spirit of her white baby. Leaving the punishers "curse-free / In [her] broken heart's disdain!" (*RSPP* lines 252–53), the slave again absolves herself; though they be cursed, they have brought the curse upon themselves and their descendants. In warning her persecutors of their own curse, the slave performs the role of prophet; in writing her story as a warning to slavers, the poet is doing the same.

"A Curse for a Nation" follows Landow's described pattern of sage discourse most closely, omitting only the last step of promised reward should the prodigal nation choose to repent. The *indictment* comes in section 1 with a series of parallel accusations ("Because you have broken . . . Because yourselves are standing . . . Because ye prosper in God's name . . . [*CWEBB* 3:356.53, 59, 65]); the *curse* in section 2 begins with a triad of prophecies, each beginning "Ye shall watch . . ." While prospering in God's name as "Freedom's foremost acolyte," America has completed Satan's work most perfectly, earning for herself the scorn of fools, the enmity of the just, a curse upon her own soul (*CWEBB* 3:356.61). The female prophet (like Moses when told to confront Pharaoh and lead the people out of Egypt) expresses herself unworthy and unwilling: "If curses must be, choose another / To send thy curse . . ." (*CWEBB* 3:354.7–8). But no other voice (or pen) is found to absolve the woman/prophet from the mission, which, significantly, comes not from herself, but from an "angel." As is the case with St. John on Patmos, who "heard a voice from heaven saying unto me, Write," the responsibility of agency is removed by this ploy (Rev. 14:13). The curse was "enjoined on me," and thus the amanuensis notes "the curse / Of God's witnessing Universe," the curse that, as the runaway slave says, the Americans have brought upon themselves (*CWEBB* 3:356.51, 358.116–17). By placing herself in the company of St. John (and Swedenborg, who also writes at divine dictation), Barrett Browning again wraps herself in the mantle of the sanctified prophet—convicting of sin, speaking God's disfavor and God's curse. Stone notes that, though she appears to surrender to the authority of the patriarchy (that is, the male angel), the poet liberates herself to pronounce the type of curse women were conventionally forbidden to utter. One might add that not only is she like the female prophets Miriam and Cassandra, as Stone notes, but she has also tapped into the sage discourse tradition devised and developed by the masculine literary discourse of her nation.[30]

"A Song for the Ragged Schools of London" (published first in a pamphlet in 1854 but appearing again posthumously in *Last Poems*) condemns England for her "[r]agged children, hungry-eyed" and huddled on doorsteps, her "[s]ickly children" whining low, her prostitutes "leering through the gas" (*CWEBB* 6:24.53, 25.69, 24.41), again reminding one of Blake's "new born Infants tear" and "youthful Harlots curse" in *Songs of Experience*[31] as well as of Barrett Browning's comments in *Aurora Leigh* that vice

> . . . slurs our cruel streets from end to end
> With eighty thousand women in one smile,
> Who only smile at night beneath the gas."
> (*AL* 8.413–15)

Though England is—in reputation—"strong," "rich," and "righteous," the speaker of "A Song for the Ragged Souls" insists that "England's cruel" (*CWEBB* 6:22.2, 5, 9, 15). The "Lordly English" take pride in their military might ("cannons on your shore"), their "free Parliament," and their unrivaled wealth ("Princes' parks, and merchants' homes"), justifying the poverty within the kingdom as the by-product of empire and progress (*CWEBB* 6:23.33–37).

> "Is it our fault?" you reply,
> "When, throughout civilisation,

30. Stone, "Cursing," 167, 166.
31. Blake, "London," in *Complete Poetry and Prose*, 27.15, 14. Barrett Browning's concern for prostitution is evidenced too in her correspondence, such as a reference to the forty thousand "wretched women" in London who live by selling their bodies (*LEBB* 2:213).

Every nation's empery
Is asserted by starvation?
(*CWEBB* 6:26.93–96)

Barrett Browning insists that the ragged and starving children—learning to become "[b]egging, lying little rebels"—will never learn the mercy of God through the hardness of the English (*CWEBB* 6:24.58). It is a great irony to be consoled by Christ's covenant while being ground under the social contract of English materialism, mercantilism, and empire. As she writes in "A Curse for a Nation," it is vain to pray that "Christ may avenge His elect"; rather, the prophet charges, the nation must consider itself elected to eradicate the curse and thus redeem its own soul (*CWEBB* 3:357.93). Like America, England has brought the curse upon herself.

Barrett Browning's poems of social protest are of varied effectiveness, "The Runaway Slave at Pilgrim's Point" being the most interesting among them. The others, however, are worth attention in that, just as surely as Eve is God's apologist in *A Drama of Exile* or Geraldine the example of classlessness in "Lady Geraldine's Courtship," they represent an important recurring strategy in the Barrett Browning canon. In these works the "inspired" prophetess or sage raises her poetic voice to condemn, counsel, prophesy, and curse. The female Wisdom as God's prophet in these works serves as predecessor of Barrett Browning's ultimate Athena/Sophia figure in *Aurora Leigh*.

V

Aurora Leigh is not, like Esther Summerson of *Bleak House,* a wisdom figure fully formed. Nor is she, like George Eliot's Dorothea, a Victorian woman yearning after wisdom that she is never to attain. Rather *Aurora Leigh* is a bildungsroman about a woman's *evolving* into wisdom. She attains wisdom not when she discovers herself capable of independence and female subjectivity, but when she fully understands the Swedenborgian text of divine wisdom and divine love. Barrett Browning's female hero is compared to the goddess Aurora of the dawn, blue-eyed Minerva, the Hebrew prophetess Miriam, Apollo's prophetess Cassandra, the male prophet Elisha and high priest Aaron, and Io and Danae who attracted the desires of Zeus (godly inspiration). Though she aspires to mortal and divine wisdom, however, she misunderstands both herself and God and must suffer in order to discover divine love and divine truth, to accept that divine works are *of the heart, the hands, the head* (which both she and her cousin Romney Leigh have, in their different ways, vainly tried to compartmentalize). She finally understands that humility and love will be her salvation both as woman and as poet. The lessons thus learned are Christian, Platonic, and Swedenborgian.

Several contemporary critics have noted that understanding Barrett Browning's intellectual quest is central to full comprehension of *Aurora Leigh*. Deirdre David sees Barrett Browning as a conservative poet whose art is "servant to patriarchy"; she argues that the ideology of *Aurora Leigh* is a marriage of art and politics, an "epithalamium for the essentialist sexual politics formed through Barrett Browning's . . . apprenticeship to male modes of intellectual training and aesthetic practice." Marjorie Stone notes that *Aurora Leigh* follows (and modifies) the tradition of Victorian sage in that Aurora is a prophetic speaker, and the work incorporates biblical allusion, typological patterning, polemical sermonizing, strategies of persuasion, and a vision of a new spiritual order. Stone goes on to praise Barrett Browning's "gynocentric adaptation" of sage strategies.[32] As David notes, Barrett Browning did accept the notion of the intellectual inferiority of women; as Stone insists, Aurora does, nevertheless, evolve into Victorian sage (as her creator has done). But it is also the case that Barrett Browning was more concerned with issues of spirituality than of gender; Aurora Leigh attains success as female intellectual and poet, yet is still questing for wisdom. She does not become wise until she understands—mind and soul—God's kingdom of divine wisdom, divine love, and divine use.

The first line of *Aurora Leigh,* "Of writing many books there is no end," is an allusion to the disenchanted seeker after wisdom in Ecclesiastes (12:12), and the last lines paraphrase John's apocalyptic vision of the new Jerusalem in Revelation (21:19–20). The biblical allusions, Old Testament and New, frame Aurora's story, as well as her quest for wisdom and for love. In thus framing her story, "blue-eyed Aurora" slyly puts herself in the company of the Old Testament and New Testament apocalyptic speakers for God, a bold and presumptive position, but then Barrett Browning had already occupied the Pythian tripod for some time.

32. David, *Intellectual Women,* 157; Stone, *Elizabeth Barrett Browning,* 138.

Barrett Browning places her novice poet who aspires after wisdom not only in the company of biblical and classical prophets but also among numerous female wisdom figures of the nineteenth-century British novel. (And, it should be noted, the poet was herself an avid reader of novels.) In Harriet Martineau's novel *Deerbrook,* which Barrett Browning knew and admired, Maria Young is wisdom personified, wisdom as equated with patience, stoicism, and pure love of truth. Lame and learned, "sensible" and "wise," Maria (whose name recalls the Virgin) lives in quiet solitude on the fringes of poverty, teaches her young students by means of Socratic inquiry (which his female teacher Diotima allegedly demonstrated to Socrates), befriends her neighbors and forgives their indiscretions and foibles, even rejoices when the heroine accepts the hand of Maria's childhood love, patiently accepting that no suitor will come calling for her; instead, "there are glimpses of heaven for me in solitude as for you in love. . . ."[33] Like the biblical Mary she serves as contemplation and as wisdom.

In Charles Dickens's 1853 novel *Bleak House,* Esther Summerson, whose name recalls the biblical savior of her Jewish nation, aspires to wisdom, which she defines as insight, prudence, and common sense, as well as being "industrious, contented, and true-hearted" and "useful, amiable, serviceable in all honest, unpretending ways." In fact Esther is called "Wisdom" and "my dear Minerva," by those who admire her equanimity, tact, modesty, forbearance, simplicity, compassion, and talent for contentment. At the novel's end the final mark of Esther's wisdom is her submission to suffering and to the wisdom of Providence, God's "Eternal wisdom."[34]

Charlotte Brontë's works also reveal another view of woman-as-wisdom. In *Shirley,* Shirley Keeldar and Caroline Helstone represent, respectively, goddess and prophetess, though both display human frailties (Shirley of the masculine variety and Caroline of the feminine). The "manly" Shirley (a tigress, she-eagle, and leopardess) thinks of herself as a Titaness, and a new Eve; the timid Caroline is given as dialogue some of Brontë's most eloquent thoughts about feminism. Caroline reads theology, studies Rousseau, and speculates why women should not have some creative purpose in life. She reinterprets St. Paul's injunction of

33. Martineau, *Deerbrook,* 45, 479.
34. Dickens, *Bleak House,* 1:27, 2:176, 262, 204.

"Let the woman keep silent" to "Let the woman speak out whenever she sees fit to make an objection." At seventeen she reads Shakespeare's *Coriolanus* aloud to Robert Moore, ostensibly to help the French speaker with his English, but actually for the political education of the man whom she loves and who represents "unwisdom." A "pretty priestess" and "little pastor," she is rewarded (by her new husband and the author) with the establishment of a woman's charity that she, along with other females, will administer. In *Villette* the English teacher Lucy Snowe is facetiously called "Mother Wisdom" and "Madame Minerva Gravity"; she seeks Truth, the "Titaness among deities." Like Martineau's Maria she philosophically accepts the loss of her first love to a more attractive friend; like Esther Summerson she offers example and counsel to those wise enough to take note. Janet Larson convincingly argues that not only Caroline and Shirley, but all Brontë protagonists speak as "sermonic prophets," echoing the voice of the novelist herself in "sage narrative."[35]

Charles Kingsley's Eleanor (Lady Ellerton) in *Alton Locke* speaks with the "low, half-abstracted voice" of Socrates' Diotima, her message that which Mary Magdalene learned at the feet of Jesus. Born rich, precocious, beautiful, and privileged, Eleanor longs to become philanthropist, philosopher, or feudal queen. Early in life she studied history and social science, Bentham and Malthus, Fourier and Proudhon. Mistakenly she gives to charities that serve but to keep the poor in degradation, she later concedes. From philanthropist and Chartist, she is converted to a "new Chartism": that of loving humankind as Christ has loved them. Dying, she selects a noble soul (Locke) and, following Carlyle's teaching, shows Locke his heavenly birthright and consecrates him to heaven. The final chapters of the novel are Lady Ellerton's extended sermon on Christ as Creator, Word, Inspirer, perfect Artist, Fountain of genius, great reformer, true King and demagogue, causing one to wonder whether Kingsley confuses wisdom and loquacity. Her mystic song endorses her Christian values and elevates herself to wisdom goddess:

> Own no rank but God's own spirit—
> Wisdom rule! and worth inherit!

35. Brontë, *Shirley*, 2:13, 1:101, 314; *Villette*, 1:108, 2:64, 276; Larson, "'Who Is Speaking?': Charlotte Brontë's Voices of Prophecy," in *Victorian Sages and Cultural Discourse*, ed. Morgan, 74, 78.

Work for all and all employ—
Share with all, and all enjoy—
God alike to all has given
Heaven as earth, and earth as heaven.[36]

Like Eleanor and Tennyson's Ida, Aurora Leigh is a seeker after wisdom, but she is also an aspiring poet and speaker of truth ("aspire" being one of the chief verbs illustrating her life). In the first blush of youth hers is the wisdom so-called of callow naïveté: "I felt so young, so strong, so sure of God! / So glad, I could not choose be very wise!" (*AL* 2.13–14). Like Eleanor, she errs in seeking wisdom on the wrong path.

Like the young Elizabeth Barrett, Aurora is early on an aspiring young scholar. Her earliest recollections are of a human father who attempted to teach love and wisdom. Before his death Leigh bequeathed his daughter a legacy of worldly and spiritual wisdom. The worldly wisdom is contained in his "[b]ooks, books, books" in which the young girl buries herself (nibbling away like a mouse at a mastodon) when she is removed from sunny Italy to cold England (*AL* 1.832, 837–38). The spiritual wisdom is his dying blessing, "Love, my child, love, love!" (*AL* 1.212). Marjorie Stone perceptively notes that the love and instruction given Aurora by her father, his "large / Man's doublet" in which she wraps herself, is to make the daughter his double, but that it is itself double in nature, signifying the wisdom of the Heart and wisdom of the Head, a connection Stone sees also in "George Sand, a Desire" (with Sand addressed as "large-brained woman and large-hearted man").[37] But Aurora is not yet ready to absorb the lesson of heart and head; she must make her way in the world worshiping at the altar of art, though it turns out that she must earn her mundane way by turning her hand in Grub Street as well.

When Romney invites Aurora to become his helpmeet, he tells her that life is serious business and that one's full engagement (head and heart) is required to conduct it seriously. But he is essentially recommending to her what Swedenborg calls the kingdom of use: a life devoted to charity work. Years later Romney is still harping on the same note: when she expresses disappointment in her art, he tells her once more that at least

---

36. Kingsley, *Alton Locke,* 2:289, 280.
37. Stone, "Genre Subversion and Gender Inversion: *The Princess* and *Aurora Leigh,*" 117–18.

she could have chosen to have been of use in the world. In Romney's marriage proposal to an idealistic young poet, he certainly fails to make his offer irresistible in telling her that her gender is weak for art but strong "for life and duty" (*AL* 2.357). It is the term *duty* (along with *use*) that ensures Aurora will not accept the proposal; she does not intend to be "used" by anyone.

In Swedenborgian wisdom—which Aurora at this stage of self-centered youth has failed to attain—God is the Divine Soul and Divine Man. He is source of Divine Wisdom and Divine Love, the true and the good, a person's voluntary life of love proceeding back to the good, the intellectual life going back to the true. There is a Platonic aspect to Swedenborg's thought in that in the spiritual world is the ideal reality to which concrete objects and human experiences correspond in the natural. Thus, even a human's love or knowledge is but reflection (or emanation) of the Lord's. God's kingdom is of Divine Wisdom, Divine Love, and Divine Use (encoded in *Aurora Leigh* in the words *head, heart,* and *hand*). Wisdom, love, and use all emanate from God and are experienced by humans via the influx (or inflow) from the divine. People who love turn toward the Lord but also toward neighbor, the celestial love being inward (that is, toward God), the spiritual love flowing outward, toward fellow persons as God's love flows from God's person into human souls.[38] Finally the central characters, Aurora and Romney, attain wisdom in that they understand these concepts and in their reunion piece together the Swedenborgian gospel, parts of which each has known intuitively from the beginning. As James Borg says, Barrett Browning finds in Swedenborg not only the most satisfactory gloss on Revelation and the life of Jesus (the Swedenborgian Jesus being, in Borg's view, a feminine Christ), but also a means of interpreting the Bible through the principles of love and wisdom.[39] Barrett had long affirmed the deity as source of Love and Wisdom; to a friend she notes, "May He who is the Beloved in the sight of His Father & His Church be near . . . & cause you to *feel* as well as *know* the truth, that what is sudden sorrow, to our judgments, is only long prepared mercy, in *His* will whose names are *Wisdom* & *Love*" (*BC* 3:162).

---

38. Swedenborg, *Heaven and Hell,* 31, 80; Swedenborg, *Angelic Wisdom,* 183.
39. Borg, "The Fashioning of Elizabeth Barrett Browning's *Aurora Leigh,*" 135. In his dissertation Borg emphasizes that Swedenborg's "Divine Man" is androgynous (5) feminine (128), Apollonian (69), and Promethean (80).

Barrett Browning's play upon the word *hand,* then, emphasizes the *Gospel of Good Works* earlier espoused by Eve.[40] In Swedenborgian terminology, it is the kingdom of use. If she were to undertake Romney's dream at the dawn of her adulthood, however, her "use" would not be an emanation of celestial love, but only duty (the kind that Aurora sees in her "caged bird" aunt who always insists that young Aurora never sit with empty hands). But Aurora does not want her hands employed in Romney's kingdom of use:

> My right hand teaching in the Ragged Schools,
> My left hand washing in the Public Baths,
> What time my angel of the Ideal stretched
> Both his to me in vain.
>
> (*AL* 2.795–98)

According to Swedenborg, works of the hand may not necessarily correspond to "divine use," for there can be many motivations (even selfishness) for doing civic or social good.[41] Romney *thinks* his motivations are entirely unselfish, and he *feels* that with Aurora at his side he will rise to the best humanitarianism of which he is humanly capable. (In his way, he also stands on tiptoe and "aspires.") He senses something of the influx of God, however imperfectly, when he tells Aurora that if they two enjoy conjugal love, their love will outflow to the suffering and degraded masses whom he wishes to save: "love . . . generates the likeness of itself / Through all heroic duties" (*AL* 2.423–25).

But Aurora is at the point in her quest when she must hold out for the kingdom of the mind, for divine inspiration. Or she hopes to engage mind and heart in her poetic endeavors without realizing that, closing her heart's door to Romney, she is engaging only a fragmented part of her human love. She rejects Romney because she does not know she loves him, does not think he is capable of loving anything except his social theories. For Aurora, it is better to stand on tiptoe as poet/priestess with both arms reached out, straining upward to burn down the god of inspiration.

---

40. In *Aurora Leigh,* there are the touches of the hands of Aurora's father, Romney, the angel, God, Zeus (all in the biblical sense of "laying on of hands"), but also there are references to reaching hands, proposal (and refusal) of hands in marriage, union of "hand in hand," and the work of one's hand in art or in charity.

41. Swedenborg, *Angelic Wisdom,* 122.

At this point in her wisdom quest, Aurora bears a resemblance to woman as failed or incomplete wisdom, to Victorian figures like Ida and Dorothea, in Alfred, Lord Tennyson's *The Princess* and George Eliot's *Middlemarch*, respectively.[42] The iconography of Ida's university/utopia in Tennyson's poem makes clear the values it will uphold: a bust of Pallas, a brooch with the device of Diotima teaching Socrates, a satin tent wrought with the triumph of the poetess Corinna over Pindar, bronze valves embossed with the queen Tomyria who slew Cyrus the Great, oaths administered in the name of St. Catherine of Alexandria who confuted the fifty wise men sent to convert her from Christianity. Thus, woman's ascendancy in wisdom, in metaphysics, in art, in logic and rhetoric, even in treachery. But the university is infiltrated from the outside and undermined by internal jealousy, and when the aggressors are wounded, Ida converts her university to a hospital. (No doubt Barrett has Tennyson's poem in mind when, skeptical of the role of Nightingale and the Crimean nurses, she says, "Since the siege of Troy and earlier, we have had princesses binding wounds with their hands . . ." [*LEBB* 2:189].) Ida admits her failure: that she has "sought far less for truth than power / In knowledge."[43] Learning does not fulfill all of life's longings; nor does it ensure wisdom. As Aurora puts it when she is unable to find happiness and truth in the library of her dead father:

> . . . the world of books is still the world,
> And worldlings in it are less merciful
> And more puissant.
>
> (*AL* 1.748–50)

Like the Princess, Aurora fails to discover ultimate meaning in knowledge. In her books the wicked are winged like angels, the beautiful seems right because of beauty, the feeble wrong because of weakness, and it is nearly impossible to separate wheat from chaff.

Eliot's Dorothea Brooke searches for wisdom in intellectual knowledge as well as in good works; she "wished, poor child, to be wise herself."

---

42. Of the nineteenth-century works mentioned in this section, Barrett Browning knew all except *Middlemarch*, published after her death. It is included, not as a formative influence on *Aurora Leigh* but as illustration of the age's preoccupation with woman as aspiring wisdom or wisdom attained.

43. Tennyson, 7.221–22, in *Poems of Tennyson*, 837.

Considered a Christian Antigone, a St. Catherine, a Laura or Beatrice, and like Eliot's Romola possessing the aura of the Virgin Mary, Dorothea is finally a St. Theresa who turns out to be "foundress of nothing." Her reading list resembles that of the youthful Elizabeth Barrett. A self-taught scholar of sorts, Dorothea has read Pascal and Jeremy Taylor, would have married either of the great men Hooker or Milton because she longs for a husband who like a father can teach her to read Greek. She takes as husband the dried-up scholar Edward Casaubon and as her example Milton's daughters who read (or rather pronounced) Greek and Latin for their blind father but could not understand what they read. But when she becomes Casaubon's amanuensis, he refuses to share knowledge with her. Dorothea cannot imagine Milton would have behaved in such a way (although if he had, she could no doubt have forgiven Milton). Repeatedly she is dissuaded from grandiose social reform schemes by "wiser" men. Sensing that her considerable wealth is a burden unless she does something worthwhile with it, she puts a new bell on the schoolhouse and befriends the doctor and various Middlemarchers of middling abilities. George Eliot is bemused, remarking that when everybody is healthy and has flannel and nobody's pig has died, what is there for a well-intentioned woman of wisdom in the village.[44]

Like Dorothea, Aurora experiences spiritual longings. As Romney has sensed that he needs Aurora for his (and her) spiritual completion, Aurora has also experienced intuitions of the soul. Neither as would-be education reformer like Ida nor would-be social reformer like Eleanor and Dorothea (with hands employed in the kingdom of use), she knows intuitively that she has been called by the divine calling of poet. In this regard, she appropriates the strength and inspiration of mythic wisdom figures also inspired (or called or possessed) by God or Jove, among them Io/Isis, the Pythian of Apollo, Cassandra, and the biblical Miriam. For example, in Romney's dismissing Aurora's works as "innocent distraction" (*AL* 4.1117) to entertain youths and maidens, he rather contemptuously suggests that she, like the prophetess Miriam, can play the cymbal and compose a song of victory once the modern Moses (presumably himself) has delivered the masses from poverty and want (*AL* 2.171). Aurora, however, undermines the implied criticism by appropriating the Miriam figure into her own litany of female heroes: Aurora will—like the Hebrew

44. Eliot, *Middlemarch: A Study of Provincial Life,* in *Writings of George Eliot,* 12:2, 14:444.

composer—sing the song of her choice. In the words of Alicia Holmes, she "trivializes Romney's trivialization of herself."[45] Further, Aurora dares to confront Romney about his unwise mistakes just as Miriam chastises Moses for his marriage of a foreign woman. Finally, however, Romney acknowledges her wisdom as "My Miriam," the voice of wisdom and salvation he has heard through reading her poems (*AL* 8.334).

Aurora dons the mantle of not only the female prophet (Cassandra and Miriam) but also the male, just as surely as Elizabeth Barrett had in her earliest efforts chosen her models from the ranks of male literary poet/prophets. Aurora is an Elijah, but also an Aaron (her aspirations to the role of Moses' brother as high priest combined with Moses' sister as poet/prophetess serve as foil to Romney's aspiration to the role of Moses/messiah). When she is in Florence suffering from writer's block and dearth of inspiration, she fears to "jingle bells upon [her] robe / Before the four-faced silent cherubim . . ." (*AL* 7.1303–4), the allusion to the bells and pomegranates of Aaron's robe (and Robert Browning's poems).[46] And when she gives up hope of marriage, she feels like Aaron doffing his robe in death.

Aurora, even while still seeking wisdom, senses that the poet/prophet has a mission to keep open the paths between the divine and the material, the seen and unseen, the inner and outer person. Her intimations of immortality inform both of preexistence (like that of Wordsworth's "Intimations" ode) and of eternity.

> . . . There's not a flower of spring
> That dies ere June but vaunts itself allied
> By issue and symbol, by significance
> And correspondence, to that spirit-world
> Outside the limits of our space and time,
> Whereto we are bound.
>
> (*AL* 5.120–25)

Aurora's poems will not be merely of nymphs and maidens, flowers and trees, but will express a higher truth, imbued with

45. Holmes, "Elizabeth Barrett Browning: Construction of Authority in *Aurora Leigh* by Rewriting Mother, Muse, and Miriam," 601.

46. For this insight I am indebted to Margaret Reynolds's "Critical Introduction" in her edition of *Aurora Leigh*, 46, and her footnote, 659. As readers of Robert Browning are aware, bells and pomegranates are embroidered on Aaron's priestly robe.

> motions of imperfect life
> . . . oracles of vital Deity
> Attesting the Hereafter
> (*AL* 1.822–24)

She knows that poets are

> The only speakers of essential truth,
> Opposed to relative, comparative,
> And temporal truths . . .
> (*AL* 1.860–62)

Taking issue with Locke's tabula rasa theory, Aurora also argues that the soul is not a "clean white paper," but rather a "palimpsest, a prophet's holograph" defiled, erased, and covered with an obscene text almost obliterating the strokes of alpha and omega signifying our inheritance from God (*AL* 1.825–32). She senses too that the inner life in some way informs the outer and that the inner is the dwelling place of soul. She will live so the inner life will inform the outer, will strive to rain Zeus (or the angel) down so that her flesh

> Thrills inly with consenting fellowship
> To those innumerous spirits who sun themselves
> Outside of time.
> (*AL* 1.913–15)

But in choosing her separate, single life she has "cleft the twain in half"; she has erred in attempting to prove that the woman's soul, like the man's, can "carry the whole octave" (*AL* 2.1186). She has also allowed the gender issue (which is to Barrett Browning of secondary importance) to displace the highest understanding of heart and mind, that is, divine wisdom and divine love. Let Romney live by his partial systems, his "sorry shifts / Of hospitals, almshouses, infant schools . . ." (*AL* 2.1223–24), she says, but *she* will live completely—mind and spirit.

> . . . Observe—"I," means in youth
> Just *I*, the conscious and eternal soul
> With all its ends, and not the outside life,
> The parcel-man, the doublet of the flesh,
> The so much liver, lung, integument,

Which make the sum of "I" hereafter when
World-talkers talk of doing well or ill.
(*AL* 3.283–89)

Joyce Zonana, in arguing that Aurora becomes her own muse, says that Romney as virile actor in the world is making a "gendered commitment" to the material, while Aurora makes an "equally gendered choice" for the spiritual: he the male path of the body and she the female path of the spirit.[47] This argument, though fascinating, misses two points: one, that in Barrett Browning either gender can make either choice; two, that either art or charity can be motivated by selfhood or by celestial love. While either gender can be dedicated to aesthetic strivings or to charitable duty, in Victorian literature it is usually the male who, as in Barrett's "The Poet's Vow" or Tennyson's "Palace of Art," resolves to live for art alone. Conversely, it is usually *woman,* not man, who is assigned (as mother, wife, daughter, nurse, or nun) to ease suffering, a "duty" and "use" of which Barrett Browning, like Aurora, is skeptical. In *A Drama of Exile,* Adam makes the mistake of assigning to woman the works of charity (certainly not to him a virile commitment), but—as noted in an earlier chapter—the poet insists that all are to work in God's kingdom. In *Aurora Leigh* she holds out for the union of soul and body, works inspired by head and heart, the whole Christian person united and complete—internal and external.

        . . . Natural things
And spiritual,—who separates those two
In art, in morals, or the social drift,
Tears up the bond of nature and brings death,
Paints futile pictures, writes unreal verse,
Leads vulgar days, deals ignorantly with men,
Is wrong, in short, at all points.
(*AL* 7.763–69)

When Aurora rejects Romney, she leaves him to his "social figments, feints, and formalisms" (*AL* 3.18), and these are not enough to engage a man's heart and soul. At the time of his marriage proposal to Marian

47. Zonana, "The Embodied Muse: Elizabeth Barrett Browning's *Aurora Leigh* and Feminist Poetics," 250.

Erle, he no longer believes in "mutual love" but only "common love," people working in pairs whether in "galley-couplings or in marriage-rings" (*AL* 4.334). Although Romney in his proposal of marriage to Aurora has declared that life means "[b]oth heart and head,—both active, both complete, / And both in earnest" (*AL* 2.131–32), Aurora in refusing his offer has deprived him of the engagement of his heart; thus he proceeds to do his work of the hands, minus the inflow of love from the heart. Aurora, who thinks herself so much the wiser of the two, accuses him of living by diagrams and systems, having memorized the doctrines of socialist theorists, together with statistical tables about poverty and want. But she is not wise enough to see that he lives so because, in failing to love him, she has inadvertently precluded his spiritual completion. His is now a purely rational approach to solving the inequities he sees around him. On his side, he accuses Aurora of thinking too much with the heart rather than the head when he reminds her that a woman weeps for individual evils rather than the greater scope of cosmic poverty and despair.

Thus with his own two good hands, his considerable wealth and influence, his pamphlets and his voice in the Commons, and his dedication to the "systems" that he has discovered, Romney sets out to renovate the decaying world and liberate the dying from the graves of poverty and despair. We know the result. Because he tries to work alone (without the squires or the church), because he arrogantly believes *his* system the best (that is, he puts his faith in his own *proprium*), because he has tried to save human bodies without illuminating their souls with the divine wisdom and love of God, he is from the beginning doomed to failure.

As for Aurora, she earns success, the critics and her public praising her when she does bad things well, good things indifferently. Her acquaintances (both admirers and detractors) recognize in her the aspiration to prophecy (as Barrett Browning's critics and biographers recognize in her a similar aspiration), and they award her with verbal laurels: Lord Howe calling her Pallas and prophetess of Delphi, Kate Ward wishing to inherit her prophet's mantle as Elijah does from Elisha (*AL* 3.54), Aurora herself calling her own premonitions a "prophet in my heart" (*AL* 6.962), Romney hailing her as prophetess Miriam, even her enemy Lady Waldemar greeting her as a "youthful prophetess," her blue eyes following the gray flight of doves between temple columns (*AL* 3.485–88).

As intellectual and poet Aurora works the work of the heart and head, although there is an indefinable something missing because, as the reader knows and Aurora later learns, she has closed the door to Romney's love as an emanation of God's divine love. It is not until her heart moves her to accept Marian and the illegitimate child that she begins the move outward from self and into the kingdom of use, the "use" being to take Marian in and create a home for her, and to assist in parenting the baby (along with Marian, serving as "father and mother"), an enormous burden (or blessing) for one who has like Aurora in the past decade lived alone, answering to no whims but her own. It should be added that, because Romney is still missing from her life, she is still unfulfilled. Although she tells herself she *should* be happy, "Tenderly / And mournfully [she] lived" (*AL* 7.1052–53). Nor will she be happy until she is fully engaged heart, mind, and soul, and for Barrett Browning that means love of God, of Romney, of her work, and of all fellow creatures.

In contrast to the educated, well-read Romney and Aurora, Marian is the "natural person," a nettle that grows unaided. Her innocence is untainted by the intellectual arrogance and stubbornness seen in Romney and Aurora. Being innocent she is—as Swedenborg would say—in the kingdom of wisdom and love (though it is, like childhood, a natural wisdom and love, not a celestial). When Aurora half regrets not marrying Romney, she says that if she had done so, she would by this time have had chubby children hanging on her neck to "keep me low and wise" (*AL* 2.517), the kind of lowness and wisdom that come from natural innocence and love, the kind that Marian will portray, the kind that the "hard old King" of *The Princess* insists to be woman's *only* allowed form of wisdom: "The bearing and the training of a child / Is woman's wisdom."[48] But Aurora is incapable of attaining "low wisdom" because she has already cultivated too far the intellectual knowledge and accompanying arrogance that lead away from innocence and, if not disciplined by love and use, lead to the hell of selfhood.

A dramatic instance reveals Marian's innocent and natural love. When the seamstress Lucy Gresham is dying, Marian feels she cannot lavish her handiwork on a lady's garment (in the workshop where Romney has set her up as seamstress), for perhaps "God has a missing hand" needed to give Lucy a cool drink or to hold the "lamp of human love arm-high . . . Until the angels, on the luminous side / Of death had got theirs ready" (*AL* 4.41, 46, 48–49). When Marian has eased the

48. Tennyson, 5.457, 455–56, in *Poems of Tennyson,* 815.

deaths of Lucy and Lucy's ungrateful crone of a grandmother, laid out the corpses, and swept the floor clean of coffin sawdust, Romney in "putting out his hand to touch this ark" (of Godly love) (*AL* 4.147) finds a woman's hand that, though untutored, is engaged in God's kingdom of use. Jesus taught that inasmuch as one ministers unto the least in the kingdom, that action is done unto Jesus himself. Marian's charity is therefore not motivated by self-love, desire for reputation, or formula derived from socialist speculation. That Marian's soul is radiant and saintly makes her rape all the more heinous and sympathy for her all the more sentimental. Thus, Victorian readers often preferred her to Aurora, and modern critics (especially feminist critics) are intrigued with her as Mariology or as source of spiritual renovation for Aurora, avenue for Aurora's subjectivity. Marian's attraction is in her innocence and selflessness, in biblical terminology her love pure and unblemished before the world. It is the humble, uncomplicated, natural love Romney desires (and now thinks he requires) to complete his practical "thumbnail" plan to alleviate human ills. In his second marriage proposal, Romney thinks not only to restore the social classes of rich and poor slashed apart by the tyrannous sword that pierced Christ's heart; he also plans to yoke his man's conscience *(of the head)* with (Marian's) woman's love *(of the heart)*. It is to his credit that he senses he is incomplete; it is his error in choosing a woman whom he does not truly love.

When Aurora and Romney are united, however, both are ready to live out the physical life as influenced by soul, to assist humankind in bringing about the New Jerusalem (to Swedenborg, as to Barrett Browning, a kingdom based on Divine Wisdom and Divine Love). But the two principals must come to one another (and before the deity) in humility because both have been proud. Aurora acknowledges that it would not have hurt her to have shown a "gentler spirit" and "less arrogance"(*AL* 8.497), and she is now a decade later "perforce more wise" although also sadder (*AL* 8.534). She sees that she put herself on a level face-to-face with God ("As He and I were equals" [*AL* 9.634]), while Romney was— in her judgment—beneath her. She now regrets that she scorned him for having "sought a wife / To use . . . to use!" and she invites him to "take my love / And use it roughly, without stint or spare . . ." (*AL* 9.671–72, 9.674–75). Romney, not to be outdone in contrition, stands "worthier of contempt, / Self-rated, in disastrous arrogance . . ." (*AL* 8.696–97). Like Tennyson's Ida and the prince who are wiser when they agree that together they can work to elevate woman's position, Aurora and Romney will bring a combined fervency to their own work: that of saving social systems by renovating souls.[49]

As for humility as an avenue to wisdom, the connection is made in Barrett's theological reading even predating her Swedenborgian period. For example, the English theologian Jeremy Taylor, whom Barrett had known since youth, warns against pride:

> First, That pride is like a canker and destroys the beauty of the fairest flowers, the most excellent gifts and graces; but humility crowns them all. Secondly, That pride is a great hindrance to perceiving the things of God, and humility is an excellent preparative and instrument of spiritual wisdom.[50]

Barrett Browning claims, however, that her primary source in religious faith and doctrine is not to be found in theologians, but rather in her reading of the Bible. The connection between humility and wisdom is well established in the wisdom literature of the Old Testament; for example, "When pride cometh, then cometh shame: but with the lowly is wisdom" and "The fear of the Lord *is* the instruction of wisdom; and before honour is humility" (Prov. 11:2, 15:33). New Testament doctrine emphasizes the contrast between intellectual wisdom and the simplicity of Christian parable and preaching. For example, Paul in his famous sermon on Mars Hill denies the Greek gods and affirms the "unknown God" (as Elizabeth Barrett was to do in "The Dead Pan"). New Testament doctrine warns to distinguish between "earthly, sensual, devilish" wisdom and that which "descendeth from above" (James 3:15). Aurora realizes that there is nothing high that was not first low, that "[m]y humbleness, said One, has made me great!" (*AL* 9.857).

The temptation to pride was the same fight that the young child Elizabeth Barrett fought. At fifty Elizabeth Barrett Browning is still face-to-face with God, still struggling with the same issues (suffering, grace, work, humility, redemption, rebirth). In the Leigh cousins the Christian poet dramatizes her own struggles. In humility, the reborn Romney will

---

49. In *The Princess,* the male sums up the goal and the female assents: the Prince says man should gain from woman increased sweetness and moral height, while woman gains in mental breadth, but does not abandon "childward care." They will exist "side by side, full-summed in all their powers" (7.267, 272, in *Poems of Tennyson,* 839).

50. Taylor, *Rule and Exercises,* 126.

work with "Christ's little ones" and Aurora will "work for two," the two understanding:

> . . . Beloved, let us love so well,
> Our work shall still be better for our love,
> And still our work be sweeter for our work,
> And both commended, for the sake of each,
> By all true workers and true lovers born.
>
> (*AL* 9.924–28)

Such is the path to Divine Wisdom and Divine Love, preparing the receptive soul for transcendence—for her face-to-face with God.

There was less than universal approbation among critics when Barrett Browning published *Aurora Leigh*—although much praise from her reading public. In some circles, however, the ailing poet remained a sibyl, a latter-day apostle John. The Brownings' intimate friend Isa Blagden considers *Aurora Leigh* a "Revelation," and Robert Lytton (Owen Meredith) calls it the great epic of the age, placing Barrett Browning in the company of Dante and Milton for having taken the weight of the whole age upon her shoulders, "yet you stand erect and full height under the weight of it, Atlantean indeed!"[51] From the successes of *Aurora Leigh* the poet turned her final poetic energy to the question of Italian unification; by dabbling in politics she risked her reputation as prophetess and saint. But then one could never accuse Barrett Browning of intellectual or spiritual (or, for that matter, political) timidity.

The first chapter of this study explored the struggle of the young poet Elizabeth Barrett to abandon pride even though she wished to become Prometheus. She took to heart the Christian injunction against the seventh deadly sin. It is a lesson that Aurora Leigh struggles to learn, even while she stands on tiptoe and aspires to draw down the holy fire of inspiration. Elizabeth Barrett Browning, like Aurora, fought the perpetual battle against hubris, and the tension between pride and humility is everywhere apparent in her work. In part she is the humble Christian accepting that she is unworthy of grace, accepting suffering and servanthood in God's kingdom; in part she is God's holy witness of

---

51. Earl of Lytton, *Letters from Owen Meredith (Robert, First Earl of Lytton) to Robert and Elizabeth Barrett Browning*, 132, 130.

the true—a rather exalted position. A spokeswoman for God who dresses herself in the priestly robe of Aaron, rebukes in tones of Elijah, echoes the visions of St. John, and undertakes to explain St. Paul is, on the one hand, a presumptuous vessel for God's divine inspiration. But just as surely as she felt called to be a Christian, she was called to be a poet. And, to her, all true poetry is but religion.

Conclusion

In 1861 when Elizabeth Barrett Browning died, the English poet
Dora Greenwell wrote a sonnet praising the woman whom Chris-
tina Rossetti called "the Great Poetess of our own day and nation."
Greenwell's sonnet closes with a personal testimony:

> . . . I only loved thee, only grew,
> Through wealth, through strength of thine, less poor, less weak;
> Oh, what hath death with souls like thine to do?[1]

Despite the syntactic clumsiness of the final line, the sonnet testifies
to the esteem in which female poets of Victorian England held Barrett
Browning: great of soul and powerful in influence. The young Elizabeth
Barrett had looked everywhere for poetic grandmothers and found none;
Elizabeth Barrett Browning had become, at the end of her life, a poetic
godmother for a generation of aspiring British female poets. (Through
her prolific correspondence, however, we know what Barrett Browning
thought of many Victorian "poetesses," and in most cases she was less
impressed with them than they were awed by her.) Among her immediate
predecessors and successors were also several who, like Barrett Browning,
were devoutly Christian in their personal lives and in their verse. In
some cases their religious poetry is grounded in Scripture; in some,
liturgy, homily, or sermon; in others (notably Christina Rossetti) there is a
decided influence from the tradition of devotional poetry (Dante serving
as poetic grandfather for Rossetti as Milton, among others, did for Barrett
Browning); and with the exception of Felicia Hemans and Mary Howitt
(both older than Elizabeth Barrett Browning), these leading female poets
of religious verse also looked to the works of Barrett Browning and saw
themselves as writing in a tradition that dated from her (in the sense that

---

1. Rossetti, preface to *Monna Innominata,* in *Complete Poems of Christina Rossetti,* 2:86;
Greenwell, "To Elizabeth Barrett Browning in 1861," in *Poems,* 193.12–14. Greenwell
dedicated the 1867 volume to Barrett Browning.

she was to them *the* British female poet who wrote devotional verse worth imitating).

Though Barrett Browning shares with these several poets an intensity of religious faith and calling, she introduces certain ideas—in both religious and secular verse—that others do not. For example, she is singular among them in positioning herself as priestess/prophet/sage; none of the others use (poetic) sage discourse to pronounce condemnation and exhortation, curses and warnings, as vehemently and effectively as she does (though Greenwell entered the political fray, and Rossetti was hailed by admirers as a divine prophetess and inheritor of Barrett Browning's mantle). None except Barrett Browning professed Swedenborgian views on resurrection and the proximity of departed souls, the doctrine of correspondences, and Divine Wisdom, Divine Love, and Divine Use (especially important in *Aurora Leigh*). None wrote as extensively on politics. Her religion, in fact, prompted Barrett Browning to speak out boldly on contemporary politics (notably in *Casa Guidi Windows* and *Poems before Congress*). Greenwell daringly follows Barrett Browning in writing several overtly political works, while Rossetti deliberately avoids the risk of accusation that she is too political and therefore too masculine.[2] Among women poets of the age none is as consciously allusive to classical and scholarly tradition, though most allude to the Bible (both Old and New Testaments) with great intimacy. Excepting perhaps Rossetti, few studied theology and the Church Fathers as Barrett Browning did. (Rossetti was knowledgeable on contemporary Anglican theology and had read Catholic and Protestant theologians—from Augustine to Hooker—and quotes or paraphrases them in verse and devotional prose.[3] She also knew the Tractarians; the pamphlets that Aurora Leigh calls "tracts *against* the times" are, for Rossetti, tracts *for* the times.)

Several Victorian women poets, nonetheless, were interested in theological concepts that preoccupied Barrett Browning throughout her career. For instance, several wrote of Christian humility and personal unworthiness to accept grace (some recalling the Mary Magdalene story as personal analogue for Christ's redemption of womanhood). Among them the theme of religious exile is frequently invoked (not only in Eve's story,

2. Deploring the suffering of war (in "The German-French Campaign, 1870–1871"), Rossetti adds an apology that her aim is "expressing human sympathy, not political bias" (*Complete Poems of Christina Rossetti,* 1:214).

3. See the preface of Rossetti's *Called to Be Saints,* for example, in which she quotes from Hooker's *Laws of Ecclesiastical Polity.*

but also in other exiles of ballad, dramatic monologue, and poetic exemplum). Frequently they warn that this is a vain and crumbling world that the Christian pilgrim ought not to love too fondly. Especially memorable in this regard is Christina Rossetti, who proclaims in Solomon's phrase that this world is "vanity of vanities," a realm of "hope deferred." The renunciation of earth's vain pleasures is perhaps best exemplified in the "convent threshold" poems of Rossetti, works in which the persona chooses a holy life as the bride of Christ. Closely allied to the theme of exile (with its attendant concepts of suffering, unworthiness, obedience, repentance, and humility) is that of invitation to repent (often to discipleship through "works" and faith as antidote to sin and exile). Finally, the doctrine of resurrection recurs throughout the works of woman poets of Victoria's era. None of them expresses the idea that the prophesied Apocalypse is merely the end of a political era, as Barrett Browning does (noted in Chapter 3), but Rossetti apparently also subscribed to an unusual belief in regard to Apocalypse. Specifically, she accepted the doctrine of millenarianism and soul sleep: that there is an initial judgment upon death, but the soul is dormant until the final judgment when each person is rewarded in eternal resurrection with the elect. This doctrine enjoyed only brief coinage in nineteenth-century Anglicanism.[4] Several female poets, however, describe the joys of the Christian heaven and incorporate resurrection theology to mirror transformed life in Christ in this present world. Finally, in the works of some of Barrett Browning's successors, especially Rossetti, are contained several illuminating treatments of woman's spirituality.[5]

I

Felicia Hemans (1793–1835) shares with Elizabeth Barrett Browning an early devotion to poetry and to religion, as well as the conviction that the two cannot be separated. At the age of nine little Felicia Browne

4. Jerome J. McGann speculates that Rossetti's poetry did not enjoy the attention of such writers as Hopkins because the doctrine of soul sleep is unorthodox ("The Religious Poetry of Christina Rossetti," 135–41).

5. The following wrote religious verse or hymns: Caroline Bowles Southey, Charlotte Elliott, Felicia Hemans, Sarah Flower Adams, Frances Anne Kemble, Charlotte Brontë, Anne Brontë, Jean Ingelow, Anna Letitia Waring, Dora Greenwell, Adelaide Anne Procter, Christina Rossetti, Frances Ridley Havergal, Alice Meynell. (Not all receive attention in this study.)

addressed to God a poetic prayer for virtue, and at twelve a hymn petitioning for "energetic fire" in raising thankful praise.[6] Her prayer must have been answered: the adult Hemans, having suffered no lack of creative energy, published well over three hundred works. One of Hemans's volumes *(Records of Woman)* is on female experience, numerous works feature soldiers and heroes on the world's stage *(Lays of Many Lands, Tales and Historic Scenes, Songs of the Cid, Greek Songs)*, some poems are meditative verse, but a great many of the works in all volumes are religious, in the form of invocations to God, narratives of exemplary religious forbears both biblical and secular, and Christian reassurance (of redemption, resurrection, grace, the efficacy of faith). Like the young Barrett, Hemans was a romantic poet. Influenced by Wordsworth and, chiefly, Byron, she was drawn to accounts of freedom struggles and epic quests. As surely as her heroes of warfare, treachery, assassination, crusade, and rebellion inevitably fight for God and freedom, they are just as surely rewarded with posthumous heroes' laurels and eternal rest on the "Sabbath shore." Death is, in fact, a central motif in the Hemans canon: in elegy, ode, dirge, and requiem she celebrates and laments dead warriors, heroes, lovers, wives, poets, children, martyrs, and monarchs, whom she assures of eternal life in the heavenly mansions of a land beyond the grave, beyond the clouds.

A comparison of the orthodoxy of Hemans's patriotism and religion reveals that, in both, she propounded simple "truths." For example, in "The Homes of England" English houses (and households) are idyllic, stately, merry, and blessed; church bells toll on the Sabbath, and children are taught to love their nation and their God. (Such a picture of happy and protected childhood is a remarkable contrast to Barrett Browning's "The Cry of the Children," as well as to poems on child labor by Mary Howitt, Eliza Cook, and Caroline Norton, and a depiction of Victorian England as God's chosen nation is certainly at odds with the testimony of more skeptical observers.) In Hemans's elegy "On the Death of Princess Charlotte," the dead princess is not only a fair vision and cherished flower, but by analogy is also compared to England, a "beacon-tower" guiding Europe. In "Stanzas to the Memory of George the Third," Death ("blest messenger of Heaven's relief") has taken England's Father, the "departed saint" who now rests in God, "immortally secure." In Hemans,

6. Hemans, "Hymn," in *Mrs. Felicia Hemans,* 3.

English parents and English monarchs (and England herself) are dutifully Christian, poetic protagonists are saints, and salvation is assured. Heroines of *Records of Woman,* for example, never doubt, never disobey God, are never guilty of pride or rebellion. Rather, Gertrude consoles her martyred husband, "We have the blessed Heaven in view, / Where rest shall soon be won," Arabella Stuart says to William Seymour, "We shall o'ersweep the grave to meet," and dying Edith assures her parents that "one happy lot / Awaits us, friends! upon the better shore. . . ."[7]

Like Barrett Browning, Hemans wrote poems of exile, the best among them emphasizing prodigality instead of eviction. Examples are "The Voice of Home to the Prodigal" and "The Forsaken Hearth." (Hemans adds to Jesus' *father* of the "prodigal son" parable, a father *and* mother longing to receive prodigal children.)[8] And, also like Barrett Browning, she is interested in the theology of Resurrection. Images of the Resurrection predominate in works such as the lyric "Breathings of Spring," in which the melody of spring produces "strange yearnings" for loved ones now deceased. As nature bursts its sleep and tremblings "gladden many a copse and glade," humans long for eternal reunion—or at least communion. Hemans in fact parallels Barrett Browning's belief in intimacy with those who have passed beyond the "thin veil" (or "filmy screen") that separates living and dead. In "A Spirit's Return" the persona is granted a dream vision of blessed communion "face to face" with the "Departed," whom she loved.[9]

One of Hemans's most thoughtful (and atypical) works, is "The Sceptic," in which a "proud Stoic" recognizes that all existence is mutability, doubt, and danger and that humankind is the nursling of pain and sorrow. Reason and Philosophy can provide only mockery and doubt; Faith and Hope, though considered illogical by the standards of Reason, offer the only escape from despair and damnation. The ways of God, Hemans admits, are beyond mere human understanding; thus she calls for faith

---

7. Hemans, "On the Death of the Princess Charlotte," in *Mrs. Felicia Hemans,* 467; Hemans, "Stanzas to the Memory of George the Third," in ibid., 470, 473; Hemans, "Gertrude; or, Fidelity till Death," in ibid., 373; Hemans, "Arabella Stuart," in ibid., 361; Hemans, "Edith," in ibid., 381. (Page numbers are cited; lines are not numbered in this edition.)

8. In Hemans the emphasis in the "prodigal" poems is upon an invitation; in C. Rossetti it is upon *acceptance* of the invitation ("I Will Arise" and "A Prodigal Son").

9. Hemans, "Breathings of Spring," in *Mrs. Felicia Hemans,* 597; Hemans, "A Spirit's Return," in ibid., 410, 412.

beyond rationality. Of all her works, this is perhaps the one that best acknowledges the void of nihilism.

> Seraph and man, alike in weakness stand,
> And countless ages, trampling into clay
> Earth's empires on their march, are but a day;
> Father of worlds unknown . . .
> . . . .
> Look on us, guide us!—wanderers of a sea
> Wild and obscure, what are we, reft of Thee?
> . . . .
> A breeze may waft us to the whirlpool's brink,
> A treacherous song allure us—and we sink![10]

Contemporary critics are rediscovering Felicia Hemans, but sometimes find her works melodramatic or maudlin, narrow or predictable, and little attention has been paid to the religious strain in the Hemans canon. The young Elizabeth Barrett also had reservations, writing of Hemans:

I admire her genius—love her memory—respect her piety & high moral tone. But she always does seem to be a lady rather than a woman, & so, much rather than a poetess—her refinement, like the prisoner's iron . . enters into her soul. She is polished all over to one smoothness & one level, & is monotonous in her best qualities. We say "How sweet & noble" & then we are silent & can say no more—. (BC 6:165–66)

Mary Howitt (1799–1888) wrote a number of religious poems, excelled at the ballad form, and made a favorable impression on Elizabeth Barrett, who particularly admired the ballads, remarking that she would prefer having Howitt's genius to that of either Felicia Hemans or Letitia Landon (BC 2:109). Howitt insisted that religion and humanitarianism formed the core of her poetic work; she wrote in an 1846 preface that she had always retained "that love of Christ, of the poor, and of little children, which always was and will be a ruling sentiment of my soul." Among Howitt's ballads are several works adapted directly from the Bible: "The Younger Son" is a ballad version of Jesus' parable of the prodigal, and "Dives and Lazarus" repeats his parable of the rich man and beggar who,

10. Hemans, "The Sceptic," in *Mrs. Felicia Hemans*, 246.

upon death, go respectively to torment and to the fellowship of Abraham. Other ballads depict dangers on the high seas and in the old-world forest of Robin Hood, the new-world forest of unknown natives (in Howitt, a less threatening breed than the European settlers). An uncomplicated love for parent, child, and sibling, as well as the beneficent mercy of God, sustains her characters in danger. For example, in the sentimental "Lilien May" (an "Easter Legend"), a lost toddler is restored to her parents on the very day upon which Christ arose to his divine Father. On the other hand, those who do not love usually perish. In "The Sin of Earl Walter," for example, the marauder Walter sacks a convent, a crime for which he and his entire family suffer for an entire lifetime. Unlike Hemans, Howitt does avoid English chauvinism. For example, in "The Rich and the Poor" the persona formerly believed in English progress and the good English King George, but is enlightened by a ten-year-old girl who works long hours in a factory. The child, having replaced an older brother crippled for life by the engine wheels, then runs away to work as the ringing factory bell "cut[s] down" her childhood joy. In still other Howitt poems the speakers of monologues describe God's sustaining of widows, returning of lost exiles to their kin, comforting of martyrs. Among these monologues are "The Preacher's Story," in which starving settlers in the New World are fed by means of a miracle recalling Jesus' feeding of the thousands from loaves and fishes. Specifically, a herd of deer come into the camp at morning light, offering their lives to feed the camp, " . . . a true sacrifice, a living store / Sent by their God and ours." In addition to these tales, ballads, and narratives, however, Howitt also presents a theory of the nature of the poet's work as God's work in "The Spirit of Poetry." Poetry is a spirit sent from divine source into human hearts (like the heart of that "blind old man" who wrote *Paradise Lost*). Thereby the poet, by God's grace, restores us to the fabled Golden Age, our near glimpse of lost Eden.

> What art thou? A glad spirit,
> Sent down, like Hope, when Eden was no more,
> From the high heavenly place thou didst inherit,
> An Eden to restore.[11]

11. Howitt, preface, in *Ballads and Other Poems,* viii; Howitt, "The Rich and the Poor," in ibid., 314; Howitt, "The Preacher's Story," in ibid., 357; Howitt, "The Spirit of Poetry," in ibid., 266 (lines are not numbered).

Jean Ingelow (1820–1897) wrote of lamentation and resurrection, together with the sanctified role of Christian poet in a troubled world. Her religious poetry is often moralistic and sentimental, as in, for example, the cautionary tale "The Dreams that Came True" (in which a justice dreams about the old hag whom he sent to jail for stealing his wood and awakens remorseful, too late to save her life, though not the lives of others whose sufferings he now vows to relieve). In "Brothers, and a Sermon" Ingelow merely preaches in the thinly disguised voice of a revered old pastor who warns his seafaring congregation against the despair of thinking oneself too wretched to receive God's grace. "Lamentation" depicts a different kind of despair, the grief of losing a child to death. The persona recalls a dream vision of a Jacob's ladder with prayers, rather than angels, ascending, and in her own prayer acknowledges that she had forgotten God while she was happy. Now that she grieves, though, she accepts with resignation: "O, God, thy will be done," an attitude that the persona recommends to the grieving mother in Mary Howitt's "The Mother and the Angels."[12] This patient acquiescence is rather like that of Barrett's persona in "Isobel's Child":

> "I changed the cruel prayer I made,
> And bowed my meekened face, and prayed
> That God would do His will . . .
> (*CWEBB* 2:28.528–30)

Also like Barrett's poem it seems too facile an acceptance of almost incomprehensible pain. In neither poem is there rage nor doubt of God's justice. Rather, submitting to the loss of a child is a foregone conclusion, like the patient loss of one's love in Hemans's "Edith," "Gertrude," and "Arabella Stuart."

Ingelow's meditative dialogues are more sophisticated than her didactic narratives. Among them, "Scholar and Carpenter" incorporates two motifs familiar to readers of Barrett Browning: first the longing to return to Paradise (as experienced by Eve then by all her children), and second the poet's *particular* longing for Eden, the notion that "[l]oss made us poets." (As Barrett Browning says of Philosophical Thought, "The loss of Eden has touched his brain" [*CWEBB* 6:354].) In "Gladys and Her

---

12. Ingelow, "Lamentation," in *Poetical Works of Jean Ingelow*, 397 (lines are not numbered).

Island," which is not a religious poem but about a poet's finding her calling, Gladys visits a beautiful island replete with exotic birds, fruits, and snowcapped mountains. This is, of course, the land of the poetic imagination: "For this, you know, / Was Eden." In Gladys's panoramic vision are in fact various settings familiar to readers of Western poetry, and the teacher/poet Gladys learns that a poet must experience troubles "And take them home and lull them into rest / With mournfullest music." Similarly, in "The Star's Monument" (like "Scholar and Carpenter," a dialogue) a poet, wondering whether he is also to be forgotten, asks an aged astronomer about a falling star that he compares to his poet's song; he is chastised that it is not his right to know how the future will unfold, but only to fulfill his work as poet: "Work is heaven's hest; its fame is sublunar: / The fame thou dost not need—the work is done." Religious or secular, creative or perfunctory, "How fine, how blest a thing is work!" Ingelow says in "Reflections."[13] (Here, the particular task is that of a milkmaid going about her chores on a pristine morning.) As noted in Chapter 2, the admonition to find one's work and do it (the Gospel of Work) is a central tenet in the religion of Barrett Browning (as well as of Carlyle and many other Victorians). Ingelow, like Barrett Browning, sees work as a blessing.

Jean Ingelow's finest work, the twelve-book epic *A Story of Doom*, is for her what *A Drama of Exile* is to Elizabeth Barrett: a uniquely female revision of a familiar biblical myth. In *A Story of Doom*, Ingelow narrates the dramatic story of the single-minded preacher Noah and his wife, the skeptical Niloiya. Heidi Johnson sees Niloiya's story as a gradual submission to the will of her master (the "Master-shipwright" Noah and the patriarchal God), representative of the desires women must repress in Christianity (Ingelow's yearnings for feminism in spite of herself).[14] Ingelow's interpretation of woman in Scripture is, in fact, rather orthodox: in "Remonstrance" she tells the "Daughters of Eve" that they will be perpetually lower than men because Eve fell lower than Adam; in "Brothers, and a Sermon" Mary Magdalene depicts humility in washing

---

13. Ingelow, "Scholar and Carpenter," in ibid., 55; Ingelow, "Gladys and Her Island," in ibid., 378, 390; Ingelow, "The Star's Monument," in ibid., 78; Ingelow, "Reflections," in ibid., 87.

14. Johnson, "'Matters That a Woman Rules': Marginalized Maternity in Jean Ingelow's *A Story of Doom*," 85, 76.

Jesus' feet and weeping at his cross; in *A Story of Doom,* matriarchy gives way to patriarchy as Japet, youngest son of Niloiya and Noah, grows to maturity. Interestingly, however, in the couple's references to their first parents Eve is credited with greater acumen than Adam in that while he understands the birds and beasts, she is endowed with the ability to understand the languages of men.

Finally Ingelow, like most other Christian poets of the age, treats the Resurrection as poetic subject. Her ode "Song for the Night of Christ's Resurrection," subtitled "A Humble Imitation," imitates and parallels Milton's famous ode "On the Morning of Christ's Nativity." As is the case in Elizabeth Barrett's elaborate apology in the preface of *A Drama of Exile,* Ingelow's boldness is chastened by the "anxiety of authorship" that results from writing in Milton's shadow. But Ingelow acquits herself rather well in manipulating the Miltonic imagery and the complex metric form required by the genre. In Milton's nativity ode the heavens are alive with the songs of cherubim and seraphim, and the poet prophesies that hell will pass away and truth and justice come to humankind by means of the cross and Resurrection. The Babe in swaddling bands controls the damned crew of infernal spirits and pagan gods, indicative that Christianity will supersede the religions of antiquity (the triumph that Barrett presents in "The Dead Pan" at "the hour when One in Sion / Hung for love's sake on a cross" [*CWEBB* 3:154.182–83]). At the close of Milton's ode the infant falls asleep in the Virgin's arms while all about "Bright harness'd Angels sit in order serviceable." Milton celebrates the birth, but anticipates the death and Resurrection of Christ; Ingelow celebrates Resurrection, but recalls the Incarnation and birth. In her work the tomb has been sealed, and Heaven and Hades are emptied of spirits who have come to watch the tomb, tier above tier of angels hovering over the scene (reminding one of Ador and Zerah and their companions in Barrett's *The Seraphim*). Among the gathered hosts are also the Greek powers and deities whom Milton places upon the scene in "Christ's Nativity," but Night flees, Dis is banished, and a mighty angel is sent by God to rend the rocks and wake the Savior from a rest as peaceful as that of infancy. Angels attend the risen Christ as in Milton they had the infant Jesus:

> The earliest smile of day
> Doth on His vesture play,
> And light the majesty of His still brows;

While angels hang with wings outspread,
Holding the new-won crown above His saintly head.[15]

In ode, epic, exemplum, sermon, allegory, parable, dialogue, and dream vision, Ingelow demonstrates Christian faith and doctrine. Her theology and her verse, however, are conventional, a fact that may account for her enormous popularity during her lifetime, as well as the comparative indifference to her work in the current century.

Dora Greenwell (1821–1882) produced a sizable body of religious prose considered both spiritual and mystical; her verse might accurately be termed a poetry of consolation and exhortation. Even her ostensibly nonreligious works are often moralistic, extolling nostalgic (and orthodox Christian) values of a simpler past, of home and familial love, of saintly life, of love and charitable deeds. Her poems of consolation are often in the form of "Hope," a personification or abstraction appearing in "A Vision of Green Leaves," "Amid Change, Unchanging," "A Comparison," "The Babes in the Wood," and in the sonnet "Hope" leading humankind to heaven as Moses led the Israelites into the Promised Land. Along with the gospel of comfort, though, Greenwell also insists upon the trials of faith: that the sanctified have been baptized in water, blood, and fire (in "A Song Which None but the Redeemed Can Sing"). For her, Christianity is also a life of uncompromising demands (specifically, of work and of moral responsibility as one's brother's keeper). It is in this regard that Greenwell enters the world of political discourse.

Among the female religious poets here considered, Greenwell is more aggressively political than any except Barrett Browning. And like Barrett Browning's, Greenwell's politics are colored by her religious faith. Greenwell's acquaintance and editor William Dorling referred to her as a "somewhat ardent politician" who "relished . . . opportunity for improving her acquaintance with the schemes and movements of political parties." Among causes she supported were benevolence for the poor and mentally incompetent, suffrage and employment rights for women, the eradication of child labor (an issue she shared with Barrett Browning), the

---

15. Milton, "On the Morning of Christ's Nativity," in *Complete Poems and Major Prose,* 50.244; Ingelow, "Song for the Night of Christ's Resurrection," in *Poetical Works of Jean Ingelow,* 355. Ingelow's verse form is not an exact duplication of Milton's: his is seven-line iambic pentameter *ababbcc;* hers an eight-line stanza *aabccbdd,* with line lengths from trimeter to hexameter.

Italian-liberation question (another burning issue for Barrett Browning), and antivivisection (for which Christina Rossetti also campaigned).[16] Although Greenwell did not produce as substantial a body of political works as did Barrett Browning (and certainly nothing of the length and complexity of *Casa Guidi Windows*), her canon does, however, include political issues both domestic and international. "The White Crusade" takes up the banner for Italian liberation, and "The Cleft" (1861) champions the cause of the North in the American Civil War. In "A Dialogue in 1863" two neighbors discuss effects felt among the Lancashire weavers unemployed because in the United States "they've given up growing their cotton." The outcome is a didactic charge to let charity begin at home: "We must be like the woman our Saviour praised," alleviating the suffering closest at hand. In "A Song to Call to Remembrance (A Plea for the Country Ribbon-Weavers)" the looms are still, the only guests at the weaver's cottage are "Want and Care," and again Greenwell exhorts Christian British subjects to action. In "The Gang-children" she attacks a recommendation that needy children be impressed for farm labor: "Hollow the harvest joy / Of the land where the reapers mourn."[17]

Like Hemans, Greenwell was interested in the particular experience of the woman saint; thus her poetic depictions of female martyr, idealized mother, poet/songstress, servant of God. Like Ingelow, she also produced several poetic conversion narratives or monologues. Among these parallels to Ingelow's "The Dreams that Came True" are "Conversion," "The Wife's Answer," "A Good Confession," and "Basilides," in which the martyrdom of a Christian virgin Potaminca prompts the repentance of the Roman soldier Basilides. Greenwell's best work of this "confession" category, however, is "Christina," about a dying Magdalene-type character who has come to salvation through the efforts of Christina, the female messiah figure whose rhetoric echoes that of the New Testament Jesus. The poem is bold in that the fallen woman is presented compassionately, not condemned, and especially in that Jesus is presented *in the person of the woman Christina.* "Christina" is in fact packed with biblical allusions from both Testaments: the speaker/narrator is the Prodigal Son from

---

16. Dorling, introduction to *Poems by Dora Greenwell,* by Greenwell, xx.

17. Greenwell, "A Dialogue in 1863," in ibid., 91, 92, 95; Greenwell, "A Song to Call to Remembrance," in ibid., 95; Greenwell, "The Gang-children" in *Selected Poems,* 171 (lines are not numbered in either edition).

Jesus' parable and Belshazzar who sees the handwriting on the wall; Christina enfolding her fallen childhood companion before the altar at the great Minster is Elijah raising the dead son of the poor widow of Zarephath; the two women together are Naomi and Ruth, as well as Lazarus and Dives. The central pattern of allusion, however, is to Jesus and Magdalene: Christina reenacting the Christ figure by seeking and leading the fallen woman into resurrected life. This allusiveness works in three ways. First, the symbolism fits: Christina has given her friend a crucifix (recalling Christ's death and Moses' brass serpent that healed the stings of venomous serpents and foreshadowed the Crucifixion). Second, Christina lives out the parables of Jesus; like the shepherd looking for the lost sheep or the woman for the precious coin, she will not give up until the fallen woman is found and reclaimed. Finally, she speaks as Jesus does, setting Madgalene's feet on a highway "strait and narrow" to a "goodly inn" where a good Samaritan will bind her wounds. Christina claims the Magdalene as Daughter, telling her to "Go and sin no more," as Jesus told the woman taken in adultery (John 8:11).[18] That Greenwell's gentle savior of the poem is a female friend and not the Father/confessor to whom the monologue is spoken reveals much about her view of female spirituality, as well as of sisterhood among women. Also, it is yet another example of the Victorian Christ-as-feminine, female-as-Christ penchant noted at several points in this volume.

A very different study of woman and religion is presented in the prose poem "Desolate, but not Forsaken," a countermyth of the "sudden rise of the female character" debased by paganism but ennobled by the Gospel. Woman (princess/diviner/witch/prophetess) vaguely remembers the voice of the Father and Brother at evening in Eden, but has been abandoned by her chieftain/father and learned the secrets of healing from her "mighty" Mother (Earth, Nature). For this act she has come to trial. A prophetess like the Old Testament Miriam with her timbrel, formerly Woman "wore the embroidered tilma" and "led for them the war-dance of the arrow, bells swung with the swaying of [her] robe"; now she is held in derision by her people. Her Brother (Jesus), who has—unknown to her—redeemed her, will now serve as her advocate. The poem concludes with Woman's anthem of celebration: "And my soul rushes free to meet you, for it also is winged and plumed . . . now shall it shine as doth the

---

18. Greenwell, "Christina," in *Poems*, 18, 19 (lines are not numbered).

silver, and its feathers be even as the gold!"[19] The prophetess whose word
has been stifled has again found her voice.

"Pax in Novissimo," reportedly Greenwell's favorite work, parallels
"Desolate, but not Forsaken" in several ways, though not in form or
style. "Desolate" sounds much like the style of biblical prophecy, "Pax in
Novissimo" like a Wordsworthian ode. (Nature is the kindly nurse who
teaches "God's glorious Book shut in between the eves / And glowing
morns.") Like Christiana in *The Pilgrim's Progress,* the female persona has
received a message that death is imminent, the "soul by cords invisible /
Is drawn the surer unto One unseen." Reviewing her life, she admits that
God's ways have often seemed grievous, that she has not always recognized
her (divine) Brother, and that at the brink of departure she finds herself
loving Earth/Nature all the more. She concludes, however, that "things
Divine / Are imaged by the earthly" and that "it was meet" to gather
in the soul "these sweet, / Long-parted, childish fancies" to light her on
her journey to the "One unseen."[20] This anticipation for immortality is
prevalent also in Barrett Browning and Rossetti.

The work of Christina Rossetti (1830–1894) treats a wide range of
religious ideas, among them: the Sacraments (sometimes baptism or Eu-
charist, but most frequently a wedding with Christ as the Bridegroom and
the speaker as Bride); a world-weariness and desire for death; soul sleep
and glorious resurrection in New Jerusalem; life as pilgrimage (bearing the
cross in pain and sorrow); the Passion of Christ (his suffering making the
only possible sense of human suffering); the soul's unworthiness of grace
and its humble acceptance of a place in the "lowest room"; renunciation
(of earthly love, worldliness, and sin); and the temporal versus the eternal.
Rossetti was most prolific; she wrote about a thousand poems, at least
half of which could be considered devotional pieces. Because her work
is richly crafted—its obvious simplicity and grace on the surface belying
the brilliance of its core—this cursory overview will not do justice to
Rossetti, but only delineate some obvious religious ideas as parallel to
Barrett Browning's. Several scholars, in fact, have written on the religion
of Rossetti. As noted earlier Jerome McGann reveals that the doctrine
of soul sleep serves as analogue for the spiritually moribund condition

19. Greenwell, "Desolate, but not Forsaken," in *Selected Poems,* 113, 116, 119–20.
20. Greenwell, "Pax in Novissimo," in ibid., 48, 45, 51. (In her preface Greenwell
quotes from the summons of death to Christiana in *Pilgrim's Progress.*)

of Victorian England. (In Rossetti's works, in fact, *all* human existence seems to be sleepwalking: in "A Daughter of Eve" the speaker sleeps through noontime/summer, awakes at night/winter when it is too late, and in " 'Behold a Shaking' " she explores the paradox "Surely our life is death, our death is life.") Antony H. Harrison's *Christina Rossetti in Context* traces the influence of Tractarian poets John Keble and Isaac Williams in Rossetti's use of the natural world as analogical mode of perceiving divine truth, as well as in her use of medieval topoi and literary forms and her revival of the sonnet; he also illustrates that *vanitas mundi,* the central concern of St. Augustine's *Confessions,* is echoed in Rossetti's adaptation of the Augustinian paradigms of repentance and conversion: in rejection of worldly pride, intellectual pride, worldly fame, and sensuality. David A. Kent illustrates the importance of the devotional poetry of George Herbert as influential in Rossetti's technique (symmetry, rhyme, and so on), in grouped patterns of Christian spiritual experience as a method of ordering her poems, in the sense of calling and commitment, and in the intimacy that "puts the reader in the position of overhearing the poet's colloquy with God."[21]

In Rossetti's works there is an insistent tension that one must not love the world and yet cannot leave the world, cannot "get quit of earth and get robed for heaven"—at least not presently. This world is "vanity of vanities" for one who indulges in life's sensual pleasures, for no matter how enticing they seem, they are at best empty and hollow, at worst devilish and destructive. In "The World," from Rossetti's first volume, she describes the insidious charms of this seductive, Duessa-like world.

> By day she wooes me, soft, exceeding fair:
>   But all night as the moon so changeth she;
>   Loathsome and foul with hideous leprosy
> And subtle serpents gliding in her hair.

In "Ascension Day" the apostles lift weary eyes to Heaven, wishing to join their savior, for "Earth is one desert waste of banishment, / Life is

---

21. Rossetti, " 'Behold a Shaking,' " in *Complete Poems of Christina Rossetti,* 2:157.2.11; Harrison, *Christina Rossetti in Context,* 76, 79, 125, 133, 100; Kent, " 'By thought, word, and deed': George Herbert and Christina Rossetti," in *The Achievement of Christina Rossetti,* ed. Kent, 266.

one long-drawn out anguish of decay." In "A vain Shadow" the world is "[m]ouldy, worm-eaten, grey. . . ." At best the world is for the travel-weary a road that winds "up-hill all the way."[22] Barrett Browning, of course, also finds the world wearying as "link by link" she goes on counting all the chains of life, at least this is the case until love resurrects her to new life in this present world (*SP* 20.5, in *CWEBB* 3:236).

If life is the perpetual bearing of a heavy cross that nearly crushes us, as Rossetti claims, then one might assume that work—either poetic creation or Christian charity—would give life purpose. But neither form of work is to Rossetti the same blessing that it is to Barrett Browning or to Ingelow (although Rossetti worked at both poetry and service with apparent energy and commitment and although she acknowledges that work is essential and every Christian a worker). Work is in the Rossetti poetic canon, however, part of the whole wearying existence we call life. In Barrett Browning works produce results; in Rossetti they merely fill up time. In the sonnet "Work," Barrett says, "And God's grace fructify through thee to all," expressing confidence that younger fellow workers will be the better for one's toil (*CWEBB* 2:232.12). (As noted in a previous chapter, although work was [after Adam] a curse, it became [after Christ] a blessing.) But in Rossetti one works throughout life's short "working day" and anticipates rest, "unworking night." Work is insistent and strenuous; it must be done "[a]t once with all my might." It is tedious and perpetual: "Day after day I plod and moil." And it brings no sense of accomplishment to the worker:

> Why should we hasten to arise
> So early, and so late take rest?
> Our labour is not good. . . .

In Barrett's "Work and Contemplation" a woman sits singing at her spinning wheel, proving work "[t]he better for the sweetness of our song" (*CWEBB* 2:235.14), and Rossetti may well have had Barrett's sonnet in mind when she wrote "Repining," in which the female persona sits in solitude, "[s]pinning the weary thread away," from sunrise to sunset,

---

22. Rossetti, "Saints and Angels," in *Complete Poems of Christina Rossetti*, 1:229.6; Rossetti, "The World," in ibid., 1:76–77.1–4; Rossetti, "Ascension Day," in ibid., 2:232.9–10; Rossetti, "'A vain Shadow,'" in ibid., 2:260.2; Rossetti, "Up-hill," in ibid., 1:65.1.

wishing for Christ to come and liberate her from labor.[23] Finally—after a vision in which a Jesus-like figure awakens her to an illuminating tableau of the horrific suffering in the world—she repents her death wish, asking merely strength to go back and work out life's day (that is, weaving out the thread of her own existence).[24] If work bears any blessing in Rossetti, it is only in that her Lord loves the willing worker, and one works because she loves him in return. In " 'Take Care of Him,' " her answer to Jesus' "How dost thou love?" is "In prayer, in toil, in earthly loss, / In a long-carried cross."[25] When Rossetti's poems are petitions, the speaker frequently asks for grace, not for guaranteed salvation, a life of ease, or blessings galore, but to endure work, pain, or martyrdom, to love and trust as one ought, to await patiently for death and resurrection.

As Barrett Browning speaks of her "face to face with God," Rossetti anticipates a face-to-face with Jesus, for "This Face . . . of Jesus Christ" thrills with awe as the face of Love and of her beloved. In " 'God is our Hope and Strength' " she petitions:

> O Jesus, Who lovest us all, stoop low from Thy Glory
> above:
> Where sin hath abounded make grace to abound and to
> superabound
> Till we gaze on Thee Face unto Face, and respond to
> Thee love unto Love.[26]

Rossetti wrote infrequently to God, but her works are filled with intimate petitions to Jesus, to whom she rarely referred by the imperial term *King*, but who is more frequently lover, betrothed, or bridegroom. Among the major Victorian women poets, Rossetti alone incorporates the wedding

---

23. Rossetti, " 'Judge nothing before the time,' " in ibid., 2:296.21; Rossetti, "In the Willow Shade," in ibid., 2:108.52, 50; Rossetti, "Weary in Well Doing," in ibid., 1:182.12; Rossetti, "A Testimony," in ibid., 1:78.49–51; Rossetti, "Repining," in ibid., 3:17.2.

24. Sharon Leder and Andrea Abbott believe that Rossetti is encoding the politics of pacifism and expressing isolation from war's insanity (*The Language of Exclusion: The Poetry of Emily Dickinson and Christina Rossetti*, 67, 96). Rosenblum argues that the vision chastens endurance, isolation, and repression (*Christina Rossetti: The Poetry of Endurance*, 178).

25. Rossetti, " 'Take Care of Him,' " in *Complete Poems of Christina Rossetti*, 2:159.7–8.

26. Rossetti, "The Descent from the Cross," in ibid., 2:154.8; Rossetti, "God is our Hope and Strength," in ibid., 2:206.8–10.

imagery of the New Testament as explicit (and repeated) statement of
woman's spirituality. In the Gospels, Christ is referred to as Bridegroom,
while the Church is his holy bride. In Jesus' parable of the ten virgins at
the wedding, for example, five brought an adequate supply of oil to keep
their lamps burning in the event of the bridegroom's delay; the other five
were closed out of the marriage ceremony because they were ill-prepared
and their flames had burned out (Matt. 25:1–13). In "Easter Tuesday"
Rossetti notes that those with oil for their lamps are those who "watch
and pray." None of these ten maidens, however, was the bride; clearly
they were members of the wedding party. But there is no mistaking that
(although she frequently alludes to this parable) Rossetti most often uses
the term *Bride* to refer to an individual soul—usually her own—awaiting
the Apocalypse. In "Advent Sunday" the speaker exhorts:

> Behold, the Bridegroom cometh: go ye out
> With lighted lamps and garlands round about
> To meet him in a rapture with a shout.

Here the Bride is not the persona (not "I" but "she"), and could well be
the church, or body of the elect. In "A Portrait" the bride is also "she,"
a dying maiden answering the Bridegroom's call. In " 'Is it well with
the child?' " "God's daughter fetched and carried" is also "Christ's bride
betrothed and married"—either the church or the individual receptive
soul. But in "Come unto Me" the virgin with "my lamp lightened and
my robe [of] white" is bride/lover of Christ, and the persona as well. Still
more unambiguously passionate is "Till Tomorrow" in which Rossetti
expresses "longing and desire" for "my Heavenly Lover." For her the
prophesied rapture is that "The Bridegroom cometh, cometh, His Bride
to enfold," and the eternal union with her deity is described in terms of
conjugal bliss: "I full of Christ and Christ of me."[27] As noted in Chapter
4, the yearning of the female ascetic or mystic for God (or Jesus) is
especially personal. In Barrett Browning's *Aurora Leigh* rape fantasy is a
code for possession by God, but also for poetic inspiration; in Rossetti,

27. Rossetti, "Easter Tuesday," in ibid., 2:231.9; Rossetti, "Advent Sunday," in ibid.,
2:211.1–3; Rossetti, " 'Is it well with the child?' " in ibid., 2:292.5–6; Rossetti, "Come
unto Me," in ibid., 3:34.7; Rossetti, "Till Tomorrow," in ibid., 2:101.2, 14; Rossetti,
" 'Whither the Tribes go up, even the Tribes of the Lord,' " in ibid., 2:299.10; Rossetti,
" 'The heart knoweth its own bitterness,' " in ibid., 3:266.56.

however, the love is never violent, always tender, whether she is expressing, formally, the Church's relationship to Christ or whether she is, in Kent's words, engaged in "personal colloquy." Rossetti's Bridegroom died for the Bride; the Bride longs to rise with the Seraphim and rest cradled in the Bridegroom's arms.[28]

A central motif of Rossetti is what Dolores Rosenblum terms "the unofficial sisterhood of renunciation," that is, the spiritual relationship among women (nuns and ascetics) who renounce sensuality and worldliness for religion. Just as compelling in Rossetti, however, is the spiritual sisterhood of woman *for* woman. Though her insights may be open to debate on some grounds, the younger sister of "The Lowest Room" teaches and demonstrates to the persona a life of Christian contentment, goodness, and wisdom. Sisterhood is, of course, best exemplified in Rossetti's most famous work *Goblin Market,* in which Lizzie, stained by goblin fruit but not having partaken (like Christ bearing sin to the cross but himself sinless), bids her sister Laura join her in eucharistic communion:

> Hug me, kiss me, suck my juices
> Squeezed from goblin fruits for you
> . . . .
> Eat me, drink me, love me;
> Laura, make much of me.

This feminization of the Passion is quite remarkable even in nineteenth-century Protestant theology in which, as Rosemary Ruether notes, "Christ himself becomes essentially a mariological figure. . . ." Rossetti reverses the figure: instead of Jesus as woman/mother, the woman/sister is Christ. Or, rather, the two are interchangeable. A eucharistic relationship between Jesus and woman is expressed again in "A Better Resurrection," in which the female penitent pleads, "O Jesus, drink of me."[29]

Not only sisterhood but also motherhood takes on spiritual importance in the works of Rossetti. Specifically, mother Eve—who represents also

---

28. In "Christus et Ecclesia," Greenwell also explores the biblical metaphor of the church as bride. With her amber, ivory, and coral, her robe of purple, gold, and scarlet, the apostate church is the woman set upon the Dragon in John's Revelation and as clear a representative of Catholicism as Duessa in *The Faerie Queene.*

29. Rosenblum, *Christina Rossetti,* 184; Rossetti, *Goblin Market,* in *Complete Poems of Christina Rossetti,* 1:23.468–72; Ruether, *New Woman, New Earth,* 24; Rossetti, "A Better Resurrection," in *Complete Poems of Christina Rossetti,* 1:68.24.

grace, penitence, and humility—depicts motherly love as a holy attribute. Like Barrett Browning, Rossetti is fascinated by Eve. In "Shut Out" an exile (not named Eve but certainly *an* Eve) looks back into the garden guarded by an implacable "shadowless spirit" and regrets her loss. In "Sexagesima" Eve *and* Adam (not Eve alone) have brought death and shame to their progeny. In *Later Life: A Double Sonnet of Sonnets*, Rossetti concludes that Eve and Adam no doubt forgave one another for the sin that produced expulsion because they loved and love is impossible without forgiveness. In "Bird or Beast?" the exiled pair grieve but will receive grace through the sacrifice of Christ, the Lamb of God. (If God loves, then God forgives because divine mercy must of necessity exceed the human variety.) In "An Afterthought," "Eve now slumbers there forgiven" at the very gate of Heaven. Diane D'Amico is accurate in noting that in Rossetti, Eve is a more significant maternal figure than the Blessed Virgin, adding that it is "as grieving mother that Rossetti portrays Eve most movingly."[30] In "Eve" the "sad mother" weeps for a loss greater than her own exile. That anguish is nothing in comparison to seeing one of her sons slain by the other and realizing that her own disobedience has precipitated violence and death among all human descendants for all time.

> "I, Eve, sad mother
> Of all who must live,
> I, not another,
> Plucked bitterest fruit to give
> My friend, husband, lover;—
> O wanton eyes, run over;
> Who but I should grieve?—
> Cain hath slain his brother:
> Of all who must die mother,
> Miserable Eve!"

In Rossetti's view Adam and Eve share the responsibility for having ushered sin and death into the world. But Eve's guilt, remorse, and vicarious suffering illustrate penitence, as well as her special tenderness and

---

30. Rossetti, "Shut Out," in *Complete Poems of Christina Rossetti,* 1:56.9; Rossetti, "An Afterthought," in ibid., 3:243.45; D'Amico, "Eve, Mary, and Mary Magdalene: Christina Rossetti's Feminine Triptych," in *The Achievement of Christina Rossetti,* ed. Kent, 177. D'Amico believes that Rossetti was more attracted by Mary's humility than her virginity (182), the trait that Mary shares with both Eve and Mary Magdalene.

transcendent love for her children. Virginia Sickbert says that Rossetti's Eve exhibits "Christ-like virtues" in that she is gracious, accessible, and eager to teach truth.[31] Certainly Eve's anguish for the yet-unborn mirrors the biblical Christ's agony for the city of Jerusalem and for those who will suffer in the human upheavals that he sorrowfully prophesies. (Or, for that matter, Barrett's Christ whose tears, "dropt too fast," salted the brackish waters of our temporal sorrows [*CWEBB* 2:330.546].) Or Greenwell's "Brother" (Jesus) who weeps for his sister in "Pax in Novissimo." Among Victorian women poets Christina Rossetti—by means of her depiction of the receptive female soul as Bride, sister, and mother—illuminates the role of female spirituality with the greatest clarity.

It would be an error to conclude that Rossetti, any more than Barrett Browning, professes a Christianity without trials. As the young Barrett struggles with hubris (the lure of "Moloch fame") and the "reptile moods" of her Promethean stage (noted in Chapter 1) and as Aurora Leigh despairs when neither knowledge nor art (nor, for that matter Moloch fame) sustains her, Rossetti also acknowledges the dark night of the human soul. In one of her most striking and troubling poems, "An Old-World Thicket," the persona in dream or trance discovers a wood in which nature is positively giddy with life. Rather than heartening her, though, the scene shocks her to consider the human plight in which "Death hangs, or damage, or the dearth of bread." Paralyzed by wrath, gloom, and agony and drowning in a tide of "helpless misery," she finally realizes the real issue is death—her own. The mother bird with feathered brood "[s]afe in some leafy niche" is illusion: they and she are born to be gnawed by worms. In the golden glow of day's end, however, the dreamer witnesses a flock of peaceful sheep led by "patriarchal ram" and journeying "[m]ild face by face, and wooly breast by breast" toward the sunset. By the flock's submissiveness, the comfort of its patriarch, its acceptance of death, its oneness (like that of the Church), or the notion that the sheep are "at peace / With one another and with every one," the poem closes with an implication that there *should* be some amelioration. An implication, but not an assurance. Although it is implied that the persona *ought* to be comforted, the pastoral closure does not negate the terror. Rossetti leaves the reader stunned and horrified by her or his own mortality.[32]

31. Rossetti, "Eve," in *Complete Poems of Christina Rossetti,* in 1:157.26–35; Sickbert, " 'Beloved Mother of Us All': Christina Rossetti's Eve," 292–93.

32. Rossetti, "An Old-World Thicket," in *Complete Poems of Christina Rossetti,* 2:125.40, 126.100, 124.4, 128.171, 178, 169–70.

Like several Victorian women writers, Rossetti reclaims the female biblical figures Eve and Magdalene as expression of woman's dignity and spiritual worth. Like Barrett Browning she believes in humans' free will, pays tribute to grace but preaches a Gospel of Work, struggles for humility, deals with the Resurrection (often in apocalyptic terminology from Revelation), and is at times sick of life and hopeful for death. Although both anticipate the rapture, the tone of both is hopeful more than ecstatic. As Rossetti says, "O hope deferred, hope still."[33]

Elizabeth Barrett Browning consciously opposed the spirit of her age, which she called "counting-house Utilitarianism" and a "rail road instead of a Via Sacra!—" (*BC* 3:241). She insisted that any poetry, however creative, that excludes the soul and its God and "takes life in its conventionality denuded of its inner mystery" is in the end one-sided and insufficient as art and "deficient in the elements of greatness" (*BC* 7:214). Her correspondence in fact reveals a gentle feud between herself and her cousin John Kenyon on the subject of religion in art: he apparently preferred that she banish religion from her poetry, but to her the poet's duty is to elevate the public mind, not to achieve popularity (*BC* 7:21), and if one elevates the mind, God is the ultimate elevation as God (the first Poet) is also the ultimate source. Furthermore, the religion of Christianity is poetry: "Oh what an unspeakable lovely poetry there is in Christ's religion! But like the lovely poetry of inferior things, men look on it coldly because without understanding, & do not even cry aloud for an interpreter" (*BC* 3:179). Barrett Browning was bold enough to fancy herself such an interpreter, and this poetic and religious calling makes her work intriguing.

Also intriguing is the marriage between creative impulse and religious ideology in the work of other Victorian women poets. Looking around them for godmothers, they found only one. Religious poetry (Dante, Milton, Herbert, Donne) was masculine. So were prophecy and wisdom writing (Elijah, Solomon, St. John), and preaching and exhortation (most notably St. Paul). So too was Anglican theology (Hooker, Taylor, Pusey, Keble). But Victorian women writers wasted little energy lamenting the shackles of patristic and poetic tradition. Instead they were creating their own icons for sainted womanliness, examining Scripture and theological pronouncements on womanhood, finding their own voices as

33. Rossetti, " 'Vanity of Vanities,' " in ibid., 2:317.16.

prophetesses for God, appropriating female figures (biblical, historical, and literary) and claiming their lives and words as paradigms for female spirituality, revising masculine-created myths to make them resonate with woman's truths, even recontextualizing the masculine Jesus and giving him more feminine qualities, making him the tender feminine Sister as well as beloved masculine Brother. They looked to Elizabeth Barrett Browning as their example and liberator. Having identified herself with the Promethean Satan, revised Milton (and Genesis), applied the religion of Christ to international politics, speculated upon resurrection and immortality, and considered the spiritual nature (and spiritual needs) of woman, she legitimized their own striving and made possible their respective poetic attempts to confront the deity face-to-face.

Works Cited

***

Primary Sources

Aeschylus. *The Complete Greek Tragedies.* Ed. David Grene and Richard Lattimore. 7 vols. New York: Modern Library, 1942–1956.

Aesop. *Aesop without Morals: The Famous Fables and a Life of Aesop.* Trans. and ed. Lloyd W. Daly. New York: T. Yoseloff, 1961.

Apollodorus. *The Library.* Trans. James George Frazer. 2 vols. Cambridge: Harvard University Press, 1921. London: William Heinemann, 1939.

Aristotle. *Politics.* Trans. Benjamin Jowett. Oxford: Clarendon Press, 1905.

Arnold, Matthew. *The Poems of Matthew Arnold.* Ed. Miriam Abbott and Robert H. Super. 2nd ed. London: Longman, 1979.

———. *The Works of Matthew Arnold in Fifteen Volumes.* 1903–1904. Reprint, New York: AMS Press, 1970.

Augustine, Saint Aurelius. *City of God.* Trans. John Healy. London: J. M. Dent and Sons, 1931.

Bacon, Francis. *The Moral and Historical Works of Lord Bacon.* London: George Bell and Sons, 1901.

Blake, William. *The Complete Poetry and Prose of William Blake.* Ed. David Erdman. Garden City, N.Y.: Anchor Books, 1982.

Brontë, Charlotte. *Shirley: A Tale.* 2 vols. The Shakespeare Head Brontë. Boston: Houghton Mifflin, 1931.

———. *Villette.* 2 vols. The Shakespeare Head Brontë. Boston: Houghton Mifflin, 1931.

Browning, Elizabeth Barrett. *Aurora Leigh.* Ed. Margaret Reynolds. Athens: Ohio University Press, 1992.

———. *"Aurora Leigh" and Other Poems.* Ed. Cora Kaplan. London: Women's Press, 1978.

———. *The Brownings' Correspondence.* Vols. 1–8, ed. Philip Kelley and Ronald Hudson. Vols. 9–13, ed. Philip Kelley and Scott Lewis. Winfield, Kans.: Wedgestone Press, 1984–1995.

———. *Casa Guidi Windows.* Ed. Julia Markus. New York: Browning Institute, 1977.

———. *The Complete Works of Elizabeth Barrett Browning.* Ed. Charlotte Porter and Helen A. Clarke. 6 vols. 1900. Reprint, New York: AMS Press, 1973.

———. *Diary by E. B. B.: The Unpublished Diary of Elizabeth Barrett Browning, 1831–1832.* Ed. Philip Kelley and Ronald Hudson. Athens: Ohio University Press, 1969.

———. *Hitherto Unpublished Poems and Stories with an Inedited Autobiography.* Ed. H. Buxton Forman. 2 vols. Boston: Bibliophile Society, 1914.

———. *The Letters of Elizabeth Barrett Browning.* Ed. Frederic G. Kenyon. 2 vols. New York: Macmillan, 1898.

———. *The Letters of Elizabeth Barrett Browning to Mary Russell Mitford 1836–1854.* 3 vols. Ed. Meredith B. Raymond and Mary Rose Sullivan. Waco: Armstrong Browning Library of Baylor University, 1983.

———. *Letters of the Brownings to George Barrett.* Ed. Paul Landis with Ronald E. Freeman. Urbana: University of Illinois Press, 1958.

———. *Letters to Her Sister, 1846–1859.* Ed. Leonard Huxley. London: John Murray, 1929.

———. *Poems by Elizabeth Barrett Browning: (From the Last London Edition Corrected by the Author).* 4 vols. New York: James Miller, 1862.

———. *The Poets' Enchiridion: A Hitherto Unpublished Poem.* Boston: Bibliophile Society, 1914.

———. *Prometheus Bound Translated from the Greek of Aeschylus. And Miscellaneous Poems, by the Translator.* London: A. J. Valpry, 1833.

Browning, Robert. *The Poems.* 2 vols. Ed. John Pettigrew. Harmondsworth, Middlesex, England: Penguin Books, 1981.

———. *The Ring and the Book.* Ed. Richard D. Altick. Harmondsworth, Middlesex, England: Penguin Books, 1990.

Byron, Lord, George Gordon. *The Complete Poetical Works of Lord Byron.* Ed. Jerome J. M. McGann. 5 vols. Oxford: Clarendon Press, 1980–1986.

———. *The Works of Lord Byron: Letters and Journals.* Ed. Richard Henry Stoddard. 16 vols. Boston: Francis A. Niccolls, 1900.

Calvin, John. *Institutes of the Christian Religion.* Trans. Henry Beveridge. 2 vols. Grand Rapids, Mich.: William B. Eerdmans, 1957.

Carlyle, Thomas. *The Works of Thomas Carlyle in Thirty Volumes.* New York: AMS Press, 1969.

Coleridge, Samuel Taylor. *Coleridge's Prose Works (Miscellanies, Aesthetic and Literary).* Ed. T. Ashe. 6 vols. London: George Bell and Sons, 1892.

Comte, Auguste. *Auguste Comte and Positivism: The Essential Writings.* Ed. Gertrud Lenzer. Chicago: University of Chicago Press, 1975.

Dante Alighieri. *The Convivio of Dante Alighieri.* London: J. M. Dent and Sons, 1912.

———. *The Divine Comedy.* Trans. Charles S. Singleton. 6 vols. Bollingen Series 80. Princeton: Princeton University Press, 1970–1975.

———. *A Translation of the Latin Works of Dante Alighieri.* London: J. M. Dent, 1904.

———. *The Vita Nuova and Canzoniere of Dante Alighieri.* London: J. M. Dent and Sons, 1933.

de Staël, Anne-Louise-Germaine. *Corinne; or, Italy.* Trans. Isabel Hill. Metrical versions of the odes by L. E. Landon. New York: A. L. Burt, n.d.

Dickens, Charles. *Bleak House.* 2 vols. London: Chapman and Hall, n.d.

———. *Hard Times.* Vol. 3 in *The Works of Charles Dickens.* 20 vols. New York: Brown, n.d.

Eliot, George. *The Writings of George Eliot Together with the Life by J. W. Cross.* Warwickshire Edition. 25 vols. Boston: Houghton Mifflin, 1908.

Emerson, Ralph Waldo. *Essays and Lectures.* Ed. Joel Porte. New York: Library of America, 1983.

Euripides. *Trojan Women.* Trans. Shirley A. Barlow. Westminster, Wiltshire, England: Aris and Phillips, 1986.

Ficino, Marsilio. *The Philebus Commentary.* Trans. Michael Allen. Berkeley and Los Angeles: University of California Press, 1975.

Fourier, Charles. *Social Destiny of Man, or Theory of the Four Movements.* Trans. Henry Clapp Jr. New York: Gordon Press, 1972.

Fulgentius, Fabius Planciades. *Fulgentius the Mythographer.* Trans. Leslie George Whitbread. Columbus: Ohio State University Press, 1971.

Fuller, Margaret. *Woman in the Nineteenth Century and Kindred Papers Relating to the Sphere, Condition and Duties, of Woman.* Boston: John P. Jewett, 1855.

Gaskell, Elizabeth. *North and South.* Ed. Dorothy Collin. Harmondsworth, Middlesex, England: Penguin Books, 1970.

————. *Ruth.* Ed. Alan Shelston. Oxford: Oxford University Press, 1985.

Goethe, J. Wolfgang von. *Goethe's Popular Works.* Trans. John Oxenford. Cambridge Edition. 10 vols. Boston: Estes and Lauriat, 1883.

Golding, Arthur. *The XV Books of P. Ovidious Naso, entytuled Metamorphoses, translated oute of Latin into English meeter by Arthur Golding, Gentleman.* 1567. Reprint, Norwood, N.J.: W. J. Johnson, 1977.

Greenwell, Dora. *Poems.* London: Alexander Strahan, 1867.

————. *Poems by Dora Greenwell.* Ed. William Dorling. London: Walter Scott, 1889.

————. *Selected Poems.* London: H. R. Allenson, 1906.

Hawthorne, Nathaniel. *The Works of Nathaniel Hawthorne.* Centenary Edition. 20 vols. Columbus: Ohio State University Press, 1962–1988.

Hemans, Felicia. *Mrs. Felicia Hemans.* Chicago: M. A. Donohue, n.d.

Homer. *The Odyssey of Homer.* Trans. Alexander Pope. Introduction by Theodore Alois Buckley. New York: Thomas Y. Crowell and Company, n.d.

Hooker, Richard. *The Works of That Learned and Judicious Divine, Mr. Richard Hooker: With an Account of His Life and Death by Isaac Walton.* Arranged by John Keble. Revised by R. W. Church and F. Paget. 7th ed. 3 vols. New York: Burt Franklin, 1970.

Horace. *Horace's "Odes" and "Epodes."* Trans. David Mulroy. Ann Arbor: University of Michigan Press, 1994.

Howitt, Mary. *Ballads and Other Poems.* London: Longman, Brown, Green, and Longmans, 1847.

Hunt, Leigh. *The Indicator, and the Companion; A Miscellany for the Fields and the Fire-side.* London: Edward Moxon, 1840.

Hyginus. *The Myths of Hyginus.* Trans. and ed. Mary Grant. Lawrence: University Press of Kansas, 1960.

Ingelow, Jean. *The Poetical Works of Jean Ingelow.* New York: Thomas Y. Crowell, 1894.

Johnson, Dale A., ed. *Women in English Religion 1700–1925.* Studies in Women and Religion, vol. 10. New York: Edwin Mellen, 1983.

Jung, C. G. *Phenomena Resulting from the Assimilation of Consciousness: Two Essays on Analytical Psychology.* Trans. R. F. C. Hull. New York: Meridian Books, 1956.

Keble, John. *The Christian Year.* Philadelphia: Henry Altemus, 1899.

Kingsley, Charles. *Alton Locke: Poet and Tailor.* Bideford Edition. 2 vols. New York: The Co-operative Publication Society, 1898.

————. *Yeast.* Bideford Edition. New York: The Co-operative Publication Society, 1899.

Leighton, Angela, and Margaret Reynolds, eds. *Victorian Women Poets: An Anthology.* Oxford: Blackwell, 1995.

Locke, John. *Two Treatises of Government.* Ed. Thomas I. Cook. New York: Hafner Publishing, 1947.

Lucian of Samosata. *Lucian.* Trans. A. M. Harmon. 8 vols. Cambridge: Harvard University Press, 1913–1967.

Lytton, Earl of. *Letters from Owen Meredith (Robert, First Earl of Lytton) to Robert and Elizabeth Barrett Browning.* Ed. Auralia Brooks Harlan and J. Lee Harlan Jr. Waco, Tex.: *Baylor University's Browning Interests.* Series 10. *The Baylor Bulletin* 39:3–4 (1936).

Macaulay, Thomas Babington. *Macaulay: Prose and Poetry.* Ed. G. M. Yong. Cambridge: Harvard University Press, 1970.

Martial. *Selected Epigrams of Martial.* Ed. Edwin Post. Boston: Ginn and Company, 1908.

Martineau, Harriet. *Deerbrook.* London: Edward Moxon, 1843.

————. *Harriet Martineau's Autobiography.* Ed. Maria Weston Chapman. 2 vols. Boston: James R. Osgood, 1877.

————. *Society in America.* 4th ed. 2 vols. New York: Saunders and Otley, 1837.

Miles, Alfred H., ed. *The Poets and the Poetry of the Nineteenth Century.* 12 vols. London: Routledge, 1905–1915.

Mill, John Stuart. *The Collected Works of John Stuart Mill.* Ed. J. M. Robson. 33 vols. Toronto: University of Toronto Press, 1984.

Milton, John. *Complete Poems and Major Prose.* Ed. Merritt Y. Hughes. New York: Odyssey, 1957.

————. *The Complete Prose Works of John Milton.* Ed. Don M. Wolfe et al. 8 vols. New Haven: Yale University Press, 1953–1982.

————. *The Prose Works of John Milton: Containing His Principal Political and Ecclesiastical Pieces.* Ed. George Burnett. 2 vols. London: John Miller, 1809.

Napoleon III. *The Political and Historical Works of Louis Napoleon Bonaparte, President of the French Republic.* 2 vols. 1852. Reprint, New York: Howard Fertig, 1972.

Nietzsche, Friedrich. *The Birth of Tragedy or Hellenism and Pessimism.* Trans. William A. Haussmann. Edinburgh: T. N. Foulis, 1910.

Nightingale, Florence. *"Cassandra" and Other Selections from "Suggestions for Thought."* Ed. Mary Poovey. Washington Square: New York University Press, 1992.

Ovid. *Metamorphoses.* 1732. Reprint, New York: Garland Publishing, 1976.

Pausanius. *Guide to Greece.* Trans. Peter Levi. 2 vols. New York: Penguin Books, 1971.

Plato. *The Dialogues of Plato.* Trans. B. Jowett. 4th ed. 2 vols. Oxford: Clarendon Press, 1953.

Poe, Edgar Allan. *Edgar Allan Poe: Essays and Reviews.* Ed. G. R. Thompson. New York: Library of America, 1984.

Pope, Alexander. *The Poems of Alexander Pope.* Ed. John Butt; translations of Homer edited by Maynard Mack. London: Methuen, 1967.

Propertius, Sextus. *Poems of Propertius.* Trans. and ed. Ronald Musker. London: J. M. Dent and Sons, 1972.

Proudhon, Pierre Joseph. *Œuvres Complètes de P.-J. Proudhon.* Ed. C. Bouglé and H. Moysset. 23 vols. Paris: Librairie des Sciences et Sociales, 1923–1974.

———. *Selected Writings of Pierre-Joseph Proudhon.* Ed. Stewart Edwards. Trans. Elizabeth Fraser. Garden City, N.Y.: Doubleday, 1969.

Richardson, Samuel. *Clarissa or, The History of a Young Lady.* Shakespeare Head Edition. 8 vols. Oxford: Basil Blackwell, 1930.

Rossetti, Christina. *The Complete Poems of Christina Rossetti.* Ed. R. W. Crump. Variorum Edition. 3 vols. Baton Rouge: Louisiana State University Press, 1979–1990.

Rossetti, Dante Gabriel. *The Collected Works of Dante Gabriel Rossetti.* Ed. William M. Rossetti. 2 vols. London: Ellis and Elvey, 1887.

Ruskin, John. *The Crown of Wild Olive and Lectures on Art.* New York: A. L. Burt, n.d.

———. *The Queen of the Air: Being a Study of the Greek Myths of Cloud and Storm.* London: Smith, Elder, 1869.

———. *Sesame and Lilies.* Philadelphia: Henry Altemus, 1896.

Sandys, George. *Ovid's Metamorphoses Englished, Mythologized and Represented in Figures.* New York: Garland Publishing, 1976.

Schaff, Philip, ed. *A Select Library of the Nicene and Post-Nicene Fathers of the Christian Church.* 14 vols. Grand Rapids, Mich.: William B. Eerdmans, 1956.

Shakespeare, William. *The Riverside Shakespeare.* Ed. G. Blakemore Evans et al. 2nd ed. Boston: Houghton Mifflin, 1997.

Shelley, Mary. *Frankenstein; or, the Modern Prometheus.* Ed. James Rieger. 1818. Reprint, Indianapolis: Bobbs-Merrill, 1974.

Shelley, Percy Bysshe. *The Complete Works of Percy Bysshe Shelley.* Ed. Roger Ingpen and Walter E. Peck. 10 vols. New York: Gordion Press, 1965.

————. *Shelley's Prometheus Unbound.* Ed. Lawrence John Zillman. Variorum Edition. Seattle: University of Washington Press, 1959.

Spenser, Edmund. *The Works of Edmund Spenser.* Ed. Edwin Greenlaw, Charles Grosvenor Osgood, Frederick Morgan Padelford. Variorum Edition. 11 vols. Baltimore: Johns Hopkins University Press, 1949.

Stowe, Harriet Beecher. *Uncle Tom's Cabin; or, Life among the Lowly.* Boston: Houghton Mifflin, 1879.

Swedenborg, Emanuel. *Angelic Wisdom Concerning Divine Love and Wisdom.* Trans. George F. Dole. New York: Swedenborg Foundation, 1986.

————. *The Apocalypse Revealed; Wherein Are Disclosed the Arcana There Foretold, Which Have Heretofore Remained Concealed.* Philadelphia: J. B. Lippincott, 1925.

————. *The Delights of Wisdom Pertaining to Conjugial Love.* New York: American Swedenborg Society Printing and Publishing, 1909.

————. *Heaven and Hell.* Trans. George F. Dole. 1758. Reprint, New York: Swedenborg Foundation, 1984.

Taylor, Jeremy. *The Rule and Exercises of Holy Living.* Ed. Thomas S. Kepler. 2 vols. Cleveland: World Publishing, 1956.

Tennyson, Alfred, Lord. *The Poems of Tennyson.* Ed. Christopher Ricks. London: Longmans, Green, 1969.

Tristan, Flora. *The London Journal of Flora Tristan 1842.* Translation of *Promenades dans Londres,* by Jean Hawkes. London: Virago, 1982.

Wollstonecraft, Mary. *A Vindication of the Rights of Woman.* Ed. Carol H. Poston. 2nd ed. New York: W. W. Norton, 1988.

Wordsworth, William. *The Poetical Works of Wordsworth.* Revised by Paul D. Sheats. Cambridge Edition. Boston: Houghton Mifflin, 1982.

Secondary Sources

Alaya, Flavia. "The Ring, the Rescue and the *Risorgimento:* Reunifying the Brownings' Italy." *Browning Institute Studies* 6 (1978): 1–41.

Albrecht-Carrié, René. *Italy from Napoleon to Mussolini.* New York: Columbia University Press, 1950.

Anderson, Amanda. *Tainted Souls and Painted Faces: The Rhetoric of Fallenness in Victorian Culture.* Ithaca: Cornell University Press, 1993.

Armstrong, Isobel. *Victorian Poetry: Poetry, Poetics and Politics.* London: Routledge, 1993.

Aschkenasy, Nehama. *Eve's Journey: Feminine Images in Hebraic Literary Tradition.* Philadelphia: University of Pennsylvania Press, 1986.

Auerbach, Nina. *Woman and the Demon: The Life of a Victorian Myth.* Cambridge: Harvard University Press, 1982.

Barthes, Roland. *A Barthes Reader.* Ed. Susan Sontag. New York: Hill and Wang, 1982.

Bloom, Harold. *The Anxiety of Influence: A Theory of Poetry.* New York: Oxford University Press, 1975.

Borg, James M. W. "The Fashioning of Elizabeth Barrett Browning's *Aurora Leigh.*" Ph.D. diss., Northwestern University, 1979.

Brady, Ann P. *Pompilia: A Feminist Reading of Robert Browning's "The Ring and the Book."* Athens: Ohio University Press, 1988.

Carr, Anne, and Elisabeth Schüssler Fiorenza, eds. *The Special Nature of Women?* Concilium 6. London: SCM Press, 1991.

Cooper, Helen. *Elizabeth Barrett Browning, Woman and Artist.* Chapel Hill: University of North Carolina Press, 1988.

Dally, Peter. *Elizabeth Barrett Browning: A Psychological Portrait.* London: Macmillan, 1989.

Daly, Mary. *Beyond God the Father: Toward a Philosophy of Women's Liberation.* Boston: Beacon, 1973.

David, Deirdre. *Intellectual Women and Victorian Patriarchy: Harriet Martineau, Elizabeth Barrett Browning, George Eliot.* Ithaca: Cornell University Press, 1987.

Davis, Lloyd, ed. *Virginal Sexuality and Textuality in Victorian Literature.* Albany: State University of New York Press, 1993.

de Beauvoir, Simone. *The Second Sex.* Trans. and ed. H. M. Parshley. New York: Modern Library, 1968.

de Rougemont, Denis. *Love in the Western World.* Trans. Montgomery Belgion. New York: Pantheon Books, 1956.

Donaldson, Sandra Marie. "Elizabeth Barrett Browning's Poetic and Feminist Philosophies in *'Aurora Leigh'* and Other Poems." Ph.D. diss., University of Connecticut, 1976.

Dowell, Susan. "A Jealous God? Towards a Feminist Model of Monogamy." In *Sex and God: Some Varieties of Women's Religious Experience,* ed. Linda Hurcombe. New York: Routledge and Kegan Paul, 1987.

Dworkin, Andrea. *Intercourse.* New York: Free Press, 1987.

Falk, Alice. "Elizabeth Barrett Browning and Her Prometheuses: Self-Will and a Woman Poet." *Tulsa Studies in Women's Literature* 7:1 (1988): 69–85.

Forster, Margaret. *Elizabeth Barrett Browning: The Life and Loves of a Poet.* New York: St. Martin's Press, 1988.

Gerard, Jessica. "Lady Bountiful: Women of the Landed Classes and Rural Philanthropy." *Victorian Studies* 30:2 (1987): 183–209.

Gilbert, Sandra M. "From *Patria* to *Matria:* Elizabeth Barrett Browning's Risorgimento." *PMLA* 99:2 (1984): 194–211.

Gilbert, Sandra M., and Susan Gubar. *The Madwoman in the Attic: The Woman Writer and the Nineteenth-Century Literary Imagination.* New Haven: Yale University Press, 1979.

Hardwick, Elizabeth. *Seduction and Betrayal: Women and Literature.* New York: Random House, 1970.

Harrison, Antony H. *Christina Rossetti in Context.* Chapel Hill: University of North Carolina Press, 1988.

———. *Victorian Poets and Romantic Poems: Intertextuality and Ideology.* Charlottesville: University Press of Virginia, 1990.

Haskins, Susan. *Mary Magdalene: Myth and Metaphor.* New York: Harcourt Brace, 1993.

Hayter, Alethea. *Mrs. Browning: A Poet's Work and Its Setting.* London: Faber and Faber, 1962.

———. "Windows toward the Future." *Browning Institute Studies* 1 (1973): 31–36.

Hewlett, Dorothy. *Elizabeth Barrett Browning: A Life.* New York: Octagon Books, 1952.

Hickok, Kathleen. *Representations of Women: Nineteenth-Century British Women's Poetry.* Westport, Conn.: Greenwood, 1984.

Holloway, John. *The Victorian Sage: Studies in Argument.* New York: W. W. Norton, 1965.

Holmes, Alicia E. "Elizabeth Barrett Browning: Construction of Authority in *Aurora Leigh* by Rewriting Mother, Muse, and Miriam." *The Centennial Review* 36:3 (1992): 593–606.

Horne, Richard H. *A New Spirit of the Age.* 2 vols. London: Smith, Elder, 1844.

Irvine, William, and Park Honan. *The Book, the Ring, and the Poet: A Biography of Robert Browning.* New York: McGraw Hill, 1974.

Johnson, Heidi. " 'Matters That a Woman Rules': Marginalized Maternity in Jean Ingelow's *A Study of Doom.*" *Victorian Poetry* 33:1 (1995): 75–88.

Karlin, Daniel. *The Courtship of Robert Browning and Elizabeth Barrett.* Oxford: Clarendon Press, 1985.

Kent, David, ed. *The Achievement of Christina Rossetti.* Ithaca: Cornell University Press, 1987.

King, Ursula. *Women and Spirituality: Voices of Protest and Promise.* Houndmills, Basingstoke, England: Macmillan, 1989.

Kris, Ernst, and Otto Kurz. *Legend, Myth, and Magic in the Image of the Artist: A Historical Experiment.* New Haven: Yale University Press, 1979.

Landow, George P. *Elegant Jeremiahs: The Sage from Carlyle to Mailer.* Ithaca: Cornell University Press, 1986.

Leder, Sharon, with Andrea Abbott. *The Language of Exclusion: The Poetry of Emily Dickinson and Christina Rossetti.* New York: Greenwood, 1987.

Leighton, Angela. *Elizabeth Barrett Browning.* Bloomington: Indiana University Press, 1986.

———. *Victorian Women Poets: Writing against the Heart.* Charlottesville: University Press of Virginia, 1992.

Lerner, Gerda. *The Creation of Feminist Consciousness.* New York: Oxford University Press, 1993.

Lootens, Tricia. *Lost Saints: Silence, Gender, and Victorian Literary Canonization.* Charlottesville: University Press of Virginia, 1996.

Markus, Julia. *Dared and Done: The Marriage of Elizabeth Barrett and Robert Browning.* New York: Alfred A. Knopf, 1995.

Martin, George. *The Red Shirt and the Cross of Savoy: The Story of Italy's Risorgimento (1748–1871).* London: Eyre and Spottiswoode, 1969.

Mazzaro, Jerome. "Mapping Sublimity: Elizabeth Barrett Browning's *Sonnets from the Portuguese.*" *Essays in Literature* 18:2 (1991): 166–79.

McColley, Diane Kelsey. *Milton's Eve.* Urbana: University of Illinois Press, 1983.

McGann, Jerome J. "The Religious Poetry of Christina Rossetti." *Critical Inquiry* 10 (1983): 127–44.

Mermin, Dorothy. *Elizabeth Barrett Browning: The Origins of a New Poetry.* Chicago: University of Chicago Press, 1989.

Miller, Jonathan. "Spiritualism: The Victorian Cult." *Sunday Times Magazine.* 16 January 1966, 26–27.

Moers, Ellen. *Literary Women.* Garden City, N.Y.: Doubleday, 1976.

Morgan, Thaïs, ed. *Victorian Sages and Cultural Discourse: Renegotiating Gender and Power.* New Brunswick, N.J.: Rutgers University Press, 1990.

Orr, Augusta (Mrs. Sutherland). *A Handbook to the Works of Robert Browning.* 5th ed. London: George Bell and Sons, 1890.

Pagels, Elaine. *Adam, Eve and the Serpent.* New York: Random House, 1988.

Phillips, John A. *Eve: The History of an Idea.* San Francisco: Harper and Row, 1984.

Plaskow, Judith. *Sex, Sin and Grace: Women's Experience and the Theologies of Reinhold Niebuhr and Paul Tillich.* Washington, D.C.: University Press of America, 1980.

Plaskow, Judith, and Carol P. Christ, eds. *Weaving the Visions: New Patterns in Feminist Spirituality.* San Francisco: HarperCollins, 1989.

———. *Womanspirit Rising: A Feminist Reader in Religion.* San Francisco: Harper and Row, 1979.

Porter, Katherine H. *Through a Glass Darkly: Spiritualism in the Browning Circle.* Lawrence: University Press of Kansas, 1958.

Prins, Yopie. "Elizabeth Barrett, Robert Browning and the *Différance* of Translation." *Victorian Poetry* 29:4 (1991): 435–51.

Radley, Virginia. *Elizabeth Barrett Browning.* Boston: Twayne, 1972.

Raggio, Olga. "The Myth of Prometheus: Its Survival and Metamorphoses up to the Eighteenth Century." *Journal of the Warburg and Courtauld Institutes* 21 (1958): 44–62.

Riede, David G. "Elizabeth Barrett: The Poet as Angel." *Victorian Poetry* 32:2 (1994): 121–40.

Ritter, Alan. *The Political Thought of Pierre-Joseph Proudhon.* Westport, Conn.: Greenwood, 1969.

Rosenblum, Dolores. "*Casa Guidi Windows* and *Aurora Leigh:* The Genesis of Elizabeth Barrett Browning's Visionary Aesthetic." *Tulsa Studies in Women's Literature* 4:1 (1985): 61–68.

———. *Christina Rossetti: The Poetry of Endurance.* Carbondale: Southern Illinois University Press, 1986.

———. "Face to Face: Elizabeth Barrett Browning's *Aurora Leigh* and Nineteenth-Century Poetry." *Victorian Studies* 26:3 (1983): 321–38.

Ruether, Rosemary Radford. *New Woman, New Earth: Sexist Ideologies and Human Liberation.* New York: Seabury, 1975.

———. *Sexism and God-Talk: Toward a Feminist Theology.* Boston: Beacon, 1983.

Sickbert, Virginia. " 'Beloved Mother of Us All': Christina Rossetti's Eve." *Christianity and Literature* 44:3–4 (1995): 289–311.

Smith, Dennis Mack. *Italy: A Modern History.* Ann Arbor: University of Michigan Press, 1959.

Steinmetz, Virginia. "Images of 'Mother-Want' in Elizabeth Barrett Browning's *Aurora Leigh.*" *Victorian Poetry* 21:4 (1983): 351–67.

Stephenson, Glennis. " 'Bertha in the Lane': Elizabeth Barrett Browning and the Dramatic Monologue." *Browning Society Notes* 16:3 (1986–1987): 3–9.

———. "The Vision Speaks: Love in Elizabeth Barrett Browning's 'Lady Geraldine's Courtship.' " *Victorian Poetry* 217:1 (1989): 17–32.

Stone, Marjorie. "Cursing as One of the Fine Arts: Elizabeth Barrett Browning's Political Poems." *The Dalhousie Review* 66 (1986): 155–73.

———. *Elizabeth Barrett Browning.* New York: St. Martin's Press, 1995.

———. "Genre Subversion and Gender Inversion: *The Princess* and *Aurora Leigh.*" *Victorian Poetry* 25:2 (1987): 101–27.

Taplin, Gardner A. *"Aurora Leigh:* A Rehearing." *Studies in Browning and His Circle* 7:1 (1979): 7–23.

———. *The Life of Elizabeth Barrett Browning.* New Haven: Yale University Press, 1957.

Taylor, Barbara. *Eve and the New Jerusalem: Socialism and Feminism in the Nineteenth Century.* New York: Pantheon Books, 1983.

Toksvig, Signe. *Emanuel Swedenborg: Scientist and Mystic.* New Haven: Yale University Press, 1948.

Warner, Marina. *Alone of All Her Sex: The Myth and the Cult of the Virgin Mary.* New York: Alfred A. Knopf, 1976. Reprint, New York: Vintage Books, 1983.

———. *Monuments and Maidens: The Allegory of the Female Form.* London: Weidenfeld and Nicolson, 1985.

Weintraub, Stanley. *Four Rossettis: A Victorian Biography.* New York: Weybright and Talley, 1977.

Welsh, Alexander. *The City of Dickens.* Oxford: Clarendon Press, 1971.

Wittreich, Joseph. *Feminist Milton.* Ithaca: Cornell University Press, 1987.

Zonana, Joyce. "The Embodied Muse: Elizabeth Barrett Browning's *Au-rora Leigh* and Feminist Poetics." *Tulsa Studies in Women's Literature* 8:2 (1989): 241–62.

Index

Aaron, 194, 203
Adam, 3, 49, 53, 57, 59, 60, 66, 72, 135, 231
Adams, Sarah Flower, 214n5
Aeschylus: influence on *The Seraphim,* 13, 18, 19, 36–39; influence on "The Tempest," 30; mentioned, 17, 19, 24–25, 27, 41, 43, 59, 167, 190
Aesop, 20
Albert, Prince, 97, 125, 139
Angel: as female, 63, 181, 182; as lover/muse, 24, 143, 144, 145, 146, 159, 192; as Napoleon III, 111, 147, 148
Angels: and death, 207; fall of, 29; in "Lay of Brown Rosary," 84; in Milton, 36, 41; in resurrection, 161, 221; in romantic love, 143–45; in "Runaway Slave at Pilgrim's Point," 192; in *The Seraphim,* 37–48; Swedenborgian, 39, 72, 141
Anglicanism, 12, 155, 214
Apocalypse, 13, 14, 22, 89, 110, 131, 154, 213
Apollodorus, 20
Aristotle, 87, 102
Arminianism, 12, 70
Arnold, Matthew, 5–6, 8, 188
Athena/Minerva, 171, 172, 174, 175–76, 186, 194
Augustine, Saint, 25, 26, 55n8, 87, 213, 226
Aurora Leigh: androgyny, 166–67; education of, 11, 198; as prophetess/wisdom, 14, 171, 185, 198, 201, 203–4, 206, 207; on rape, 167–68; on work(s), 73, 127, 199, 206
Austria, 103, 107, 113, 116

Bacon, Francis, 176, 186
Bandieri, the, 100

Barrett. *See* Moulton-Barrett
Bentham, Jeremy, 128, 197
Benthamites, 108, 129
Blagden, Isa, 2, 126, 210
Blake, William, 36, 61, 63, 64, 142, 165, 170, 188, 193
Blanc, Louis, 14, 119, 125, 128
Boccaccio, Giovanni, 94
Bowles, Caroline. *See* Southey, Caroline Bowles
Boyd, Hugh Stuart, 24, 180
Brontë, Anne, 214n5
Brontë, Charlotte, 62, 67, 124, 175, 181, 187, 196, 214n5
Browne, Charlotte Elizabeth, 187
Browne, Thomas, 2
Browning, Elizabeth Barrett: on Apocalypse, 89, 92; art/poetry as religion, 9, 15, 17, 43, 48, 78, 168, 233; as Athena/Minerva, 171–72, 175, 176–79, 183, 206; and ballads, 79–84; and Bible reading, 10, 32, 44, 138; on capitalism/materialism, 107–8, 122, 134–35; as Cassandra, 186; on Catholicism, 11, 12, 13; and class prejudice, 122, 129, 157, 168, 194; and communism, 117; on Auguste Comte, 108; as conservative, 89, 195; criticism of, 17, 26, 37, 39, 52, 180, 183, 210; and curses, 192–94; and the dead, 134, 136–37; and death, 132–138 passim, 142, 143, 169, 151, 212, 226; on democracy, 96, 98, 110, 112, 114–15, 118, 129; on duty, 200, 205; education/reading of, 9, 10, 51, 88, 116, 122, 176–77; and Eve/exile, 49, 62, 84–85; on Charles Fourier, 117, 119; on freedom, 87, 91, 104, 108, 117–18; on Elizabeth Gaskell, 158–59; as goddess,

172; on grace, 53–57, 63–65, 133; on Felicia Hemans, 24, 217; on heroes, 93–94, 99–101, 104–6, 110, 129, 212; on Mary Howitt, 218; on immortality, 134, 135; inconsistency of, 88–89, 99, 101, 111–14, 129–30; influence of, 212–13; on inner/outer man, 109–10, 127, 204, 205–6; as intellectual, 8, 98; on Italy, 113–14; on Charles Kingsley, 116, 127–28; on marriage, 120–22, 129, 163–66; on mesmerism, 139–40; on John Milton, 11, 36, 60–62, 114; on monarchy, 97, 98, 102; on Gregory Nanzianzen, 31; on Napoleon III, 98, 105, 111, 112, 114; and New Jerusalem, 47–49, 115–16; on people and rulers, 88–89, 96–99, 105, 110–11, 114; on (political) messiah, 96–99, 104–6, 111; as political observer, 45–48, 90, 110–11, 125; on politics as religion, 88–89, 91–92, 99, 107, 114, 118, 213; on pride/humility, 32–34, 36, 47–48, 60–62, 208–10, 232; as Promethean, 18–19, 21–23, 29; as prophetess, 14, 18, 45–49, 78, 90, 116, 147, 171, 172, 173, 178, 180, 181, 183–95 passim; 213; and quest, 5, 13, 195; on rape, 150–70 passim, 229; on religions/sects, 8–12, 84, 107; on resurrection, 3, 141, 143, 144, 146–66, passim, 150, 159, 169; as revisionist, 39, 49–73 passim; as sage, 188–95 passim; as saint, 2, 186; on Samuel Richardson, 157, 158; and séances, 136; self-criticism, 19, 176, 184; on Percy Shelley, 38*n24;* on sin, 30–31, 87–89; on slavery, 190–93; on socialism, 91, 92, 116, 118, 121, 125–27, 129; on social issues, 19, 124, 128, 131, 173, 187–90, 192–94; and suffering, 39, 40, 42, 49, 50, 74–75, 78, 84, 106; and Swedenborg, 2, 11, 141, 142, 173, 213; on teacher/messiah, 105–6, 107, 110; and theology, 213; as translator, 19, 22, 26, 190; on Tuscany, 105, 108; on tyranny, 101–2; on unity, 90, 115, 149–50; on Victoria, 96–97; on wisdom, 5, 14, 172–78 passim, 184–85, 194; on women, 91, 185, 212; on work, 13, 50, 65–73 passim, 84, 121, 168, 200, 220, 227, 233

—works: "Adequacy," 77; "The Appeal," 187; "An Apprehension," 1; "An August Voice," 103; *Aurora Leigh,* 13, 14, 25, 32, 62, 68–69, 86, 78, 92, 108, 115–31 passim, 121, 135, 150–70 passim, 193, 194–211 passim; "Battle of Marathon," 177–78; "Bertha in the Lane," 80–82; *The Book of the Poets,* 36; *Casa Guidi Windows,* 13, 14, 89, 92–115 passim, 129, 146–47, 213; "Catarina to Camoens," 145; "Christmas Gifts," 107; "Comfort," 62; "Confessions," 132; "Crowned and Wedded," 97; "The Cry of the Children," 129, 188–89, 191; "The Cry of the Human," 189–90; "A Curse for a Nation," 186, 187, 194; "The Dead Pan," 48, 78, 221; "De Profundis," 76, 77, 133; "The Deserted Garden," 74, 76; *Diary by E.B.B.,* 17*n1,* 37; "Discontent," 75; *A Drama of Exile,* 8, 13, 17, 22, 37, 42, 44, 48, 49, 50–73 passim, 180, 205, 221; "Earth and her Praisers," 74; "An Essay on Mind," 2*n1,* 27, 88, 133, 179; "Exaggeration," 77; "Felicia Hemans," 24; "First News from Villafranca," 86, 112; "A Forced Recruit," 113; "Garibaldi," 113; "To George Sand, a Desire," 198; *The Greek Christian Poets,* 31, 84; "The Greek Slave," 191*n28; Hitherto Unpublished Poems,* 17*n1;* "Idols," 32; "Insufficiency," 75, 134; "Irreparableness," 75; "Isobel's Child," 74, 219; "Italy and the World," 107, 115, 147–49; "Lady Geraldine's Courtship," 145, 180–82, 189, 194; *Last Poems,* 2, 92, 96, 98, 113, 161, 193; "Lay of the Brown Rosary," 83–84; "The Lost Bower," 77; "Memory and Hope," 74; "Mother and Poet," 113; "Napoleon III. In Italy," 95, 97–98, 110, 113, 148, 114; "Night and the Merry Man," 74; "On laying Hooker under my pillow at night," 88; "On Poverty," 187; "Past and Future," 75; "Perplexed Music," 78; *Poems, 1833,* 27; *Poems, 1850,* 19; *Poems before Congress,* 13, 14, 95, 110, 115, 147, 213; "The Poet's Vow," 74, 205; *Prometheus Bound* (translation), 16, 19, 27; "The Prisoner," 75, 77; "Rhyme of the Duchess May," 62; "A Romance of the Ganges," 74;

"The Romance of the Swan's Nest," 76; "The Romaunt of Margret," 74; "The Romaunt of the Page," 79–81; "The Rhyme of the Duchess May," 79–80; "The Runaway Slave at Pilgrim's Point," 190–92, 194; "A Sea-side Meditation," 35–36, 40; "The Seraph and the Poet," 76; *The Seraphim,* 13, 16, 17, 18, 25, 26, 36–48 passim, 52, 62, 73, 75, 180, 221; "Song for the Ragged Schools of London," 193–94; *Sonnets from the Portuguese,* 13, 14, 76, 134, 143, 145–47, 159, 169, 170; "The Soul's Expression," 78; "The Soul's Travelling," 74; "Stanzas on the Death of Lord Byron," 23; "Summing up in Italy," 11, 112; "Tears," 75; "The Tempest," 27–35, 39; "To a Poet's Child," 22; "Victoria's Tears," 97; "A Vision of Poets," 78, 84, 182–83, 186; "The Weeping Savior," 135; "Where's Agnes?" 161; "Wine of Cypress," 79, 185–86; "Work," 69, 227; "Work and Contemplation," 69, 227; "The Young Queen," 97

Browning, Robert: courtship/marriage, 12, 24–25, 133, 135, 143, 165, 174; influence on EBB, 25, 174, 184, 203; on politics, 71, 117, 119; on Prometheus, 25–26; and resurrection in love, 134; on spiritualism, 140; on Wisdom, 175
—works: "Easter-Day," 16; "Mr. Sludge, the Medium," 140; *Paracelsus,* 175; "Prince Hohenstiel-Schwangau," 71, 112, 119; *The Ring and the Book,* 63, 160, 175; mentioned, 6, 16, 31, 49, 132, 133

Browning, Robert Wiedemann ("Pen"), 12, 89, 134, 140, 148

Browning, Sarianna, 139, 162

Brutus, 92, 100, 104

Bunyan, John, 224

Burke, Edmund, 108

Byron, Lord (George Gordon): as influence on EBB, 19, 20, 21, 22, 23, 33, 36, 80, 105, 176, 180

Cabet, Etienne, 119, 125

Caesar, 105

Calvin, John, 87

Calvinism, 12, 88, 89

Carlyle, Thomas: influence on EBB, 14, 96, 104; on politics, 96, 99, 103–4, 105, 108, 109; on religion, 6; on work, 67–68, 70–72, 72, 220; mentioned, 110, 142, 188, 197

Cassandra, 14, 79, 172, 174, 183, 184, 185, 186, 193, 194, 202, 203

Catholicism, 11–13

Cavour, Camillo, 110, 113

Charlemagne, 105

Charles Albert of Piedmont, 94, 100, 104

Charles I, of England, 100

Chartism, 129, 197–98

Chrysostom, John, Saint: influence on EBB, 10, 46, 64, 160–61, 163

Church Fathers, 26, 55–56

Claudian, 29

Clement, 55

Coleridge, Hartley, 36

Coleridge, Samuel Taylor, 20, 23, 142, 149, 182

Coleridge, Sara, 44

Communist Manifesto, 116

Comte, Auguste, 108, 119, 120*n37,* 175

Congregationalists, 9

Considérant, Victor Prosper, 128

Cook, Eliza, 215

Corn Law League, 21, 22

"Corruption" (figure for sin), 147, 151, 160–62

Cottrell, Count, 140

Cromwell, Oliver, 104, 110

Danae, 166, 167, 194

Dante Alighieri: as hero, 93, 94, 100; influence of, 21, 37, 102, 176, 180, 181–82, 115, 210, 212; and politics, 87, 96, 100, 102, 115; as Promethean, 25, 105; and Wisdom, 176; mentioned, 41, 71, 94, 110, 132, 186, 194, 233

de Beauvoir, Simone, 3, 136–37

Demogorgon, 40–41

de Staël, Anne-Louise-Germaine, 22, 23, 82

Dickens, Charles, 7, 62, 139, 175, 194, 196–97

Dickinson, Emily, 1

Diotima, 14, 196, 197, 201

Dissenters, 7, 11, 129

"Divine Wisdom and Divine Love." *See* Swedenborg, Emanuel

Donne, John, 34, 166, 233
Dorling, William, 222

Eden: exile from, 49, 73–76, 79, 82–83;
    return to, 40, 75, 78, 218, 224
Elgin, Lady Elizabeth, 140
Elijah, 203, 206, 211, 223, 233
Eliot, George: on pride, 33; on religion, 7;
    on suffering, 75; on wisdom, 175, 180,
    194, 201–2
—works: *Adam Bede,* 75; *Middlemarch,* 118,
    180, 194, 201–2; *Romola,* 99; mentioned,
    8, 62, 75, 82, 104, 187
Elliott, Charlotte, 214*n5*
Emerson, Ralph Waldo: on Anglicanism,
    6–8; on politics, 119; on Swedenborg,
    142, 165
Engels, Friedrich, 118–19
England: and empire, 187, 192–93;
    socialism in, 116–17; wealth and poverty,
    122, 189, 192–93
Evans, Mary, 173
Eve: as empress, 60, 61, 72; as exile, 13, 52;
    the Fall, 54, 220; as grace/pity, 53, 57, 60,
    63, 65–66; as hope, 59, 60; and humility,
    48, 60, 62, 65–66; in myth, 55; and sin,
    55–56; as teacher/prophetess, 49, 50, 54,
    57, 61, 65–70, 72, 78, 194, 231; and
    women writers, 196, 220, 230–31; and
    work, 66–67, 68, 72, 77–78; mentioned,
    4, 14, 37, 50, 55, 160, 186, 213, 231,
    233

"Face to face": as motif, 1, 2, 11, 77, 84,
    143, 146, 210, 228
Ficino, Marsilio, 25, 26
Florence, 91, 94, 98–99, 100
Fourier, Charles: on socialism, 115, 118–19,
    121; on women and marriage, 116–17,
    118, 120, 122, 124; mentioned, 14, 116,
    197, 120–21, 128, 129
France, 116, 117
Fulgentius, 25, 26
Fuller, Margaret: on feminism, 118, 120,
    136, 142, 174; on wisdom, 174, 185

Gabriel, 57
Ganymede, 166–67
Garibaldi, Anita, 100
Garibaldi, Giuseppe, 100, 113

Gaskell, Elizabeth: *North and South,* 7; *Ruth,*
    158; mentioned, 187
Giotto, 94
Godiva, 14, 172, 184, 185, 186
Godwin, William, 99, 116
Goethe, Johann Wolfgang von, 19*n3,* 20,
    22, 36
Golding, Arthur, 25
Greek Christian Fathers, 10, 180
Greenwell, Dora: on EBB, 212; on politics,
    95, 213; on religion, 222–25, 232;
    on social issues, 222, 224; mentioned,
    214*n5,* 230

Hardy, Thomas, 62, 187
Havergal, Frances Ridley, 214*n5*
Hawthorne, Nathaniel: *The Scarlet Letter,*
    157–58; socialism in *The Blithedale
    Romance,* 120–21, 123
Hemans, Felicia: on art, 23; on religion,
    133, 214–17; mentioned, 22, 212, 219
Herbert, George, 2, 226, 233
Hesiod, 29
Hobbes, Thomas, 88
Home, D. D., 140
Homer, 71, 176, 186
Hood, Thomas, 129
Hooker, Richard: on females, 54, 176; on
    pride, 32, 33; on sin and grace, 8, 70;
    mentioned, 10, 202, 213, 233
Horace, 20
Horne, R. H., 183, 184, 189
Howitt, Mary: on religion, 217–18;
    mentioned, 212, 215, 219
Hunt, Leigh, 184
Hyginus, 20, 167*n32*

Ingelow, Jean: religious verse, 219–22;
    mentioned, 22, 47, 49, 214*n5*
Io, 18, 27, 166, 167, 172, 183, 184, 194,
    202
Isis, 174
Italy: as female, 95, 113, 147; politics of, 22,
    90–91, 93–94, 95, 107, 108, 122, 147,
    153

James, John Angell, 8
James, Saint, 70
Jameson, Anna, 91

Jesus: as androgynous/feminine, 4, 5, 72, 82, 174, 199, 224, 230, 234; and Apocalypse, 149–50; as Conqueror, 28–30; death and resurrection, 17, 42–45, 95, 106, 169, 226; and grace, 65, 85; as lover/Bridegroom, 144, 145, 165, 229–30; and poetry, 9, 233; and politics, 1, 92, 99, 106, 115; and Prometheus, 13, 25, 191; suffering of, 39, 42, 66n23, 75, 135, 228, 232; as Word/Wisdom, 44–45, 67, 174; on work, 73, 147, 152; mentioned, 13, 41, 44, 46, 109, 127, 129, 135, 136, 138, 145, 150, 174, 194, 197, 208, 218, 223, 224, 228
Jewsbury, Geraldine, 187
John, Saint, 15, 145, 188, 192, 195, 211, 233
Jung, C. G., 31

Keats, John, 181, 182
Keble, John, 46, 226, 233
Kemble, Frances Anne, 214n5
Kenyon, John, 21, 233
Kingsley, Charles: on socialism, 116, 127–30; on Wisdom, 175, 197–98; mentioned, 7, 11, 14
Kirkup, Seymour, 140

Landon, Letitia: on poetry, 23, 24; mentioned, 122, 217
Lazarus, 135, 150, 154
Lee, Ann, 173
Leopold, Grand Duke, 91, 94–95, 100, 101, 102, 110, 111
Locke, John, 88, 99, 102, 204
Lombard, Peter, 55n8
Lucian, 20, 167n32
Lucifer, 22, 44, 53, 60
Luther, Martin, 10, 72n30, 73
Lytton, Robert (George Meredith), 140, 142, 210

Macaulay, Thomas Babington, 108
Machiavelli, Niccolo, 94, 96
Mahony, Francis, Reverend, 184
Malthus, Thomas, 128, 129, 197
Marian Erle: death of, 14, 155–66 passim; and as Virgin, 150, 155, 165–66; mentioned, 20, 122, 124, 206
Martial, 20

Martineau, Harriet: on EBB, 190; mesmerism of, 138–39; on politics, 91, 96; on religion, 138; on woman and wisdom, 138, 175, 184, 196–98; mentioned, 8, 81, 122, 187
Marx, Karl, 5
Mary, mother of Jesus, 4, 46, 62–64, 121, 161
Mary Magdalene: and EBB, 13–14, 45–48; in Greenwell, 223–24; as humility, 18, 36, 41, 61–62, 220; as prophetess, 45–48; as Victorian womanhood, 46–47; mentioned, 4, 14, 172, 186, 196, 197, 213, 223–24, 233
Mary of Bethany, 46, 61, 62, 69, 180
Maurice, F. D., 129
Mazzini, Giuseppe, 93, 105, 111
Meredith, George. See Lytton, Robert (George Meredith)
Mesmerism, 2, 136, 138–39, 140
Metternich, Prince von, 110
Meynell, Alice, 214n5
Michelangelo, 92, 94, 100, 110
Mill, Harriet Taylor, 91, 187
Mill, John Stuart, 33–34
Milton, John: on duty, 68; on Eve, 50, 54; on government, 88; as hero, 100; influence on EBB, 13, 17, 21, 28, 29–30, 33, 34, 35, 36–37, 39, 50–52, 54–56, 67, 91, 99, 114, 177, 210, 212; influence on Ingelow, 221; on pride, 33; on religion, 11, 71; on Satan and Prometheus, 22, 27, 35; and *The Seraphim,* 16, 36–45; and "The Tempest," 28–31
—works: *Lycidas,* 107; "On the Morning of Christ's Nativity," 221; *Paradise Lost,* 8, 16, 17, 28–30, 36–45 passim, 177; *Paradise Regained,* 16, 17, 37, 40, 41, 43; *Samson Agonistes,* 37; *Tetrachordon,* 54
Minerva: and wisdom, 172, 177–78, 194, 196, 197. *See also* Athena/Minerva
Miriam: prophetess, 14, 124, 194, 202–3, 224
Mitford, Mary Russell: as correspondent 20, 21, 38n24, 99, 117, 122, 134
Moravians, 126, 127
More, Hannah, 2
Moses, 105, 203
Moulton-Barrett, Edward ("Bro"), 1, 30, 132, 135, 136

Moulton-Barrett, Edward (father of EBB),
    3, 21, 24, 30, 32, 136, 138
Moulton-Barrett, Henrietta, 136, 139, 184
Moulton-Barrett, Mary, 9
Moulton-Barrett, Sam, 135

Nanzianzen, Gregory: dualism of, 31, 34;
    influence on EBB, 10, 31
Napoleon I, 105, 148
Napoleon III: as hero/savior, 90, 94–95, 98,
    104, 106, 110–13, 148; and spiritualism,
    140; mentioned, 72n29, 125
New Jerusalem, 86–87, 90, 108, 131, 208,
    225
Newman, John Henry, Cardinal, 10, 188
Nietzsche, Friedrich, 20
Nightingale, Florence: on religion, 6, 7,
    174; on work, 33, 67, 71, 73, 95n10,
    124, 201; mentioned, 185
Norton, Caroline, 187, 189, 215

Ogilvy, Elizabeth, 158, 168
Origen, 61n18
Ovid, 20, 167n32
Owen, Robert, 14, 116, 122, 129, 139
Owenites, 131

Paine, Thomas, 88
Pandora, 55, 65
Pascal, Blaine, 2
Paul, Saint: influence on EBB, 136, 141,
    163, 169; on resurrection, 135, 141,
    142, 145, 160, 169; on women, 33;
    mentioned, 1, 5, 15, 54, 64, 70, 115,
    140, 150, 196, 209, 211, 233
Pausanius, 20
Petrarch, Francis, 93, 94
Pius IX, Pope, 94, 101–2, 106, 111
Plato, 16, 102, 103, 142, 199
Poe, Edgar Allan, 61
Pope, Alexander: influence on EBB, 21,
    166, 176–77, 180, 186
Powers, Hiram, 140, 142
Predestination, 12, 88
Presbyterians, 12
Price, Uvedale, 180
Procter, Adelaide Anne, 214n5
Prometheus: as artist/creator, 20, 25–26,
    44; and bondage, 24, 35, 190; and EBB,
    20, 48, 232; as female artist, 23–24; and

Jesus, 17–18, 25, 26–27, 36, 38, 44; and
    Satan, 22, 34, 37, 234; mentioned, 104,
    190, 210, 234
Propertius, 20
Proudhon, Pierre-Joseph: on marriage,
    120n37; on religion, 120; on socialism
    and property, 14, 116, 122, 125, 128,
    129, 197
Puritanism, 8
Pusey, Edward Bouverie, 10, 233
Pythia, 172

Quinet, Edgar, 26n13

Rape: in *Aurora Leigh,* 150–66 passim
Raphael (angel), 36, 94
Resurrection: in *Aurora Leigh,* 150–66
    passim; in Felicia Hemans, 216; in human
    love, 134, 145, 146, 154–55, 165; in
    Jean Ingelow, 219–20; in Saint Paul, 135,
    141, 142, 145, 160, 169; in politics, 95,
    146–50; in *Sonnets from the Portuguese,*
    143–46; in Swedenborg, 135, 140–41,
    169; mentioned, 3, 14, 45–56, 141, 145,
    151, 152, 154, 213, 233
Richardson, Samuel, 157
Romney Leigh: as messiah, 124, 126,
    151, 203; on pride, 127, 206, 208; on
    reform(s), 69, 87, 107, 110, 122, 126,
    131, 208; on resurrection, 141, 154; on
    socialism, 107, 122; and Swedenborg,
    165, 195; on women, 153; on work, 69,
    72, 198, 204–5; mentioned, 72, 120,
    127, 165, 203
Rossetti, Christina: on Apocalypse, 213;
    on death, 133, 232; on EBB, 212;
    on Eve/exile, 63, 213, 231; on female
    spirituality, 213, 230–31; on vanity, 213,
    227; wedding imagery of, 228–30; on
    work, 73, 227–28
—works: "Advent Sunday," 229; "An
    Afterthought," 231; "All Thy Works
    Praise Thee, O Lord," 60; "Ascension
    Day," 226; "A Better Resurrection,"
    230; *Called to be Saints,* 213n3; "Come
    unto Me," 229; "Cousin Kate," 80;
    "The Descent from the Cross," 228;
    "Easter Tuesday," 229; "Eve," 231; "The
    German-French Campaign," 213n2;
    Goblin Market, 230; "God is our Hope

and Strength," 228; "The heart knoweth its own bitterness," 229; "In the Willow Shade," 228; "Is it will with the child?" 229; "Judge nothing before the time," 228; *Later Life: A Double Sonnet of Sonnets,* 63, 231; "Light Love," 80; "The Lowest Room," 230; "An Old-World Thicket," 232; *The Prince's Progress,* 82; "Repining," 227; "Sexagesima," 231; "Shut Out," 231; "Songs in a Cornfield," 80; "Take Care of Him," 228; "A Testimony," 228; "Till Tomorrow," 229; "A vain shadow," 227; "Vanity of Vanities," 233; "Whither the Tribes go up, even the Tribes of the Lord," 229; "The World," 226; mentioned 73, 213
Rossetti, Dante Gabriel, 95, 139
Rousseau, Jean Jacques, 88, 196
Ruskin, John: on politics, 107; on women, 8, 164, 174; on work and religion, 70–71; mentioned, 142

Sand, George, 86
Sandys, George, 25, 26
Satan: as hubris, 32–33; influence on EBB, 30–31, 36; as Promethean, 28, 35–36, 234; as tempter, 41
Savio, Laura, 113
Savonarola, Girolamo, 92, 99, 104, 110
Sellon, Lydia, 47
Shakespeare, William, 36, 71, 97, 197
Shelley, Mary Wollstonecraft, 20, 23, 34
Shelley, Percy Bysshe: his Prometheus as Jesus, 25, 27, 38–39; influence on Brownings, 24, 37, 39; on love, 107; on politics, 99; and *The Seraphim,* 36–45 passim; on suffering, 39–40
—works: *Adonais,* 38n24; *Hellas,* 25; "Ode to the West Wind," 232; *Prometheus Unbound,* 13, 20, 22, 38–44 passim; 107; *Queen Mab,* 38n24; *Revolt of Islam,* 38n24, 174; mentioned, 13, 48
Siddal, Elizabeth, 139
Socrates, 196, 201
Sophia (Wisdom), 4, 14, 181n11, 194
Southcott, Joanna, 173
Southey, Caroline Bowles, 187, 215
Spence, Thomas, 116
Spenser, Edmund, 161, 182
Spiritualism, 136–42

Story, William Wetmore, 140
Stowe, Harriet Beecher: on mesmerism, 2, 140; on slavery, 129, 187, 190
Swedenborg, Emanuel: on angels, 39, 72, 141; on Apocalypse, 89; and EBB, 11, 72, 135, 136, 141, 142, 148, 169, 192, 195, 209, 213; on conjugal love, 141, 165; on correspondences, 142, 165, 169; Divine Use, 198–200, 208; Divine Wisdom and Divine Love, 13, 14, 173, 195, 199, 206–11; Heaven and Hell, 131, 141; on resurrection, 14, 135, 140–41, 169; on Selfhood, 36, 61, 154; mentioned, 5, 58, 72, 170, 171, 199

Tasso, Torquato, 133
Taylor, Harriet. *See* Mill, Harriet Taylor
Taylor, Jeremy: influence on EBB, 10; on pride, 209; on sex, 161; on works, 70; mentioned, 202, 233
Tennyson, Alfred, Lord: influence on EBB, 180; on mesmerism, 139; on wisdom, 175, 181; on woman and marriage, 164, 208–9
—works: "Godiva," 184; "The Poet," 175; *The Princess,* 181, 208–9; mentioned, 62, 184, 186, 198, 201, 205
Tennyson, Frederick, 140
Teresa of Avila, 166n31, 202
Tertullian, 26
Thackeray, William Makepeace, 62
Tractarians, 10, 11, 13, 213, 226
Transfiguration, 145
Trinitarianism, 44
Tristan, Flora, 187, 189
Trollope, Frances, 187
Tuscany, 109, 111

Utilitarianism, 12, 233

Verdi, Giuseppe, 96
Victor Emanuel, 96, 98, 101, 110, 113
Victoria, Queen, 96–97, 139
Villifranca, Treaty of, 112

Waring, Anna Letitia, 214n5
Wesley, Charles, 2
Whistler, James, 139
William I of England, 104
Williams, Isaac, 226

Wollstonecraft, Mary: influence on EBB, 51; on Prometheus, 23; on reason, 23, 34; on women, 116, 119
Womanhood (as Victorian ideal), 46–46, 63, 72
"Woman's question," 67

Woolf, Virginia, 51, 187
Wordsworth, William: and EBB, 21, 33, 180; and influence, 35, 224

Zeus, 166–68